Thirty Years
of
Liturgical Renewal

Statements of
the Bishops' Committee
on the Liturgy

Edited
with an Introduction and Commentaries
by Frederick R. McManus

Secretariat
Bishops' Committee on the Liturgy
National Conference of Catholic Bishops

In its planning document, as approved by the general membership of the National Conference of Catholic Bishops in November 1985, and again in November 1986, the Secretariat of the Bishops' Committee on the Liturgy was authorized to prepare a collection of statements of the Bishops' Commission on the Liturgical Apostolate and the Bishops' Committee on the Liturgy. The present work, *Thirty Years of Liturgical Renewal: Statements of the Bishops' Committee on the Liturgy*, edited by Frederick R. McManus, has been approved by Bishop Joseph P. Delaney, Chairman of the Bishops' Committee on the Liturgy, and is authorized for publication by the undersigned.

Monsignor Daniel F. Hoye
General Secretary
July 9, 1987   NCCB/USCC

ISBN 1-55586-154-7

Contents

Abbreviations Used

AAS   *Acta Apostolicae Sedis* ("Acts of the Apostolic See"). Periodical published at Vatican City as the official record of papal statements (Rome, 1909–   ).

DOL   *Documents on the Liturgy 1963–1979: Conciliar, Papal, and Curial Texts* (Collegeville, Minn., 1982).

EACW   *Environment and Art in Catholic Worship.* Statement of the NCCB Committee on the Liturgy (Washington, D.C., 1978).

EM   *Eucharisticum Mysterium* ("On the Worship of the Eucharist"). Instruction of the Sacred Congregation of Rites and the Consilium (Rome, 25 May 1967).

FDLC   Federation of Diocesan Liturgical Commissions. Voluntary association formed in October 1969 and comprised of representatives from diocesan liturgical commissions, offices of worship, and the NCCB Liturgy Secretariat.

GIRM   *General Instruction of the Roman Missal* (6 April 1969; fourth edition, 27 March 1975).

GS   *Gaudium et Spes* ("Pastoral Constitution on the Church in the Modern World"). Second Vatican Council (Rome, 7 December 1965).

I   *Inter Oecumenici* ("First Instruction on the Proper Implementation of *Sacrosanctum Concilium*"). Sacred Congregation of Rites (Rome, 26 September 1964).

ICEL   International Commission on English in the Liturgy. A joint commission of members of Catholic Bishops' Conferences in English-speaking countries, comprised of an Episcopal Board and an Advisory Committee on translation of texts. Organized in Rome, October 1963.

LG   *Lumen Gentium* ("Dogmatic Constitution on the Church"). Second Vatican Council (Rome, 21 November 1964).

MCW   *Music in Catholic Worship.* Statement of the NCCB Committee on the Liturgy (Washington, D.C., 1972; revised 1983).

MD	*Mediator Dei* ("On the Sacred Liturgy"). Encyclical Letter of Pope Pius XII (Rome, 1947).
MS	*Musicam Sacram* ("On Music in the Liturgy"). Instruction of the Sacred Congregation of Rites (Rome, 5 March 1967).
NCCB	National Conference of Catholic Bishops.
PG	*Patrologicae Cursus Completus: Series Graeca,* J. P. Migne, ed. (Paris, 1857–1866).
PL	*Patrologicae Cursus Completus: Series Latina,* J. P. Migne, ed. (Paris, 1844–1855).
RCIA	*Rite of Christian Initiation of Adults.* Sacred Congregation for Divine Worship (Rome, 1972).
Ritus	*Ritus servandus in celebratione Missae.* Rite to be followed in the Celebration of the Mass (Rome, 7 March 1965).
SC	*Sacrosanctum Concilium* ("Constitution on the Sacred Liturgy"). Second Vatican Council (Rome, 4 December 1963). This document is frequently referred to as simply *Constitution on the Liturgy.*
SCR	Sacred Congregation of Rites.
USCC	United States Catholic Conference.

Foreword

On December 4, 1963, the Constitution on the Sacred Liturgy (*Sacrosanctum Concilium*) of the Second Vatican Council was formally approved. Opened for discussion at the beginning of the first session of the council, it was brought to its final form in the closing days of the second session. Early in 1964, the implementing document was issued by Pope Paul VI.

Reciting these bald facts gives no suggestion of the process of liturgical renewal that it set in motion. Even those who participated in the council could not have anticipated the breadth and sweep of the changes it brought about in so brief a time. All recognized, of course, the broad principles that the constitution set forth. But it was assumed by most that the implementation of many of its proposals would lie years in the future.

Looking back from the vantage point of today's liturgical celebrations enables us to appreciate how far we have come. The rigidly ordered liturgy of three decades ago—modified significantly by actions of Pope Pius XII—is a far cry from the joyous, reverent celebration of worship now involving the entire Christian community. It is not only a matter of accidentals such as language; the spirit is different. The eucharistic liturgy is no longer the almost solitary action of the priest witnessed by individuals in the congregation. It is, instead, an action of the total community presided over by the priest. And the entire event is an expression of the understanding of Church given us by the council.

The process of change was given shape in the United States by the Bishops' Commission on the Liturgical Apostolate, formed in 1958, succeeded later in the reorganized National Conference of Catholic Bishops by the Bishops' Committee on the Liturgy. And its work continues to the present day.

An involved participant in the process was Msgr. Frederick McManus. He was close to the scene throughout its unfolding. Early on, he was active in the North American Liturgical Weeks. Once the Bishops' Commission on the Liturgical Apostolate was established, he was a valued consultant. As a *peritus* at the Second Vatican Council, he was privy to its deliberations. Later on, he rendered and continues to render an invaluable service to the Bishops' Committee on the Liturgy. With this rich and varied experience, he is well qualified to bring together for us the record of activities in the field of liturgy over these years. This he has done in this publication, *Thirty Years of Liturgical Renewal*. The work traces the historical trajectory of liturgical reform and progress from 1958 to the present day. It is the story of the work of the American bishops responding to the questions of the day, the reforms of Pope Pius XII, but most especially the implementation of the conciliar and papal reform of the liturgy begun when the council issued *Sacrosanctum Concilium*. This book, then, is about reform and renewal.

The council provided guiding principles for reform for "changes of

1

words and rites of public worship." However, more important, the council impelled the Church to a deeper renewal, which would manifest itself in every aspect of its life, its worship becoming the "hallmark" of that renewal. Msgr. McManus' commentaries on some thirty-seven statements of the Bishops' Committee on the Liturgy describe that curiosity, impatience, acceptance, and response to change and even to critical situations that arose during the course of the liturgical reform—a reform not yet completed, it should be added.

Msgr. McManus' book tells the partial story of how the American bishops have responded to that first free acceptance of renewal. It is a partial story because the history of liturgical renewal cannot be told only from one angle or point of view—that of the bishops. It must also be told from the point of view of the people—their bewilderment, their surprise, their faith, their genuine acceptance of the reform and how they have made the liturgical renewal truly their own at the deepest level of their lives. *Thirty Years of Liturgical Renewal* is really an introduction to the real story of liturgical renewal in the United States. As such, it constitutes a valuable record of historical movement. We are all indebted to Msgr. McManus for having preserved this record for us.

John Cardinal Dearden
Archbishop Emeritus of Detroit

Introduction: The Formative Years

There are any number of ways to tell the story of the last three decades of liturgical renewal in the United States. For that matter, there are any number of ways to tell the story of the Bishops' Committee on the Liturgy since November 14, 1957, when the American episcopate created a committee to study the question of a national episcopal liturgical commission.

The way chosen here to commemorate those thirty years of the Bishops' Committee on the Liturgy—called the Bishops' Commission on the Liturgical Apostolate from 1958 to 1967—is to reprint, with commentaries, the committee's statements and similar documents over that period.

Because there has never been any set pattern of issuing formal statements, the materials are very diverse in style and purpose. Collecting them, however, has revealed that they are not really dated in the positions they espouse, but only in specific reference to events and practices at the several stages of liturgical reform. Indeed, they have a remarkable consistency of outlook and purpose; they often show an unusual foresight.

The content of the statements is itself a quasi-official history of liturgical progress in the United States—at the level of the National Conference of Catholic Bishops. Of course, this differs from the history of the general liturgical renewal, or apostolate as it was called; from a record of individual diocesan pastoral-liturgical activities; and from an account of the Roman revision of the liturgical rites and books that has taken place during this time. It does not take into account directly the many other publications and promotional efforts of the Bishops' Committee on the Liturgy or its *Newsletter* published since 1965. The chief publications are listed at the end of this introduction.

The most obvious prenote to this collection and the commentaries is that the statements begin only in 1963 after the committee had been in existence and operation for five years. Its history and, in fact, its prehistory have first to be told.

A National Episcopal Liturgical Commission

The prehistory of the Bishops' Committee on the Liturgy might be traced to the first liturgical concerns of the body of bishops during the nineteenth century, whether the bishops were assembled in councils or less formally in conferences. It might even be traced back to the celebrated interest of the first bishop of Baltimore, John Carroll, in the use of the vernacular in the liturgy.

The modern concept of conferences of bishops goes back to the first half of the nineteenth century. Such conferences were understood as the regular meetings, in a style less formal than councils, of the bishops (or the diocesan bishops or the metropolitans) of a country or region. These

3

meetings inherited but did not replace the role of particular councils, which had a tradition long antedating the first ecumenical council in the year 325.

In the young Church of the United States, the strong sense of episcopal conciliarity and collegiality was reflected in the nineteenth-century series of provincial and plenary councils, but also in the meetings of the metropolitans. Formal decisions concerning church worship, however, were ordinarily confined to the canonical decrees or statutes of the councils—for example, the 1829 decision to follow *The Roman Ritual* in the United States.

After the Third Plenary Council of Baltimore in 1884, the metropolitans continued to meet annually, but it was only after the First World War that the entire episcopate—including all the diocesan and titular bishops—again assembled "in conference." Meeting in February 1919, the bishops agreed to hold annual plenary sessions and then took the first steps to set up what became, later that year, the National Catholic Welfare Council (called "Conference" from 1922), the NCWC.

The distinction between the annual meeting of the bishops and the civil entity established by the body as its instrument and agency has often, and understandably, been lost. The parent conference of bishops was very generally referred to as the NCWC, but the conference of bishops remained distinct. The assembly was, in fact, an ecclesiastical body, the kind of conference referred to years later by the Second Vatican Council as the practical application of the collegial sense or character of the episcopate. It was kept separate from the incorporated NCWC, which was the necessary agency of the conference of bishops. All the bishops were members of the NCWC, and the NCWC secretariat of departments and divisions had major accomplishments in the fields of social, educational, governmental, and other concerns of the Church in the succeeding decades. In 1966, it became the United States Catholic Conference or USCC.

All this is mentioned in summary, but it is necessary in order to understand the origin of the episcopal liturgical commission that was under consideration by the American bishops in 1957–1958. From the 1920s on, there had been extreme sensitivity, at least among a minority of the bishops, that the NCWC should keep to its charter and not enter into matters of faith or worship. There was concern too that the conference of bishops as an ecclesiastical body must have no ecclesiastical jurisdiction or compulsory authority. It was an issue that remained alive until 1963 and the promulgation of the conciliar *Constitution on the Liturgy* and even until 1965 and the promulgation of the conciliar *Decree on the Pastoral Office of Bishops in the Church*. Beginning in 1966, the conference designated itself, under new statutes, the National Conference of Catholic Bishops or NCCB.

In the 1940s and 1950s, the conference of bishops approached liturgical questions with some hesitation. The deep, if not broad, liturgical movement in this country had developed enough to hold annual Liturgical Weeks. These were first sponsored by the Benedictine Liturgical Conference and later by the voluntary association called The Liturgical Con-

4

ference. Overtures were made seeking the corporate involvement of the conference of bishops in such liturgical action, and the leaders of The Liturgical Conference, among others, recommended the formation of a national liturgical commission.

It was not so easy to avoid action in response to papal liturgical efforts or to ignore the actions of other major conferences of bishops, especially in Europe. In 1947, Pope Pius XII issued an encyclical letter on Christian worship, *Mediator Dei*. It was a doctrinal and disciplinary exposition, welcomed as the charter of the liturgical movement, but the encyclical was as minimally effective in many parts of the Church as the social encyclicals. It was followed the next year by the creation of a papal commission on general liturgical restoration—to take up the work begun, but hardly completed, by Pope Pius X at the beginning of the twentieth century.

While the papal commission set about official liturgical reform—it resulted in the rite of the Easter Vigil (1951); the restored Holy Week (1955); and further partial reforms completed only after John XXIII became pope in 1958—a parallel, less radical development was taking place under the direction of several national conferences of bishops. This was the series of bilingual rituals to introduce limited concessions of the vernacular into some of the sacramental celebrations other than the Eucharist.

In the United States, the conference of bishops, lacking a liturgical commission, had to turn to an ad hoc committee to prepare the American *Collectio Rituum* (1954), as the Latin-English ritual was called. Similarly, other issues were considered by the conference of bishops during the 1950s: the possible shortening of the Rite for the Dedication of a Church (actually a matter being worked on by the Roman commission); the use of a shorter profession of faith for the "reception of converts"; the celebration of the feast of Saint Joseph the Worker on Labor Day rather than on May 1; a "practical ceremony" for giving Holy Communion to the sick in Catholic hospitals, and the like.

A proposal different from this ad hoc approach was formally submitted to the bishops in 1957, namely, to create a national episcopal liturgical commission. The proposal was partly influenced by the increased number of canonical issues affecting the liturgy that had been brought before the assembly of bishops, partly (and more broadly) by the swelling but still small liturgical movement in the country at large.

Today, it is hard to estimate the impact of the liturgical movement or apostolate in the eyes of the bishops in the late 1950s. Rubrical aberrations and proposals of reform, especially the use of the vernacular, were viewed by many with great suspicion—and the efforts at liturgical participation and catechesis were not universally welcome by any means. Even the proportions of the movement itself are hard to estimate.

What was being said in the principal liturgical journal *Orate, fratres* (later *Worship*) was of high quality in scholarship and pastoral good sense. The same was true of the annual *Proceedings* of the Liturgical Weeks already mentioned. But, widespread impact was lacking, for example, even when the official Roman decree on the revised Holy Week was issued—although The Liturgical Conference, the Liturgical Press at Collegeville, and the University of Notre Dame's liturgical studies program made valiant efforts at catechesis and preparation for its first celebration in 1956. Very few American bishops, for another example, were among the American delegates at the International Liturgical Congress at Assisi and Rome that same year. In some ways, like the North American Liturgical Weeks, the congress was under the auspices of European liturgical scholars and promoters but was presided over by the prefect of the Roman Congregation of Rites and climaxed by a papal address.

Certainly, some of the bishops were themselves deeply involved in the liturgical movement, and others were truly interested. Thus, at the "Thirty-Ninth Annual Meeting of the Bishops of the United States" the proposal of a liturgical commission was readily accepted. On November 14, 1957, Bishop Leo Dworshak (auxiliary to the Bishop of Fargo) moved and Archbishop William Brady (Saint Paul and Minneapolis) seconded a motion "that a committee be appointed to study the competence of a liturgical commission should one be appointed by the bishops and a report of this committee be made at next year's meeting."

The motion passed, and Cardinal Edward Mooney (Detroit)—in the chair as the senior member of the hierarchy present—designated Archbishop Karl Alter (Cincinnati) as chairman of the committee, with Archbishop Brady and Bishop Dworshak as the other members. On the same day, without direct reference to this action, the conference dealt with other liturgical matters: It authorized a second edition of the *Collectio Rituum*; referred to the existing committee on the ritual the special question of the instruction to be given sponsors at baptism; and tabled a proposal to return the restored Easter Vigil to the early morning of Holy Saturday.

The planning committee of three bishops met on March 18, 1958, at the home of Cardinal Samuel Stritch, Archbishop of Chicago. They reviewed a thorough report on the reasons for establishing a national commission along the lines of such bodies in France, Germany, Spain, the province of Quebec in Canada, and elsewhere. The information about these commissions was elaborated in the material studied by the small group, but primary attention was paid to the papal character of the liturgical apostolate and to the need of the bishops to have information and assistance "to overcome reactionary influences, . . . to eliminate abuses, . . . to keep up with further reforms." Special reference was made, among these persuasive reasons for a commission, to the need for "a minimum of guidance and direction for the North American Liturgical Conference."

The committee chose Bishop Dworshak as secretary, and it is to him that the preparation of the extensive report and minutes is attributed. There was some discussion about the name to be recommended for the new committee. Cardinal Stritch suggested "Bishops' Commission (Committee) on the Liturgical Apostolate" when it was pointed out that in the encyclical *Mediator Dei* Pius XII had urged the setting up of diocesan commissions *ad liturgicum provehendum apostolatum*. The title "commission" was preferred because of its use in other countries; it was understood that the commission would be one of the committees of the conference of bishops itself.

The full report of the March 18 meeting was sent to the bishops the following September 10, along with the material studied by the ad hoc committee and a supplement about the experience of other countries. At the next general meeting of the bishops, on November 13, 1958, Archbishop Alter presented the committee's report formally, and it was accepted. The minutes describe the subsequent action:

> A motion was made by Archbishop Ritter that an Episcopal Committee for the Liturgical Apostolate, as outlined by the report, comprised of five archbishops and bishops with rotating membership be established. This was seconded by Archbishop Lucey and carried. The following names were proposed: Archbishop Ritter as Chairman, Archbishop William O. Brady, Bishops Waters, Dearden, Griffiths. Moved by Bishop McVinney and seconded by Bishop Russell, the motion was carried.

The function and competence of the new commission may be described from the report accepted by the bishops, but one point needs to be explained first. The great sensitivity to any possible infringement of the individual diocesan bishop's authority by the conference of bishops itself or by the NCWC secretariat, already mentioned, was carefully anticipated and forestalled in the report:

> If the body of bishops choose to create such a commission, it would have to be an agency of the American Hierarchy and responsible directly to it. Neither the NCWC nor its Administrative Board could formally enter into the picture.
>
> The charter or constitution of the National Catholic Welfare Conference excludes matters of doctrine and the liturgy from its competence. That does not, however, restrict the authority of the hierarchy as a group to create a commission on the liturgical apostolate if they so choose.

In 1958, the conference of bishops, as such, had neither an Administrative Committee nor an Executive Committee as it would later under the statutes of the National Conference of Catholic Bishops. The concern in 1958 was to exclude the NCWC from any role in liturgical matters and, as was made clear in the description of the new commission's competence that is quoted below, to deny any binding authority to the new commission itself or to the conference of bishops. In 1958, it was understood or supposed that conferences of bishops lacked any canonical power; in any event, the resolution of the question would have to await the decrees of the Second Vatican Council in 1963 and 1965, which recognized such power.

Two sections of the report would govern the responsibilities of the commission until the enactment of the *Constitution on the Liturgy* in 1963. The following is under the heading, "The Function of the Commission (Committee)":

1. To report to the bishops on all directives of the Holy See concerning the liturgy. Such reports would consist of the original text, a good English version and an analysis of the directive.

2. To remain on the alert for and report to the bishops decisions concerning the liturgy handed down by the SRC [Congregation of Sacred Rites] or other congregations, which are not published in the *Acta Apostolicae Sedis* but which have significance for the dioceses in the United States.

3. At the direction and on behalf of the hierarchy, to prepare and submit to the Holy See petitions for privileges, faculties, etc., which might have general application in all dioceses of the country, subject, obviously, to the final decision of the local ordinary.

4. To consider various practical matters, such as the dialogue Mass, etc., with a view to developing greater uniformity of practice and providing some protection against variations or abuses that might creep in through the imprudence of some, excessive zeal of others, or simple lack of direction on the part of the hierarchy. Gradually, as the pattern of its activities is established, the Commission could render great service in the cause of promoting the liturgical reform instituted by the Holy See.

5. If a Commission is established, one may well anticipate that an office or bureau of some kind would soon become a necessity. This would likely also involve a Roman contact to obtain and to send quickly to the Chairman of this Commission copies of important documents pertaining to the liturgy, decisions of the SRC, etc.

6. The Commission, if established, should have the power to designate one of its members, preferably the Chairman, to serve as "Episcopal Adviser" to the North American Liturgical Conference. The function of the "Episcopal Adviser" would be: (a) to remain in close contact with the activities and programs of the Conference; (b) to attend the meetings of the board of directors of the Conference; (c) to report to the bishops at their annual meeting all important developments within the Conference.

By hindsight, it is possible to see that the planning committee was not prepared for the breadth and depth of the impending liturgical reforms, perhaps not even those of 1960 (the simplified code of rubrics of missal and breviary) and 1962 (the rite of adult baptism according to the stages of the catechumenate, as well as the revised second part of the *Roman Pontifical*). Nor would the new commission itself have the immediate capacity to support liturgical changes with analyses and studies. Yet, the mandate was realistic and, as will be suggested below, was carefully fulfilled.

Another section of the 1958 report that should be quoted in full is headed "The Competence of the Commission (Committee)." It reveals the hesitations and even suspicions that the ad hoc committee felt had to be addressed:

1) The Commission would be strictly an agency to render service

to the bishops. The scope of its activities would be determined by the bishops at the annual meeting. Its relationship to other agencies of the NCWC and the American Hierarchy would also be defined at the annual meeting if any question arose on that point.

2) Under no circumstances would any report, recommendation, study, or document of any kind prepared by the Commission and distributed to the bishops have any binding force upon any ordinary or upon any person under the jurisdiction of such ordinary, even if the document had been unanimously approved by the bishops at an annual meeting. Such matters would have only such validity in a given diocese as would be determined by the ordinary.

3) Within the scope of the program outlined by the bishops at the annual meeting, individual bishops would be free to call upon the Commission for assistance in promoting the liturgical apostolate in their respective jurisdictions.

First Years of the Liturgical Commission

Under successive chairmen, beginning with Archbishop Joseph Ritter of St. Louis, the ordinary work of the new commission was carried on largely by the secretary, Bishop James H. Griffiths, auxiliary to Cardinal Francis Spellman in the latter's capacity as military vicar. The NCWC provided the commission with limited administrative support, but throughout this period, it was Bishop Griffiths who pursued the routine responsibilities of the commission until his death on February 24, 1964. Along with successive chairmen, he was faithful in participating in meetings of The Liturgical Conference; in effect, he was the adviser mentioned in the commission's charter.

In the first year after its establishment, the pattern of functions described in the founding report was followed by the commission. The extent of promotional activity, as this would be later understood, was very limited. It often involved only giving encouragement to the setting up of diocesan liturgical commissions and offering counsel to bishops on an individual basis. (Although the diocesan commissions were strongly recommended by Pope Pius XII in 1947 and required by the Holy See in 1958, they did not become widespread in anything more than a formal way until the mid-1960s.)

What may be called the canonical tasks of the commission included the preparation of (Latin) liturgical texts in accord with the 1960 code of rubrics for feasts proper to the particular calendar of the United States, as well as the control and licensing of material from the *Collectio Rituum*— a responsibility that devolved upon the commission after the ad hoc committee completed its work on the second edition. There were also various specific questions to be submitted to the plenary meetings of the bishops: the celebration of funeral Masses on certain excluded days; the transfer of the major observance or "external solemnity" of certain important feasts to Sundays; the recommended extension to hospital chaplains of the faculty to confirm; and the like.

In November 1959, Archbishop Ritter reported to the bishops on the implications of the Roman instruction on music and the liturgy, which had appeared on September 3 of the preceding year; it had been the object of study and discussion at the Liturgical Week held in August 1959 at the University of Notre Dame. He reported also on the good relationship that had been established with The Liturgical Conference at that time, and he then proposed to have only a one-year term on the commission so as to begin the rotation of membership.

Archbishop Ritter was succeeded as chairman by Archbishop John F. Dearden of Detroit. In November 1960, he was able to report to the bishops about Bishop Griffiths' efforts to stimulate the activity of diocesan commissions and to explain the responsibilities of the episcopate in light of the simplified code of rubrics just promulgated by Pope John XXIII. In particular, he reminded the bishops that the principles of general liturgical restoration had been explicitly proposed by the pope as part of the agenda of the forthcoming council. At this point, too, the commission was moving toward the enlistment of a number of liturgical scholars as its advisers.

Archbishop Dearden was followed as chairman for the next two years by Cardinal Albert Meyer, archbishop of Chicago, who had earlier chaired the committee on the Latin-English *Collectio Rituum*. At the last preconciliar meeting of the conference of bishops, in November 1961, Bishop Griffiths reported. By this time, the role of the commission was clear: it had initiated plans for the liturgical feast days proper to the United States; issues raised by individual bishops concerning liturgical regulations were regularly referred to it. And, the commission had the task of making a survey concerning liturgical progress in the dioceses; the survey had been suggested by the Cardinal Secretary of State for the benefit of the council.

The Bishops' Commission on the Liturgical Apostolate did not have a role in the preparation of the *Constitution on the Liturgy*, but the chairman of the 1957 committee that laid the plans for the commission, Archbishop Alter of Cincinnati, was a member of the Central Preparatory Commission. In the spring of 1962, he participated in that commission's meeting in Rome when it reviewed the final draft of the constitution that had been drawn up by the Preparatory Commission on the Liturgy.

During the years of the Second Vatican Council, 1962–1965, the November general meetings of the bishops were held in Rome. Archbishop Dearden returned to the chairmanship of the liturgical commission in November 1963 and held that position for the next three years, covering the period of immediate implementation of the liturgical constitution and of the establishment of a secretariat of the commission, as had been envisioned in 1958.

During the second period of the council, in the fall of 1963, as the *Constitution on the Liturgy* was nearing completion, the Bishops' Commission on the Liturgical Apostolate made plans for its implementation in the United States. Archbishop Paul Hallinan of Atlanta was a member of the Conciliar Commission on the Liturgy and chairman of its subcommittee on the sacraments other than the Eucharist (Chapter III of the constitution). He was added to the membership of the American commission, and on November 16, at the general meeting of the conference, he reported several proposals from the commission.

These recommendations were that the bishops of the United States "agree to avail themselves of the vernacular concessions" made by the council—approved by vote of 130 to 5; authorize the commission "to prepare translations for interim use"—approved 127 to 7; and authorize the United States representatives in the recently established international committee (Hallinan and Griffiths) "to work with the bishops of nine other English-speaking nations in preparing a long-range, definitive liturgical text that will win acceptance in the English-speaking world"—approved 126 to 3. It was also agreed to hold a special meeting of the episcopate on the subject of the liturgy in the following spring.

Thus, with a unanimity comparable to that of the conciliar fathers' approval of the *Constitution on the Liturgy* two weeks later (by vote of 2147 to 4), the conference of bishops set in motion the introduction of the liturgical vernacular in the American dioceses. In the following April, after a preparatory meeting of the commission at Archbishop Dearden's home in Detroit, the conference held the special plenary assembly in Washington to enact formal decrees concerning the use of the vernacular and the interim English texts for the Mass and the sacraments, for the divine office and other rites. With the exception of the Mass, in which the vernacular was still severely limited, the concessions were comprehensive, and the conference formally entrusted the commission with the "examination and control" of the liturgical books, by decree of April 2, 1964. This has been a major responsibility of the commission ever since. Along with the preparation of decrees and documentation for the conference, it has occupied as much of the commission's efforts as its promotional and catechetical activity.

The introduction of the vernacular into the Roman liturgy was only a first step in the reform that had been mandated by the Second Vatican Council, but it increased several times over the regular responsibilities of the commission. In 1964, The Liturgical Conference provided administrative assistance to the commission in the preparation of the first post-conciliar liturgical books. Then, at the recommendation of Archbishop Dearden and under his direction, a secretariat for the commission was established in 1965. In the meantime, after the death of Bishop Griffiths, Archbishop Hallinan had succeeded to the position of secretary of the commission in August 1964.

Just as important as some of these more concrete developments was the redefinition of the commission's competence in the *Constitution on the Liturgy* and later in the Roman instruction of implementation of 1964. In treating the "promotion of pastoral-liturgical action," the constitution urged the creation of national and regional liturgical commissions (art. 44):

It is advisable that the competent, territorial ecclesiastical authority mentioned in art. 22, §2 [i.e., the conference of bishops or councils] set up a liturgical commission, to be assisted by experts in liturgical science, music, art, and pastoral practice. As far as possible, the commission should be aided by some kind of institute for pastoral liturgy, consisting of persons eminent in these matters and including the laity as circumstances suggest. Under the direction of the aforementioned territorial ecclesiastical authority, the commission is to regulate pastoral-liturgical action throughout the territory and to promote studies and necessary experiments whenever there is question of adaptations to be proposed to the Apostolic See.

The recommendation of the Second Vatican Council was further refined in the first Roman instruction of implementation—along with an interim determination of the procedures to be followed by conferences of bishops in making decisions in liturgical matters. The document, *Inter Oecumenici* of September 26, 1964, provided under the heading "Liturgical Commission of the Assembly of Bishops":

44. The liturgical commission, which should be expeditiously established by the territorial authority, shall as far as possible be chosen from among the bishops themselves or at least include one of them, along with priests expert in liturgical and pastoral matters and designated by name for this office.

The members and consultants of the commission should ideally meet several times a year to deal with issues as a group.

45. The territorial authority may properly entrust the following to the commission:

a. to carry out studies and experiments in keeping with the norms of the *Constitution,* art. 40, §§1 and 2;

b. to further practical initiatives for the whole region that will foster liturgical life and the application of the *Constitution on the Liturgy;*

c. to prepare studies and resources required as a result of decrees of the plenary assembly of the bishops;

d. to control pastoral liturgy in the whole nation, to see to the application of decrees of the plenary assembly, and to report on these matters to the assembly;

e. to further frequent consultation and promote collaboration with regional associations involved with Scripture, catechetics, pastoral care, music, and art, as well as with every kind of lay religious association.

46. Members of the institute of pastoral liturgy, as well as experts called to assist the liturgical commission, shall be generous in aiding individual bishops to promote pastoral-liturgical activity more effectively in their territory.

A word or two of comment is needed to explain the application of some of the terms of these conciliar and curial texts to the American liturgical commission, before completing this account of its first years.

First, the composition of the Bishops' Commission on the Liturgical Apostolate was from the beginning exclusively episcopal, unlike the possibility envisioned in the Roman instruction as an alternative, namely, a commission with nonbishop members perhaps in the majority. The commission subsequently conformed to the structural pattern of standing committees under the NCCB statutes of 1966 and later years: instead of a designation of the full commission by the conference of bishops, with the elected members then choosing the chairman (the original procedure), only the chairman was to be elected by the conference for a three-year term, and then he was to choose, to a limit of six, the other members, also for three-year terms. The structure did permit the addition of consultant-bishops—and it became customary to add under this formality the NCCB representative on the governing or episcopal committee of the International Committee (later "Commission") on English in the Liturgy—as well as the other advisers in liturgical and pastoral matters.

Next, both the *Constitution on the Liturgy* and the Roman instruction spoke of a pastoral-liturgical institute of specialists and scholars working with the national liturgical commission. This proposal derived from the successful experiences of the French and German episcopates with such institutes or centers in Paris and Trier, respectively. In later years, there were occasional proposals to set up that kind of adjunct pastoral-liturgical institute in the United States or even a department of worship within the United States Catholic Conference. In practice, however, rather than sponsoring or creating an institute, the commission turned to advisers and individual specialists drawn from the academic programs at the University of Notre Dame and The Catholic University of America and from diocesan commissions and departments of worship; to the private resources of voluntary associations and publishing houses; and to other independent centers, especially the Notre Dame Center for Pastoral Liturgy.

Finally, in the matter of studies looking to major liturgical adaptation, the commission took its responsibility seriously enough, but the conference of bishops did not succeed in obtaining faculties from the Apostolic See to experiment in any substantive way, either at centers of research or elsewhere. The commission did supervise experiments on behalf of the Roman Consilium of Implementation and, thus, contributed to the development of the reformed rites for funerals, Christian initiation of adults, etc.

It is fair to say that the work of the commission in succeeding years satisfied the expectation of the documents quoted, although it has never undertaken "to control pastoral liturgy in the whole nation." In the concrete, the principal change that followed the conciliar constitution was not in the commission itself but in the creation of a secretariat, housed in Washington, D.C. with the NCWC. This was set up by Archbishop Dearden in January 1965, parallel to the secretariat of the new ecumenical commission, later called the Bishops' Committee on Ecumenical and Interreligious Affairs.

The new secretariat was able to carry the efforts of the commission beyond the now extensive matters of preparing documentation for the bishops and supervising the new vernacular liturgical books. Archbishop Dearden planned at once the initiation of a monthly *Newsletter,* which was directed in the first place to bishops and diocesan commissions but was available more broadly. From this point on, the *Newsletter* provides a detailed chronicle of the work of the commission. Now collected and reprinted in three volumes (1965–1975; 1976–1980; 1981–1985), it is a contemporaneous record of the activities of the commission and its secretariat. It lacks, of course, the background material submitted to the bishops each time a formal decision was to be made and the analyses and information prepared, again in the first instance, for the bishops and the commissions. This latter activity eventually developed into substantial publications of liturgical catechesis and commentary, such as the later *Study Texts* Series listed at the end of this introduction.

In May of 1965, the first steps were taken by the commission toward a structure of subcommittees. Archbishop Dearden chaired, on behalf of the commission, the first meeting of the Music Advisory Board held in Detroit May 4–5. From this developed not only the extensive work of the board in the preparation of music for the new liturgical books for the United States, but also a pattern of subcommittees such as those on liturgical adaptation and, in later years, on black and Hispanic liturgies.

Also in May 1965, the secretary, Archbishop Hallinan, formally sought the assistance of The Liturgical Conference on two projects: catechesis for the reception of communion under both kinds and formats for the general intercessions. This was the occasion for him to delineate the positive role of the pioneering society, which the commission praised warmly, while insisting on an official role reserved, at the national level, to the episcopal commission.

It was clearly a delicate matter. Eighteen months before, for example, at the general meeting of the bishops in November 1964, one bishop had strongly challenged The Liturgical Conference on grounds of impracticality and inexperience. Archbishop Dearden responded that the organization was distinct from the commission and that no official liaison existed between the two. Archbishop Hallinan's letter (written at the direction of the commission) tried, on the one hand, to leave "the whole area of creative liturgical discussion to the [Liturgical] Conference . . . for a healthy expression of opinion. . . ." On the other hand, he proposed to free the organization from "the burden of interpretation, thus avoiding the hazard of two distinct sources of authority [the official commission and the private society] in liturgical matters."

This, too, provided a pattern for the relationship of the commission to other societies and organizations, and even to centers of liturgical research—which it later recognized formally and encouraged without official sponsorship. The Liturgical Conference and the Liturgical Weeks continued to provide a place for annual information meetings held by the commission with members of diocesan commissions. When the Liturgical Weeks ceased, The Liturgical Conference dedicated more of its efforts to important publication programs, including the journal *Liturgy*, which is still an effective organ of high quality. The commission then began to co-sponsor meetings of diocesan commission members together with the new Federation of Diocesan Liturgical Commissions.

The interaction of the commission and its secretariat with other committees of the NCCB and the departments of the USCC—just as with the official diocesan commissions—clearly differs from the relationship with all kinds of other bodies and groups, whether educational or promotional, in the liturgical field, or indeed with the committees of worship of other churches and ecclesial communities. The relationship with the International Committee (later "Commission") on English in the Liturgy was also altogether different. The formal decision taken by the conference of bishops in November 1963, only a month after ICEL was established, has been quoted above. It provided the American commission with the services of a joint commission shared by the other founding members of ICEL, the principal conferences of bishops of the countries where English is spoken. The relationship was enhanced from the beginning by the role played by Archbishop Hallinan, one of the founders of ICEL.

Archbishop Dearden set the direction and policies for the new secretariat and, in fact, guided the work of the commission until November 1966. He was then elected president of the National Conference of Catholic Bishops and was succeeded as chairman of the commission by Archbishop Hallinan, who was elected to that position under the new NCCB statutes on November 17, 1966. The two had worked together closely—both were priests of the diocese of Cleveland—and their collaboration constituted a second beginning of the Bishops' Commission on the Liturgical Apostolate, called Bishops' Committee on the Liturgy after February 1967.

At this point, the early history of the commission may be broken off. It may be picked up in detail in the issues of the *Newsletter* and, even better so far as major contributions are concerned, in the statements and similar documents issued over the years from 1963 to the present.

The Statements and the Commentaries

As already suggested, the collected statements are diverse in character. They are long and short, official and unofficial, topical and theoretical, simple and complex. Necessarily, those reprinted in this volume are selected from a larger quantity of material—although all the formal statements are included, except a couple of very lengthy documents published separately and still in print, principally *Music in Catholic Worship* (1972; revised 1983) and *Environment and Art in Catholic Worship* (1978).

As collected here, the statements appear chronologically and in their original form, apart from the correction of evident typographical errors. After the indication of an individual document's precise source and date, a cross-reference to other statements on the same topic is given for convenience. A general index at the end covers the documents and the accompanying commentaries.

The commentaries that introduce each statement or document have several purposes. As is apparent, some commentaries are very brief, some lengthy—this having little to do with the significance of the document. Instead, an effort has been made first to situate the statement in the immediate and necessary context in order to offer an explanatory introduction and, perhaps, to point out the principal features and sometimes limitations. Equally, the commentaries place the individual statements in a broader context of liturgical reform and renewal—sometimes to fill in the gaps, to bring the matter or issue up-to-date, or to illustrate the relation of the American commission's work to the general reform of the Roman liturgy.

Reference to the general liturgical reform leads to another point. Much of the activity of the Bishops' Committee on the Liturgy has been properly tied to the issuance of successive liturgical books of the Roman rite and the review of the English translations submitted to the NCCB by the International Commission on English in the Liturgy. The story of these can be best followed in the journal *Notitiae*, founded as a publication of the Consilium for the Implementation of the *Constitution on the Liturgy* and now published by the Congregation for Divine Worship. Even better, the account given in the volume *La riforma liturgica (1948–1975)* by Annibale Bugnini, referred to in the commentaries, traces the Roman enterprise with great thoroughness, ritual book by ritual book. And, each Roman liturgical book has its corresponding English version prepared, in turn, by ICEL first in a provisional text and then in a definitive text; each version is submitted to the NCCB by the Bishops' Committee on the Liturgy. A guide to this sequence of official liturgical texts, first in Latin and then in English, is given in the committee's *Ritual Revision: A Status Report* (Washington, D.C.: USCC Office of Publishing and Promotion Services, 1981).

Footnotes and other apparatus have been avoided in the commentaries, and the references to other documentation have been kept to a minimum. All the quoted Roman documents are taken from the English translation prepared by ICEL and collected in *Documents on the Liturgy 1963–1979: Conciliar, Papal, and Curial Texts* (Collegeville, Minn.: Liturgical Press, 1982); they are used by permission. Such documents are cited by "DOL," together with the number of the individual document as found among the 554 texts collected in that volume. The *Constitution on the Liturgy (Sacrosanctum Concilium)*, decreed on December 4, 1963, by the Second Vatican Council, has been referred to throughout as "SC," together with the number of the article of the constitution. The English translation of the constitution is also from DOL, in which it is document no. 1.

The commentaries reflect many judgments about the significant elements in the statements as well as judgments of the surrounding events—the successes and the failures, the progress and, at times, regression of the liturgical renewal. The statements can and should speak for themselves, but—as is said often—they do demonstrate breadth and foresight.

One must not look for liturgical creativity in the statements. Not unlike the Second Vatican Council in the *Constitution on the Liturgy*, the Bishops' Committee on the Liturgy explains and exhorts and, even when cautionary in tone, remains completely open to desirable creativity and growth, which can be guided but cannot be fashioned by authority. The statements mirror a fresh life and vigor in the Roman liturgy celebrated in the local churches of the United States, in fact a life and vigor to which the Bishops' Committee on the Liturgy has made its own distinctive contribution over a period of three decades.

Frederick R. McManus
Editor

Bishops' Committee on the Liturgy: 1958–1987

Chairmen (Committee)

Joseph E. Ritter
  Archbishop of St. Louis   1958–1959

John F. Dearden
  Archbishop of Detroit   1959–1960

Albert Cardinal Meyer
  Archbishop of Chicago   1960–1963

John F. Dearden
  Archbishop of Detroit   1963–1966

Paul J. Hallinan
  Archbishop of Atlanta   1966–1968

Leo C. Byrne
  Coadjutor Archbishop of St. Paul-Minneapolis   1968–1969

James W. Malone
  Bishop of Youngstown   1969–1972

Walter W. Curtis
  Bishop of Bridgeport   1972–1975

John R. Quinn
  Archbishop of Oklahoma City   1975–1977

Rene H. Gracida
  Bishop of Pensacola-Tallahassee   1977–1978

Rembert G. Weakland, OSB
  Archbishop of Milwaukee   1978–1981

John S. Cummins
  Bishop of Oakland   1981–1984

Daniel E. Pilarczyk
  Archbishop of Cincinnati   1984–1986

Joseph P. Delaney
  Bishop of Fort Worth   1986–

Secretaries (Committee)

James H. Griffiths
    Auxiliary Bishop to Military Vicar   1958–1964

Paul J. Hallinan
    Archbishop of Atlanta   1964–1966

Executive Directors (Secretariat)

    Frederick R. McManus   1965–1975

    John E. Rotelle, OSA   1975–1978

    Thomas A. Krosnicki, SVD   1978–1981

    John A. Gurrieri   1981–

Associate Directors (Secretariat)

    Joseph M. Champlin   1968–1971

    John E. Rotelle, OSA   1970–1975

    Thomas A. Krosnicki, SVD   1972–1978

    John A. Gurrieri   1978–1981

    Ronald F. Krisman   1981–

    Alan F. Detscher   1987–

Administrative Assistant (Secretariat)

    Luanne Durst, FSPA   1976–1980

Staff Consultants

    Frederick R. McManus   1975–

    Alan F. Detscher   1986–1987

Publications of the Bishops' Committee on the Liturgy

Study Text Series

1. *Holy Communion* (under revision)

2. *Pastoral Care of the Sick and Dying* (revised 1984)

3. *Ministries in the Church* (1974)

4. *Rite of Penance* (1975)

5. *Eucharistic Concelebration* (1978)

6. *The Deacon: Minister of Word and Sacrament* (under revision)

7. *The Liturgy of the Hours* (1981)

8. *Proclaim the Word: The Lectionary for Mass* (1982)

9. *The Liturgical Year: Celebrating the Mystery of Christ and His Saints* (1985)

10. *Christian Initiation of Adults: A Commentary* (1985)

11. *Eucharistic Worship and Devotion outside Mass* (1987)

Liturgy Documentary Series

1. *Lectionary for Mass: Introduction* (1982)

2. *General Instruction of the Roman Missal* (1982)

3. *Pastoral Care of the Sick: Introduction and Pastoral Notes* (1983)

4. *Christian Initiation of Adults* (1983)

5. *General Instruction of the Liturgy of the Hours* (1983)

6. *Norms Governing Liturgical Calendars* (1984)

7. *Penance and Reconciliation in the Church* (1986)

BCL Reports Series

1. *Directory for Masses with Children* (1980)

2. *Ritual Revision: A Status Report* (1981)

Other Publications

Music in Catholic Worship (1972; revised 1983)

Bishops' Committee on the Liturgy Newsletter 1965–1975 (1976; out of print)

Environment and Art in Catholic Worship (1978)

The Cathedral: A Reader (1979)

The Environment for Worship: A Reader (1980)

Bishops' Committee on the Liturgy Newsletter 1976–1980 (1981)

Liturgical Music Today (1982)

Holy Days in the United States: History, Theology, Celebration (1984)

Liturgical Formation in Seminaries: A Commentary (1984)

This Holy and Living Sacrifice: Directory for the Celebration and Reception of Communion under Both Kinds (1985)

Bishops' Committee on the Liturgy Newsletter 1981–1985 (1986)

The Bishop and the Liturgy: Highlights of the New Ceremonial of Bishops (1986)

1

Liturgical Constitution and the Vernacular in the United States

Statement, Bishops' Commission on the Liturgical
Apostolate
Rome, December 4, 1963

(See also nos. 2, 5, 13, 16, 32, 35)

During the first two periods of the Second Vatican Council, in the fall of 1962 and of 1963, not many bishops of the United States took an active role in the refinement and development of the council's first document, the *Constitution on the Liturgy,* which goes by the name of *Sacrosanctum Concilium.* Fewer than a dozen American bishops spoke during the conciliar debate, which lasted three weeks in 1962; no more than that number submitted written interventions.

Nevertheless, the welcome to the conciliar constitution, expressed in this statement of the American commission, was genuine. The vast majority of the bishops of the United States warmly, even enthusiastically, supported the document as it moved from draft to emended text to supplementary amendments to final decree of the council, approved by 2147 votes to 4 on December 4, 1963.

Among those who had spoken in favor of the constitution were Cardinal Joseph Ritter of St. Louis, the first chairman of the American liturgical commission; Bishop Victor Reed of Oklahoma City-Tulsa, a commission member at the time; and Archbishop Paul J. Hallinan of Atlanta. The role of the latter, at whose insistence the statement was issued to coincide with the constitution's promulgation, was of greatest significance.

In the preparatory period before the council, from 1960 to 1962, three Americans, none of them bishops, had served on the drafting commission: Joannes Quasten and Frederick McManus of The Catholic University of America and Godfrey Diekmann of Saint John's Abbey, Collegeville, editor of *Orate, Fratres,* later *Worship.* During the first days of the council itself, which began on October 11, 1962, the national episcopates had the opportunity to propose candidates for membership on the conciliar commissions—after an initial dramatic rejection of the planned procedure of election. For the council's liturgical commission, the American conference of bishops nominated Archbishop Hallinan, already known for his involvement in the liturgical movement, and Bishop Leo Dworshak of Fargo, who had been the secretary of the 1957–1958 committee that made the plans for the establishment of the American commission. Hallinan was then elected by the fathers of the council to the Conciliar Commission on the Liturgy.

21

Within that commission, Hallinan played an important role, chairing the Subcommission on Chapter III (about the sacraments other than the Eucharist) and reporting to the full council on that part of the draft. Outside the conciliar commission, he played an equally important role, reporting regularly to the American bishops at their study meetings, keeping them informed of progress or lack of progress. In view of this, he was named a member of the Bishops' Commission on the Liturgical Apostolate and was largely responsible for the statement issued on December 4 as a press release.

At the same time, with the sponsorship of Archbishop Hallinan, an English version of the *Constitution on the Liturgy* was readied, with the collaboration of the American *periti* of the conciliar commission. Thus, the text was available on the day of promulgation for the wire services and the media in general; it was published immediately, for example, in the *New York Times*.

The statement, which lists the membership of the American liturgical commission at the time, deals realistically and pastorally with the constitution as a whole and with the vernacular in particular—since vernacular in the liturgy was the most evident and striking feature of the document for the Catholic community. It also took the occasion to repeat what had been announced only six weeks before: the formation of a joint commission of bishops' conferences of countries where English is spoken.

This joint commission, known as the International Commission on English in the Liturgy or simply as ICEL, had its beginnings in 1962 in the discussions of Archbishop Hallinan and a few other bishops, principally Archbishops Denis Hurley of Durban (South Africa), Guilford Young of Hobart (Australia), and Francis Grimshaw of Birmingham (England and Wales), who was the first chairman. In 1963, the body was formally constituted by mandate of ten national conferences, which designated their episcopal representatives—from the United States, Archbishop Hallinan and Bishop James Griffiths, auxiliary of the military ordinariat and then secretary of the American liturgical commission. The story has been told in *ICEL: The First Years* (Washington, D.C.: ICEL, 1981).

This development is the reason why the statement welcoming the *Constitution on the Liturgy* goes on directly to the matter of vernacular texts and explains how a whole international program would be undertaken to achieve a language worthy of the spoken and sung liturgy.

Again, this is the reason why the members of the initial ICEL governing body, the episcopal committee (later called the episcopal board), are listed at the end of the statement. A quarter of a century later, ICEL retains its relationship with the national liturgical commissions of the participating countries, submitting translated and original liturgical texts in English for the individual conferences to review and consider for official approbation.

The *Constitution on the Sacred Liturgy*, promulgated on December 4, is the first achievement of Vatican Council II. It will affect the spiritual life of prayer and worship of all Catholics; it will make the Church more comprehensible to all men. Thus, it is the first great step in the Church's inner renewal, begun by Pope John XXIII and now being carried out by all the bishops in union with the chief bishop, Pope Paul VI.

The bishops of the United States, having taken part fully in the discussion, amendment, and acceptance of this document, welcome it wholeheartedly and dedicate themselves to fulfill its purposes.

On the one hand, the constitution is a statement of the Church's doctrine and discipline. It explains the meaning of public worship. It gives a clear mandate to deepen the liturgical understanding and activity of the people: "This full and active participation by all the people is the aim to be considered before all else."

At the same time, the constitution is a document of change and revision. In broad terms, it directs a reform of rites and texts so that they may be simpler and clearer. Putting such changes into effect must await specific action by a commission set up by the Holy Father.

One important change, however, has become the immediate concern of the bodies of bishops in the different countries or regions. This is the concession of the vernacular languages in the liturgy for the sake of the people's understanding, piety, and easier participation.

Such concessions are possible without waiting for the revision of rites but depend upon the action of the bodies of bishops for the respective regions. For the Mass, the council has allowed the vernacular for the lessons and for the parts of the people; in effect, for most of the parts said aloud or sung up to the canon, and for such parts as the Sanctus, Our Father, etc. For the sacraments and sacramentals, the vernacular is allowed throughout. For the divine office, the clergy must receive permission from the individual bishops or ordinaries.

The bishops of the United States assembled in Rome have formally agreed to make full use of the vernacular concessions made by the council. They have directed the Bishops' Commission on the Liturgical Apostolate to propose English translations for the consideration of all the bishops. At a meeting of the bishops, now proposed for the spring of 1964, formal decrees will be drawn up and sent to the Apostolic See in Rome for confirmation. At the same time, official translations will be approved by the bishops for publication. Only then can a date be determined by the bishops for the actual use of English in the liturgy.

This prompt action ensures the introduction of English into public worship during the interim period while the revision of the missal, ritual, breviary, etc., is awaited. In addition, the bishops of the United States authorized their representatives to work with an international committee; this committee will ultimately propose translations based upon the reformed rites for the consideration of the respective hierarchies of the English-speaking world.

Members of U.S. Bishops' Commission on the Liturgical Apostolate

Archbishop John F. Dearden, Detroit
Archbishop Paul J. Hallinan, Atlanta
Bishop James H. Griffiths, New York
Bishop Vincent S. Waters, Raleigh, N.C.
Bishop Victor J. Reed, Oklahoma City-Tulsa

Members of the International Committee on Common English Text*

Archbishop Francis Grimshaw, Birmingham, England, Chairman
Archbishop Guilford Young, Hobart, Tasmania, Australia, Vice-Chairman
Archbishop Paul J. Hallinan, Atlanta, U.S.A., Vice-Chairman
Archbishop Denis E. Hurley, Durban, South Africa
Archbishop Gordon Gray, Edinburgh, Scotland
Archbishop Joseph Walsh, Tuam, Ireland
Archbishop Michael O'Neill, Regina, Canada
Bishop James H. Griffiths, New York, U.S.A.
Bishop Leonard Raymond, Allahabad, India
Bishop Owen Snedden, Wellington, New Zealand

---

* Editor's Note: This was the name used by the founding episcopal committe of ICEL.

2

The Use of the Vernacular at Mass

Statement, Bishops' Commission on the Liturgical Apostolate
November 1964

(See also nos. 1, 5, 13, 16, 32, 35)

This document has three parts, only the first two of which are reprinted here. Part III, entitled "Extent of Liturgical Use of English," gives a detailed enumeration of the parts of the liturgy permitted in the dioceses of the United States in the first stage of this development in 1964. A decree had been passed by the conference of bishops, meeting in Washington on April 2, 1964, and confirmed on May 1, 1964, by the new Roman Consilium for the Implementation of the Constitution on the Liturgy.

The specifics of this first, limited concession are no longer of great interest. In the case of the eucharistic rite, a kind of hybrid celebration was determined. It respected the hesitant concessions made in the *Constitution on the Liturgy* (SC 36, 54): English was permitted for the ordinary and proper chants, the readings, and the Lord's Prayer; Latin was retained for the presidential prayers, including the canon or eucharistic prayer, as well as the prayers at the foot of the altar and the last gospel (still recited at that time) and the silent prayers of the priest.

For these initial concessions of the vernacular in the Mass, the American conference of bishops approved English versions: for the ordinary chants and the responses, a rather literal translation similar to translations found in popular missals of the day, but with contemporary language; for the Scriptures (readings and psalm chants), the "Confraternity edition," later called the *New American Bible*.

The 1963–1964 concessions in the case of the other sacraments and rites were more generous, in fact, were without any limitations (SC 63a, 101). The approved texts were those found in the 1961 *Collectio Rituum*; for the largest quantity of such texts not found in that bilingual ritual, the version of *The Roman Ritual* translated by Philip Weller was adopted. For the divine office, two existing translations were made official, one published by Benziger Brothers of New York, the other by the Liturgical Press of Collegeville, Minnesota.

Part I of the statement, "Understanding Liturgical Texts in the Vernacular," is substantive and of continuing concern. It faces up to the large problem of Catholics' lack of familiarity with the Scriptures. The context is the excessive expectations aroused by the vernacular concessions. It is worth noting that there were no false expectations on the part of the commission itself: something more than hearing the English words is needed to achieve "a great advance in meaningful participation by all the people." It is not merely "a matter of vocabulary or of remembering biblical events." Rather, a grasp of the scriptural idiom and ethos is needed, and this in the light of the biblical, catechetical, and liturgical renewals of recent decades.

In these observations, there is the unspoken realization that these biblical, catechetical, and liturgical renewals had not penetrated very deeply into the life of the Catholic clergy and people of the United States. At the same time, the exhortations are put at a twofold level: catechetical study of the Scriptures and the liturgical texts and, above all, preparation "to meet with Christ as he speaks with us through the liturgical rites and the inspired word of Scripture."

What is said in Part I of this statement is applicable enough at any moment. The direct application in November 1964 was to the celebration of the Eucharist, with the introduction of the vernacular largely limited to the readings from Scripture and the chants from the psalter.

Part II of the statement deals with "Reading and Praying in the Vernacular," conscious that priests and lay readers were not prepared for the development. This part of the statement was reissued by the commission in December 1965, when the vernacular concession had been extended by the conference of bishops to the presidential prayers and the prefaces of the eucharistic prayer (effective March 27, 1966).

Two decades later, hardly a word of the recommendations in Part II would have to be changed—aside from the failure to attend to the possibility of women as readers. Much more could be said, of course, but the immediacy of concern is evident. In 1964, the tradition of hurried reading of texts in Latin needed to be corrected. Even a point is made of reading the Latin of the eucharistic prayer, still not permitted in the vernacular, in a loud, clear, and measured tone. This had been demanded by the old rubrical directions but had been easily neglected when even the best enunciation of the Latin words would be unintelligible. The vernacular development was revolutionary enough; it had to be matched by a revolutionary approach to the spoken word in celebration.

Like many of the statements collected, this one is beyond challenge or question; some elements of it are just prosaic common sense. It is one of many illustrations of the deep-seated problem, still present in the 1980s, of authentic celebration. Unhappily, there are still uninformed and unintelligible readers. Unhappily, there are still presiding celebrants who proclaim the prayers in hurried and unintelligible fashion. The cynic would say that statements from official bodies are useless; they too will go unheard. The more optimistic will hope that the very ordinary comments of the commission, at the very beginning of the vernacular development, could be repeated now for every reader, every priest.

I. Understanding Liturgical Texts in the Vernacular

The *Constitution on the Liturgy*, issued by the Second Vatican Council, states that it is of the highest importance that the faithful understand the rites because the sacraments "not only presuppose faith but by words and objects they also nourish, strengthen, and express it"; moreover, "they do indeed impart grace, but in addition, the very act of celebrating them most effectively disposes the faithful to receive this grace in a fruitful manner, to worship God duly, and to practice charity" (59). Another basic principle taught by the constitution is that "Christ is always present in His Church, especially in her liturgical celebrations." Among the ways he is present is "in His word, since it is He Himself who speaks when the Holy Scriptures are read in the Church." He is present also "when the Church prays and sings, for He promised: 'Where two or three are gathered together in my name, there am I in the midst of them'" (7).

The widespread interest in the council and particularly in the discussions on vernacular in the liturgy have prepared the people for changes. Many are filled with hope for a great advance in meaningful participation by all the people in the sacred rites. At the same time, it is evident or will soon be evident that, beyond use of the language which the people understand, there must be developed an understanding of the "language" of the liturgy in a deeper sense. No one can find the meaning in the allusions to Abraham's bosom or to Jerusalem in the funeral rites unless he knows Abraham as our father and Jerusalem as the place of God's presence with his people, the prefiguring of the Church on earth and in heaven. We all know how necessary is a grasp of scriptural idiom to understand the Epistles. This is also necessary to appreciate the use of water, oil, bread, and wine and to know the significance of such phrases as "now and eternal covenant" and "Lamb of God." The simple phrase, "through Christ our Lord," or "through Him and with Him and in Him," expresses a direction in devotion, a union with Christ's worship of the Father that is not yet the spontaneous manner of praying among our people. The same is true of praying the psalms as Christian prayers.

Understanding the liturgy is not merely a matter of vocabulary or of remembering biblical events. Christ's earthly life followed in large part its Old Testament prefigurings and he established the basic rites of his Church on the basis of meanings already indicated in the Scriptures. He made the inspired psalms and canticles his own prayers. His great act of worship and sacrifice for mankind, "the paschal mystery" (5, 6, 47, 61, 102, 106), was intended as a new Exodus, a passing from this world to the Father, and it took place at the time of the Passover celebration.

Because of the scriptural basis of liturgical language and actions, the *Constitution on the Liturgy* provides for more extensive reading of Scripture in the liturgy and also for the integration of preaching with Scripture. It states that the sermon is part of the liturgical service and that it "should draw its content mainly from scriptural and liturgical sources, and its character should be that of a proclamation of God's wonderful works in the history of salvation, the mystery of Christ, ever made present and active within us, especially in the celebration of the liturgy" (35).

The constitution also states that bible services should be encouraged (35), which include of their nature a sermon on the texts read to the people and said or sung by them. And it states that it is essential to "promote that warm and living love for Scripture to which the venerable tradition of both eastern and western rites give testimony" (24)—a love which may be possessed by

27

the simplest as well as the most learned members of the Church, as history shows us.

Since, as the constitution states, it is now a primary pastoral duty to enable the people to take their full internal and external part in the liturgy (14, 19), it is clearly our duty to equip ourselves at once to carry out this task and to begin to carry it out among our people. Providentially, the scriptural, catechetical, and liturgical renewals of recent decades have already produced an abundance of reading matter, at many levels, which can serve to enrich our basic structure of its rites and prayers and, at the same time, help us to form our people. A brief bibliography of some basic books which serve both these purposes is included herewith.

But what is most necessary of all is that we begin, if we have not begun already, to meet with Christ as he speaks to us through the liturgical rites and the inspired word of Scripture. This should best start with the use of the primal form of Christian "mental prayer" or "meditation," traditionally known as *lectio divina*—or, as we might call it in English, "praying the Bible." This means, very simply, prayerfully "hearing," by slow meditative reading, a biblical or liturgical passage as Christ's word here and now: asking ourselves, for example, what is he telling us here about himself, about the Father, about the divine plan for our own salvation and that of our people? How does he ask us to respond to this word of God's love with him, now in our prayer and also in our life?

Such a form of meditation, especially when the passages chosen are those which the priest is to explain and open out to his people in Sunday Mass, or at a baptism or wedding or funeral, or at a bible service, will, experience shows, serve to integrate the priest's prayer-life in itself and with his work for his people as "minister of the Word." Any *study* of the liturgical texts and of sacred Scripture then serves to enrich and deepen both the priest's own prayer and worship and the sermons in which he opens out God's Word to his people.

The question, obviously, is not one of making biblical scholars either of all priests or of the faithful. It is one simply of restoring that living familiarity with Scripture and, through it, with Christ, which is our rightful inheritance.

II. Reading and Praying in the Vernacular

The introduction of the common language into liturgical rites is an event of numerous and important implications. Clearly, it was the intention of the fathers of the Second Vatican Council to provide the people with rites of sacred worship which would be meaningful and intelligible to them (36, 54, 63, 101, 113). Both those parts of the liturgy which instruct the faithful and those parts which express their prayer and devotion are to be spoken or sung in the vernacular language. This reform in our custom is intended to bring the people into more effective contact with the sacred Scripture and the holy texts of the liturgy, thereby fostering deeper faith, greater knowledge, and more sincere prayer.

But these worthy objectives will not automatically be achieved by the use of the vernacular. Such prayer and readings will have to be done in a more

28

meaningful and appropriate manner than has unfortunately been employed by some priests when reciting Latin texts. To celebrate the liturgy in a manner that is apparently hasty, matter-of-fact, and without attention to the meaning of the words would, of course, be irreverent and improper no matter what the language; however when the vernacular is used, there is the greatest possibility of scandal. These observations, which must be honestly admitted, are commonly expressed whenever the vernacular is discussed and both clergy and laity are surely anxious not only to avoid the danger but, first of all, to seek the fullest advantages the vernacular can bring. For this reason, the following comments are offered on the manner of speaking the English tongue in liturgical services, in the hope that they might serve as a guide to all. For the purposes of these remarks, there is a basic difference between reading the Word of God and reading other texts.

A. Reading the Word of God

All Scripture readings are to be proclamations, not mere recitations. Lectors and priests should approach the public reading of the Bible with full awareness that it is their honored task to render the official proclamation of the revealed Word of God to his assembled holy people. The character of this reading is such that it must convey that special reverence which is due the sacred Scriptures above all other words.

1. It is of fundamental importance that the reader communicate the fullest meaning of the passage. Without exaggerated emphasis or affectation, he must convey the particular significance of those words, phrases, clauses, or sentences which constitute the point being made. Careful phrasing and inflection are necessary to enable the listener to follow every thought and the relationships among them. Patterns of speech, especially monotonous patterns of speech, must be avoided, and the pattern of thought in the text must be adhered to. The message in all its meaning must be earnestly communicated.

2. The manner of speaking and tone of voice should be clear and firm, never indifferent or uncertain. The reader should not draw attention to himself either by being nervous and awkward or by being obviously conscious of a talent for dramatic reading. It is the message that should be remembered, not the one who reads it. The voice should be reverent without being unctuous, loud without shouting, authoritative without being offensive or overbearing. The pace must be geared to understanding—never hurried, never dragged.

3. By his voice, attitude, and physical bearing, the reader should convey the dignity and sacredness of the occasion. His role is that of a herald of the Word of God, his function to provide a meaningful encounter with that living Word. Perfection in this mission may not always be achieved, but it must always and seriously be sought.

B. Praying and Speaking Aloud

When the celebrant leads the people in prayer, or speaks to them, or addresses God in their behalf, his manner of speaking will differ somewhat in each case. In every instance, however, he should convey that he sincerely means what he says. This sincerity is crucially important; it makes the difference between a matter-of-fact, ritualized, indifferent celebration and one that is truly an expression of faith and devotion.

1. *Dialogue*. In the greetings and verbal exchange between celebrant and congregation, all participants should speak their parts with meaning. When the priest says, "The Lord be with you," for example, he must convey that he is really addressing the people, that he sincerely means the greeting, and that he invites response. The tone and inflection of voice must be natural and convincing. At the same time, dialogue should never become extremely informal; all must be aware that the words they speak are part of a sacred rite. The liturgy must always be characterized by dignity and reverence as well as meaningful and sincere speech.

2. *Prayer*. When reading the orations, preface, and the like, the priest should speak in a manner befitting his sacerdotal role. His tone of voice should be more formal, more reverent; yet, he must remember he is speaking to a person, not merely reciting formulas. Note that this applies no matter which language is used in the prayer; it applies equally to the canon as to the collect or the Lord's Prayer. The latter prayer is gravely abused by a sing-song recitation which pays little attention to the praises and petitions actually contained in the words. The conclusions of prayers, although in set formulas, must never be hurried or routinely said. Since the affirmative response of the people is expected, the rhythm and tone of the priest should be sufficiently strong to encourage and facilitate the response.

3

The Reform of the Rite of Mass
The Meaning of Liturgical Change

Commentary (Conclusion), Bishops' Commission
on the Liturgical Apostolate
February 1965

(See also nos. 5, 12, 22, 23)

This commentary, comprising almost twenty pages of typescript, was issued by the commission for the information and use of the American bishops and their diocesan liturgical commissions. Its careful exposition of the rubrical details of the first stages of ritual revision of the Mass is no longer of direct interest. The concluding section, which is reprinted here, was republished eighteen months later in the August 1966 issue of the *Newsletter* under the title "The Meaning of Liturgical Change" as a "summary of the purposes of the preliminary liturgical revisions." The text illustrates the concern of the commission to introduce the reform gradually, reasonably, with attention to religious and spiritual values.

The context of the document is the "first instruction" of implementation of the *Constitution on the Liturgy,* prepared by the postconciliar body for implementation, the Consilium, and issued by the Roman Congregation of Rites. This instruction, entitled *Inter Oecumenici* (and referred to here as "I"), was dated September 26, 1964 (DOL 23). On January 27 of the next year, it was followed by the issuance of a revised Order of Mass and a description of the "Rite to Be Followed in the Celebration of Mass." These two Roman documents replaced the *Ordo Missae* and *Ritus servandus in celebratione Missae,* texts from the missal that had not been substantially altered since it was first published in 1570. The partial reform of the Order of Mass was to go into effect on March 7, 1965, the First Sunday of Lent, along with similar but lesser changes in the other liturgical services.

What this initial development meant, in the period immediately after the *Constitution on the Liturgy,* can best be understood in terms of the gradualness with which the liturgical reforms of the eucharistic rite were approached. Aside from the introduction of the vernacular (which might have been employed without any ritual changes whatever), it was possible to begin with a number of changes in the Order of Mass that did not require a new edition of the *Roman Missal.* That project of a complete new edition would involve a redoing of the presidential prayers, with a substantial increase of new texts, the reordering of the biblical readings (for the lectionary volume of the missal), and the reform of the liturgical calendar—all a matter of several years' study.

In the meantime, it was possible, simply by issuing new directions, to accomplish a first stage in the reform of the rite or *ordo* of Mass. When this was available in the Roman documents, the American commission issued a practical exposition and commentary. Its few concluding paragraphs, reprinted here, were intended to orient presiding celebrants to the initial liturgical changes in the form of celebration. The commission relied heavily and characteristically on the *Constitution on the Liturgy* and the 1964 instruction, in the obvious hope of making unfamiliar changes palatable and reasonable. While the material itself can hardly be faulted, the weakness in 1965 lay in the degree of dissemination of background information like this to the priests of the United States.

In order to understand the revisions in the rite of Mass, it is necessary to relate them to the principles of liturgical reform determined by the Second Vatican Council. Apart from minor ceremonial adjustments and simplifications, the changes serve the following broad purposes:

. . . To encourage the participation of the people, both internal and external participation, "the aim to be considered before all else" (SC 14), by means of a revision of sacred rites so that "the Christian people, so far as possible, should be enabled to take part in them fully, actively, and as befits a community" (SC 21).

. . . "To promote a warm and living love for Scripture" (SC 24). This is the reason for the emphasis upon the liturgy of the Word (cf. SC 51, 56), preaching as proclamation of the mystery of Christ (cf. SC 35, 2; 52), bible services (SC 35, 4; I 37–39), and the ambo or distinct place for the reading of the Scriptures to the people (I 96).

. . . To clarify the nature of the parts of Mass and the connection between them (SC 50). The distinct nature of the liturgy of the Word and the celebrant's presidential role in it are shown by his position at the seat, reserving the altar for the eucharistic liturgy proper (cf. SC 56); the principal prayers are emphasized by singing or loud recitation, especially the conclusion of the eucharistic prayer or canon, which is clearly distinguished from the Lord's Prayer before communion; the singing or loud recitation of the prayer over the offerings clarifies the structure of Mass: the collect-style prayer (collect, prayer over the offerings, postcommunion) completes or concludes each of the processional rites of Mass—at the entrance, at the offertory, at communion.

. . . To stress the communal and hierarchical nature of the liturgy (SC 26, 41, 42). This explains the distinctions made in the roles of celebrant, ministers, lectors, and servers, schola or choir and people, and especially the constant directions that the people should respond, recite, or sing.

. . . To allow for the diversity of circumstances in individual churches and on individual occasions, with various choices, for example, in the matter of the celebrant's position.

The appreciation of the revised rite for the celebration of Mass, which is introduced until the complete restoration of the Roman liturgy can be accomplished, thus requires the study of the *Constitution on the Sacred Liturgy* and of the Instruction on its immediate implementation.

4

Music in the Renewal of the Liturgy

Statement, Music Advisory Board of the Bishops' Commission on the Liturgical Apostolate May 5, 1965

(See also nos. 6, 10, 14, 15, 18, 24, 31)

Not long after the establishment of a secretariat of the episcopal commission in January 1965, a subcommittee of priests and lay persons, the Music Advisory Board, was set up. This was to be the first of many subcommittees, but it was something new and it was distinctive because it was asked by the parent commission to issue a formal statement at once.

The statement, slight and summary in itself, clearly forecasts the substantial document issued two years later: *The Place of Music in Eucharistic Celebrations.* The more immediate task of the music board during its first couple of years, however, was the preparation of ministerial chants, chiefly in the chant-style, for use at sung celebrations of the eucharistic liturgy in the vernacular. At this time, the first ICEL texts were not ready, and the commission itself had had to propose adaptations of the ordinary texts of Mass and, later, of the presidential texts, including the sung prefaces of the eucharistic prayer (the Roman canon). In turn, the Music Advisory Board, chaired by Coadjutor Archabbot Rembert Weakland, OSB, of Saint Vincent's Abbey, Latrobe, provided accompanying chants for interim use. (Even after the preparation of chants to accompany the ICEL texts in later years, many of the same chants were appended to the American editions of *The Sacramentary.*)

Although the statement itself is brief, it covers much of the territory of current and subsequent concerns. Positively, it insists on good music— whatever the liturgical language the music may accompany—and on suitability for the celebration of worship. This is the sense of the references to the differentiation of roles in the celebration, already adverted to in the *Constitution on the Liturgy* (SC 28), and the liturgical and literary genre and context, something often neglected, even in the great compositions of sacred music. Negatively, the statement is equally anxious that the participation of the people be respected, that they not be "denied their rightful part in worship," an unhappy characteristic of much church music of the past, and that those who provide (those who compose and perhaps those who choose and lead) music "be well informed on the nature of the liturgy and the aims of its renewal."

The Music Advisory Board membership reflected qualifications of sound musicianship, liturgical awareness, and pastoral concern. Even in this

33

preliminary statement, there is a sense of the tensions common between musicians and liturgists. Within the board itself, however, there was considerable unity, and the group was later able to develop the lengthier document mentioned already.

An immediate concern of the Music Advisory Board—and of the parent commission—is evident in the central message of the statement: "The Church calls upon the creative abilities of musicians to compose new musical settings better suited to present needs." The desire was not only for a vernacular, community shared liturgy, but also one in which the integral but serving role of music is freshly understood. This, in turn, flowed from the *Constitution on the Liturgy*, with its openness to all forms and styles of music and its radical rationale for the "holiness" of church music: "Sacred music will be the more holy the more closely it is joined to the liturgical rite, whether by adding delight to prayer, fostering oneness of spirit, or investing the rites with greater solemnity. But the Church approves of all forms of genuine art possessing the qualities required and admits them into divine worship" (SC 112). Oftentimes, the invitation to composers, made by the board on behalf of the commission, was not fully understood, but the statement was positive and encouraging.

Realizing the urgent need for music to be used in the vernacular liturgy and realizing the inadequacies of adaptations into English of music written for other languages and other cultures, the Church calls upon the creative abilities of musicians to compose new musical settings better suited to present needs. In setting themselves to this task, composers should keep in mind that:

1. A liturgical composition is to be, first of all, good music. Only true art is worthy for the worship of God.

2. Since the music in question is vocal, it is to be well suited to the words it uses. In particular, English has a distinctive accent and rhythm, a special flavor and spirit which is to be respected in any musical setting of that language.

3. The liturgy provides different roles for celebrant and ministers, cantor and choir, and the community as a whole. Each of these roles calls for its own type or kind of music.

4. The music should also have due regard for the liturgical action or moment to which it is related and the nature of the text being used (e.g., litany, hymn, confession of faith, proclamation of the Word, etc.).

All compositions of the past which have true artistic value and which contribute to the worthy celebration of the liturgy and foster the devotion of the faithful should be retained in those situations where they can be suitably rendered. Use of these works should be made in such a way that the faithful are not denied their rightful part in worship. It should also be noted that the Church's heritage of sacred music is best preserved in the language in which it was written.

In summary, then, it is of greatest importance that those who set themselves to the great work of providing music for the worship of God should be

34

competent musicians, should have a true feeling for the English language, and be well informed on the nature of the liturgy and the aims of its renewal. With these qualifications and inspired by the liturgy itself, there is no doubt that musicians of our day and of the future will make a distinct contribution to art in the worthy celebration of the sacred liturgy.

5

English in the Liturgy: Part II

Statement, Bishops' Commission on the Liturgical Apostolate
February 1966

(See also nos. 1, 2, 13, 16, 32, 35)

Just as the ritual changes, in particular those in the Order of Mass, were to be introduced gradually, so the extent of the vernacular used in the eucharistic rite was gradually enlarged. In this case, however, a different consideration was at work. It was not a matter of permitting a step-by-step assimilation of ritual liturgical change but, rather, catching up with the pastoral expectations and needs of the Catholic people.

Although Vatican II had placed no restrictions on the use of the vernacular in the sacramental celebrations and rites other than the Eucharist, its initial concession for the Eucharist was minimal. In fact, the expectation of the Conciliar Commission on the Liturgy, in reframing the texts in Chapter I (of general principles) and Chapter II (on the Eucharist) of the 1963 constitution had been that not all the conferences of bishops would make the concessions, much less seek the assent of the Roman See to a further, even total, use of the vernacular in the Mass. As things turned out, the conferences promptly made the concessions that were within their competence and almost as promptly sought the agreement of the Roman See for a further development.

The second stage of the vernacular concession authorized for the dioceses of the United States by the conference of bishops went into effect on March 27, 1966. For all practical purposes, this meant that the entire Mass might be celebrated in the vernacular, the only notable exception being that part of the eucharistic prayer after the Sanctus—since the prefaces of the anaphora were included in the second major concession.

Although the earlier statement of November 1964 (*The Use of the Vernacular*) had envisioned a further development—in its reference to the presidential prayers and the manner of their proclamation—in 1966, the commission decided to issue a further statement. It is not a reprise of the 1964 document and deals less with the use of English than with other issues of the eucharistic celebration. *English in the Liturgy: Part II* is, thus, a misnomer. The commission took an obvious occasion, as the new text demonstrates, to raise questions of silent prayer and of the distribution or allocation of (spoken and sung) parts of Mass.

The treatment of silence and specifically of the silence that should precede the presidential prayers is still valid today. Unhappily, in many, many celebrations, the invitations to pray such as "Let us pray" are still

36

followed by an immediate recitation of the appointed text. And, the rebuke expressed in the statement over "a sense of hurry at holy Mass" is almost as valid two decades later. The commission would return to this theme in connection with the second instruction of implementation in 1967 (DOL 39) and again when the completed edition of *The Sacramentary* was to be published in 1974.

The final and somewhat longer section of the statement is equally pragmatic. It is based upon a critical principle asserted in the *Constitution on the Liturgy*, article 28. The principle goes by several names: *differentiation, distribution,* or *allocation* of roles in the liturgy—on the one hand, in order to enlarge the participation of the people as a whole and the special ministerial roles, whether of the ordained deacon or of the nonordained readers, servers, cantors, singers, and the like; on the other hand, in order to limit and thus to clarify and enhance the role of the bishop or priest who presides over the eucharistic assembly.

The emphasis in the text is topical: on the proper chants of the Mass and their singing or recitation by the choir of singers and/or the assembly as a whole. This concentration becomes clearer if one remembers that in 1966, the very broad concession of substituting other song for the appointed chant texts of the Mass had not been made. What is said, however, is applicable to the later and current situation: The song accompanying the entrance and communion, whether an antiphon and psalm or hymns or other responsorial song, is not an element pertaining to the priest celebrant but, rather, to the cantor or choir and people. And the so-called intervenient chants—the responsorial psalm, which must always be psalmody in some form or other, and the acclamation before the gospel—again belong to cantors or choirs and people rather than to the priest.

What seems an odd omission from the statement's discussion of the distribution of roles is any explicit treatment of the readings proper to the deacon and to the (lay) readers. In 1966, progress in this direction was already substantial. By then, it was understood that the celebration of the Word involves the proclamation of the Scriptures by Christian worshipers other than the presiding priest. In the restored or recovered Roman liturgical tradition, the one who presides over the celebration listens to the proclaimed Word of God along with the other members of the assembly; then, ordinarily, as the norm puts it, he unfolds that Word of God in the homily after the gospel.

Even today, the full consequences of the principle in relation to the readings is not always appreciated. Sometimes, even when two readers are at hand on Sundays, one reader reads both texts, possibly as a matter of convenience, but clearly in contradiction to the principle (and the rubric) that one reader, whether instituted in the lay ministry of readers or not, reads the first reading and a second reader, if available, proclaims the second reading. As late as 1981, this point was reiterated in a second edition of the *Lectionary for Mass* (no. 52).

Similarly, the principle is not always appreciated in the case of the gospel. The priority is clear: if there is an assisting deacon—and, of course, when this statement was prepared there were no permanent deacons in the United States, much less the more than seven thousand who are now members of that sacramental order—he should always proclaim the gospel to the assembly rather than the presiding priest or a priest homilist or indeed any other priest. In the absence of a deacon, the gospel should be read by some priest other than the presiding celebrant; indeed, even if, in some special circumstances, the homily is preached by a priest or deacon other than the presiding priest, the liturgical role of gospel reader should be separate if at all possible. It is only in the absence of any other deacon or priest that the presiding celebrant should proclaim the gospel.

All this is spelled out because it is not so obvious, nor so generally observed. And, it is a rather clear omission from the statement, although it is a logical, liturgical consequence of what is well said in the statement about the differentiation of roles in the liturgical gathering.

In the same context of the distribution of roles, the commission drew attention to the new pattern of liturgical books: the sacramentary of the presiding celebrant and the lectionary of the readers. The former is for the role of liturgical presidency, exercised by the priest at the chair for the opening rite, the liturgy of the Word, and the concluding rite; exercised at the altar for the liturgy of the Eucharist. The latter is for the readers and the deacon in their liturgical roles exercised at the lectern or pulpit. It is easy to see how the commission, with whatever success, was trying to employ the signs of liturgical books and ritual placement to clarify the meaning of the partially reformed rite of Mass—and, in particular, to support and deepen the call for congregational participation with insistence on the principle of distribution of roles.

The second stage in the introduction of English into the celebration of Mass on the First Sunday of Passion Time has a twofold significance:

1. The new concession brings into the language of the people the variable prayers and prefaces, precisely those elements of the missal's prayer-text that can be of greatest value in forming the faithful spiritually.

These are the prayers (the collect, the prayer over the gifts, and the prayer after communion) that complete the three processions of Mass: the entrance rite, the preparation of the offerings, and the communion procession. They are the prayers to which the people give the response of assent and affirmation—together with the preface of the canon, which expresses the meaning of the holy Eucharist as praise and thanks to God.

2. This further concession also clarifies and simplifies the rite of Mass, eliminating the need to change from one language to another, at least so far as the people are concerned. Now, without confusion, the parts of the Mass that are proclaimed aloud or sung will be directly intelligible to the people— with the exception of the doxology of the eucharistic prayer.

To take one example, the Sanctus should be more evidently the continuation of the preface—whether the Sanctus is recited in common by all or, as the revised liturgical norms indicate, sung by the celebrant, ministers, servers, and all the congregation together. Thus, the unity and continuity of the whole eucharistic prayer or canon should be clearer—from "The Lord be with you" and the people's response at the beginning to the concluding doxology with the people's "Amen."

In this additional use of the vernacular, the obvious and immediate responsibility is that of the celebrating priest, since these parts of Mass (the prayers and preface) are recited or sung by the celebrant. They should now be intelligible to the people without other assistance or explanation (cf. SC 34). The particular problems of praying aloud in the vernacular have already been considered by the Bishops' Commission on the Liturgical Apostolate in its recommendations of November 1964 (repeated in the *Newsletter*, December 1965).

This second major step in the permission to use the vernacular at Mass may also be the occasion for further clarification and for a greater participation that is meaningful and devout. Two points may be mentioned.

"Let Us Pray" and Silent Prayer

In speaking of the parts to be said or sung by the people, the *Constitution on the Liturgy* adds the sentence: "And at the proper times all should observe a reverent silence" (art. 30). There is a religious silence in which we hear God's word, another silence in which we listen to the prayer of the priest and then respond in affirmation, and also a prayerful silence of priest and people together, recently restored to public worship.

After the invitation to prayer, "Let us pray," of the collect and of the prayer after communion—and just before the prayer over the gifts—it has been customary and desirable for a commentator to intervene, with a summary of the Latin prayer or a suggestion directing the intentions of the people. With the use of the vernacular for these prayers, this intervention of the commentator becomes unnecessary, and the new rubric of the Roman missal, issued last January, should be employed to full advantage (*Ritus servandus in celebratione Missae*, n. 32).

After "Let us pray," a brief but real pause for silent prayer should be made by the celebrating priest—and the people themselves should be prepared so that they know the meaning of this time of prayer. In it, each one, priest and people alike, may reflect briefly on the needs of one and all, on concrete and personal petitions and pleas. These petitions can be only generally summed up in the public prayer then recited aloud or sung by the priest and affirmed by the people.

A preparation for this development was found in the change (in 1956 and in 1960) by which, on certain occasions, a period of silent prayer and kneeling was restored after the direction "*Flectamus genua*—Let us kneel." Now the silent prayer is introduced into the collect-style prayers—and the new use of the vernacular makes it all the more evident how this period should be used.

With some reason, there has been concern lest too much recitation or singing by the people should create a sense of hurry at holy Mass. A meaningful silence, intended for prayer, should answer this concern on the specific occasion of the collect, the prayer over the gifts, and the prayer after communion.

Distribution of Parts

A second clarification in the rite of the eucharistic sacrifice is also provided by the circumstances of the new permission to use the vernacular for the prayers and prefaces.

For very practical reasons, the newly approved texts are being made available for liturgical use in the form of a missal supplement called a sacramentary. This contains all the prayers of the priest celebrant and the ordinary of the Mass, but not the biblical readings or the chants that are proper to the people or choir. At first glance, this may appear to create a practical inconvenience for the celebrating priest because of the multiplication of books, at least on those occasions when the chants cannot be sung or said by the people, choir or other group, cantor, commentator, or any person other than the celebrant himself.

This apparent disadvantage should be the opportunity for a new effort to achieve, at least for public Masses in which the vernacular may be used, the real distribution of parts, which is an important goal of the liturgical renewal. This is expressed in the *Constitution on the Liturgy* in these words: "In liturgical celebrations, each person, minister or layman, who has an office to perform, should do all of, but only, those parts which pertain to his office by the nature of the rite and the principles of liturgy" (art. 28).

Leaflets, booklets, and books are now available so that the four proper chants of Mass may be sung or recited by the people or a group of people or by a choir. Failing this, the recitation of these parts by the one who acts as cantor, leader, or commentator should be considered an important step toward a better understanding of the Mass.

Even the role of the commentator as leader of congregational participation in common recitation or song thus becomes clearer. There is no longer any need of the commentator's summaries of the prayers (above) or of his directions concerning standing and kneeling, now familiar to most congregations. But the importance of the "commentator" who acts as a kind of cantor or leader in the proper chants of Mass is now more evident.

The three processional chants of Mass—at the celebrant's entrance, at the preparation of the bread and wine, at the communion—may be supplemented by psalm verses, as has been frequently recommended in official documents. In fact, the brief antiphons become clear in the structure of Mass only when they are sung or recited as refrains to psalm verses. In any case, their recitation or singing does not properly pertain to the celebrating priest, when this can be avoided.

Similarly, the more important chants between the readings stand as an integral and significant part of the liturgy of the Word—whether these chants are sung or said by the people or choir, alternated with a cantor or leader, or recited by the lector who has read the epistle. Again, if at all possible, they should not be left for the priest to recite alone.

Emphasis on these parts—the proper chants—as congregational or choral rather than as priestly prayers, as they have incorrectly appeared to be in the past, can be one immediate advantage of the distinctive nature of the priest's book or sacramentary. There will always be some occasions when there will be no one but the priest to say these proper chants—as in the case of Masses celebrated privately—but the efforts already made to distinguish the roles at Mass should now be increased. When this is done, the new sacramentary or missal supplement will be the only book needed by the celebrant of Mass at his seat and at the altar; he will need the full missal or a lectionary only if, in the absence of others, he reads the epistle or gospel at the lectern.

It should not be necessary to add that each development and change in the liturgy must be explained fully to the people; nothing should change without reason. In this way, revisions such as those just mentioned may have meaning and spiritual benefit, over and above the advantages that will come from the additional use of English permitted in the eucharistic celebration.

6

Church Music

Statement, Bishops' Commission on the Liturgical Apostolate
April 18, 1966

(See also nos. 4, 10, 14, 15, 18, 24, 31)

At its April 1966 meeting, the commission issued a statement, or rather three statements, on music in the liturgy. These were made upon the recommendation of the commission's Music Advisory Board.

The first statement, *The Role of the Choir,* deals with a curious postconciliar phenomenon. As a significant element of liturgical renewal and promotion, Vatican II had forcefully urged the strengthening of church choirs: "The treasury of sacred music is to be preserved and fostered with great care. Choirs must be diligently developed, especially in cathedral churches . . ." (SC 111). It is true that the text added immediately: "but bishops and other pastors of souls must be at pains to ensure that whenever a liturgical service is to be celebrated with song, the whole assembly of the faithful is enabled, in keeping with art. 28 and 30 [on the distribution of liturgical roles and on the elements proper to the assembly] to contribute the active participation that rightly belongs to it." This injunction, like the other calls for popular participation in music throughout Chapter VI of the *Constitution on the Liturgy,* was misunderstood and misinterpreted rather widely as denigrating the role of choirs of trained singers.

The position of the council was correctly, and almost universally, understood by liturgists as, first, supporting the growth and improvement of choirs and *scholae cantorum* and, second, enlarging the role of such groups to include their leadership of congregational singing: by choirs singing with the whole assembly in the unison parts, alternating with the congregation, singing part-music with the rest of the people, and so on. Despite this, the Music Advisory Board and the parent commission recognized a great disaffection on the part of musicians and choirs following the introduction of the vernacular.

The commission's response is a clear, simple definition of the parts of the liturgical celebration, in particular the Mass, while suggesting a diversity of liturgical responsibilities (or, indeed, ministries) for the choir of singers. It also presses for the use of cantors—not only in their traditional role of singing verses in responsorial or antiphonal style but also as leaders of congregational singing, all the more important if there is no choir to sing with the people and so help them.

Because of the then limited repertoire of English hymns and other liturgical music suited to the Eucharist, composers in 1965 and 1966 had begun to offer new materials. Some of this music was in fresh styles and of sound quality; admittedly some of it reflected the poorer and weaker music of the moment. The second of the three statements, *The Use of Music for Special Groups,* approaches the problem in a sensitive and balanced manner. On the one hand, it encourages the diverse efforts and the diverse styles, with special attention to the level of music appreciation of special groups of the faithful (or, it may be added, of the ordinary parish congregation). On the other hand, it is sufficiently cautionary in suggesting that aberrations of "incongruous melodies and texts" and of instruments should be avoided. And it makes the point, already stated by the music board itself in the year before and to be expanded in the lengthy statement on *The Place of Music in the Eucharistic Celebration,* that the music itself must have "genuine merit."

Finally, the brief statement on *The Salaries of Church Musicians* has a familiar ring. It, too, was topical because the rapid expansion of musical opportunities for congregations (and choirs) to sing in the vernacular were not matched by a sufficient pool of trained and competent church musicians, who often are simply not attracted to church work because of inadequate compensation. A few years later, the pragmatic and Christian recommendations remain sound enough, except that the analogy with the compensation of public school teachers limps since they, too, are generally underpaid.

---

1. The Role of the Choir

The liturgical renewal is bringing tremendous changes in the shape of our worship of God. These changes, while creating unprecedented opportunities, present special problems. The opportunities and problems call for a reexamination of the whole role of music in the liturgy and especially the role of the choir—that part of the people of God whose special task it has been, and still is, to enrich communal prayer by all the resources of the art of music.

In the restored liturgy, it is evident that the choir will have more varied roles than in the recent past. At times, the choir, within the congregation of the faithful and as part of it, will assume the role of leadership, while, at other times, it will retain its own distinctive ministry. This means that the choir will lead the people in sung prayer by alternating or reinforcing the sacred song of the congregation or by enhancing it with the addition of a musical elaboration. At other times, in the course of liturgical celebration, the choir alone will sing works whose musical demands enlist and challenge its competence. Then the role of the congregation is to listen in a spirit of prayerful meditation.

In the framework of the present liturgy, as a general rule, the ordinary parts of the Mass will be recognized as the responsibility of the entire worshiping community. Here the choir is joined to the remainder of the congregation, leading and assisting them in a variety of ways, supporting and enhancing the worship. The distinctive musical contribution of the choir should be made

43

primarily in the proper parts of the Mass, but not to the total exclusion of the assembly. Thus, both the unity of God's people and the harmonious diversity of roles in the music of the liturgy become obvious. The choir then exercises its "true liturgical function" (SC 29), while "the whole body of the faithful [contributes] that active participation which is rightly theirs" (114).

In those instances when it is not possible for a choir to fulfill these functions in the liturgical celebration, the use of a cantor is to be highly recommended. Although he cannot enhance the service of worship in the same way as a choir, a trained and competent cantor can perform an important ministry by leading the congregation in common sacred song and in responsorial singing.

From this, it is evident that the failure to promote and encourage choirs, or at least the use of a cantor, can only hinder the realization of the goals of the *Constitution on the Liturgy* and impoverish the worship of God by the Christian community. "Only the rich harmony of experienced voices can add a note of majesty and power, and move even the poorest singers among the people to a greater love of God. . . . Membership in the choir is truly a vocation, and a call to responsibility" (*A Manual for Church Musicians,* pp. 43–44).

2. The Use of Music for Special Groups

In modern times, the Church has consistently recognized and freely admitted the use of various styles of music as an aid to liturgical worship. Since the promulgation of the *Constitution on the Liturgy,* and more especially since the introduction of vernacular languages into the liturgy, there has arisen a more pressing need for musical compositions in idioms that can be sung by the congregation and thus further communal participation.

Experience has, furthermore, shown that different groupings of the faithful assembled in worship respond to different styles of musical expression which help to make the liturgy meaningful for them. Thus, the needs of the faithful of a particular cultural background or of a particular age level may often be met by a music that can serve as a congenial, liturgically oriented expression of prayer.

In this connection, when a service of worship is conducted primarily for gatherings of youth of high school or college age, and not for ordinary parish congregations, the choice of music which is meaningful to persons of this age level should be considered valid and purposeful. The use of this music presupposes:

a) that the music itself can be said to contain genuine merit;
b) that if instruments other than the organ are employed as accompaniment for the singing, they should be played in a manner that is suitable for public worship;
c) that the liturgical texts should be respected. The incorporation of incongruous melodies and texts, adapted from popular ballads, should be avoided.

3. The Salaries of Church Musicians

To ensure the successful realization of complete and effective programs of liturgy in parishes, it is necessary for the Church to employ well-trained and competent musicians. Moreover, it is essential that such competency be recognized and compensated for in a realistic and dignified manner.

It is suggested that a full-time musician employed by the Church (i.e., one who is expected to lead the musical aspects of the liturgical program of a parish, play the organ, conduct the choir, etc.) be considered as carrying the same workload, and hence to be paid on the same salary scale, as full-time teachers in the local public school system. Length of service, experience, and academic qualifications should be likewise considered and adequately compensated for.

Musicians, on the other hand, who desire this kind of full-time employment should examine their qualifications and assure themselves that they can bring to the work the knowledge and skill that the Church demands. (As a nonpartisan norm for judging the level of their ability, it is suggested that musicians and priests alike consider the excellent and long-standing examination program annually given for just such a purpose by the American Guild of Organists whose National Headquarters is in the Rockefeller Center, New York City.)

Part-time musicians must likewise be compensated for their services in a realistic and dignified manner. The terms of their payment should be worked out to the satisfaction of those involved.

7

Concelebration

Statement, Bishops' Commission on the Liturgical Apostolate
June 1966

The statement on concelebration, which appeared in the commission's *Newsletter* in July 1966, is described as an "explanation of the concelebration of Mass, as conceded by the Second Vatican Council." The conciliar text (SC 57–58) was rather simply stated but had profound doctrinal meaning underlying it, including both liturgical and ecclesial dimensions. And, it certainly had much greater potential than the few instances of restored concelebration that were enumerated.

Several points are noteworthy about this decision of Vatican II. Like the concession of the vernacular and of communion under both kinds (to which the next statement in this collection is addressed), it is rather cautiously phrased—but would rapidly be embraced and would rather easily develop into common church usage. Any Ordinary, religious or diocesan, might permit concelebration on a regular and ordinary basis, but the regulation of its discipline was said to pertain to the diocesan bishop, who presides over all liturgies of the local Church, either personally or through a presbyter, and is the moderator and guardian of the liturgy. The freedom of priests not to concelebrate was also respected, given the anticipated problem of priests who had not been formed in the spirit of a communal liturgical life.

More important, the decree of implementation came quickly after a short period of controlled experiment; it was issued on March 7, 1965 (DOL 222). The Roman document remains valuable and is the source of the American commission's reasoning in the statement. The decree speaks of the several ecclesial unities to be signified.

First is the unity of the one sacrifice of Christ, to be manifest in the eucharistic celebration itself. The multiplicity of Masses in one place at one time works against this signification.

Another is the unity of the presbyteral order. The ordained presbyters participate in the eucharistic celebration according to their order, under the presidency of the bishop or the presbyter who represents him.

Finally, concelebration reflects and signifies the unity of the Church. This, too, is shown by the single celebration, which was spoken of by the council in terms of a principal Mass, during which all individual celebrations are proscribed. This echoes the crucial conciliar definition of the Church's "preeminent manifestation in the full, active participation of all God's holy people . . . in the same Eucharist, in a single prayer, at one altar at which the bishop presides, surrounded by his college of priests and by his ministers" (SC 41).

46

The *Constitution on the Liturgy* had carefully avoided any question of the extent or degrees of the signs of presbyteral concelebration, such as the actual association of the priests as a body, college, or order; their participation in the prayers and songs and in response to the presiding celebrant; their external vesture and gesture; and—a matter of medieval and indeed modern practice and concern—their common recitation of at least the principal parts of the eucharistic anaphora.

The document prepared by the Consilium and issued by the Congregation of Rites spelled out a simpler style of concelebration. On the basis of this new rite, different in usage and tone from concelebration (for ordinations) in the 1596 *Roman Pontifical,* the American commission offered its statement to encourage the introduction of the practice and to give it a firmer basis.

The statement indicates some of the preoccupations of the period when concelebration was being introduced, before the general and even implicit permissions of bishops and religious superiors were taken for granted. In particular, the commission was anxious that concelebration not be a matter of interest to the ordained clergy alone, certainly not a clericalization of the Eucharist; this explains the emphasis on the chief Sunday (or daily) Mass in the parish community, in which all the priests not obliged to preside over other celebrations on a given day should join, along with visiting priests to whom a eucharistic welcome is shown in the concelebrated rite.

Equally, the commission was concerned over a potential image of concelebration simply as a rite for the convenience of the ordained ministers at a meeting or gathering or as a practice largely intended for religious communities. However important to avoid a multiplication of "private Masses" at the same time, however practical to simplify the liturgy through concelebration, the purpose is deeper. It is the manifestation of ecclesial unity.

The statement does not deal directly with a misunderstanding that has arisen in later years: a misconception of a kind of co-presidency of the concelebrating priests over the Eucharist, as if a committee were in charge of the liturgical proceedings. There is an indirect allusion to this problem in the statement's mention of the role of the single presiding celebrant— the bishop or the presbyter who takes the bishop's place.

And, there is no reference to a related problem, bound up with concern for what is only one facet of concelebration, namely, the communal recitation of the institution narrative and the epicletic and anamnetic parts of the eucharistic prayer. This ritual problem is the loud proclamation of these texts when—as the rubrical norm declares—only the celebrant should be heard by the assembly. This, too, may arise from a faulty notion of shared presidency, very different from the conciliar image of celebration: the single bishop (or presbyter) presiding together with the order of presbyters, the deacons, and the whole body of Christian worshipers.

In its way, the commission's statement does anticipate what has become and remains an issue, often leading to the participation of priests in the Eucharist without any signs of their order beyond those common to the whole liturgical assembly. The issue is dealt with in terms of excessive solemnization or, as might be said nowadays, clericalization. The commission rightly detected a tendency to treat concelebrated Masses as somehow different from the one Eucharist of the Church, like a separate category of eucharistic liturgy, or as if the participation of additional presbyters according to their sacramental order was chiefly an enhancement rather than the normal means of signifying the Church at worship with its hierarchical orders (bishops, presbyters, deacons) taking part within the whole praying people.

On the other hand, the commission's hope that a refined (and still simpler) rite of concelebration would be developed—either by the Apostolic See or by regional adaptation—has not been fulfilled. Probably, this is because of a continued stress on "co-consecration" and the verbal expression of presbyteral participation. The statement's reference to the danger of interpreting concelebration as "impressive liturgical display" has unhappily come true, so much so that, in many instances, the positive sign of concelebration has had to be sacrificed in order to avoid the overwhelmingly clerical appearance of some such liturgies.

All this said, the 1966 statement of the Bishops' Commission on the Liturgical Apostolate is worth contemporary reflection. It is supportive of the usage of concelebration and this for all the right reasons, as sign of unity of the Eucharist, of the priesthood, of the Church.

In the Churches of the East, concelebration of the Eucharist has been maintained as a sign of priestly unity and of the unity of priests with people. In the West, concelebration has been limited to the Masses of ordination of priests and consecration of bishops.

The fathers of the Second Vatican Council undertook the promotion and reform of the liturgy so that the external signs of worship may not only give expression to the belief and devotion of the people of God but may also stimulate and nourish it (cf. SC 59). It is only in this context that the extension of the practice of concelebration can be understood.

Without prejudice to other forms of communal celebration which have existed in the past or may develop in the future, the rapid implementation of the *Constitution on the Liturgy* by the Holy See has provided a rite of concelebration, as the council directed (ibid., 58; *Ritus,* March 7, 1965). Some of its details are complex, but they take on meaning if the whole sense of concelebration is understood.

The Practice of Concelebration

So far as practice is concerned, it is important to distinguish the steps taken by the council. In some few instances, the concelebration of Mass was made a matter of universal norm and usage. The chief example is Holy Thursday, both for the principal parish Mass of the Lord's Supper and for the morning Mass of the Chrism in cathedrals.

The real development, however, is left to the permission of bishops and religious superiors. It would be totally wrong to understand this requirement of permission—usually granted in generous terms—as any hesitation or reluctance of the council with regard to the need or importance of concelebration. Rather, it allows the individual bishop or religious superior to promote and oversee the practice, and it provides for those circumstances where pastoral instruction or catechesis is needed for proper understanding (*Ritus*, n. 11). Where this understanding is present, there should be no obstacle to the restoration and extension of concelebration.

The *Constitution on the Liturgy,* in describing how the concelebration of the Eurcharist may spread, makes a basic distinction, which in turn helps to explain the underlying reasons for this liturgical development.

First, there is the principal Mass in any church or chapel. This may be a concelebrated Mass with the permission of the bishop or the appropriate religious superior, a permission that may be given in general and once for all, or for individual occasions. Next, there is the special concelebration at the time of a meeting of priests.

The first case is the ordinary and usual one for the daily concelebration of the principal Mass in circumstances where "the needs of the faithful do not require that all the priests available should celebrate individually" (SC 57, 1, 2a).

The obvious instance is the concelebration of the community or conventual Mass in monasteries and other houses of religious, in schools and institutions, in seminaries, etc. In the United States, this is already commonplace and has brought vitality to the forms of celebration of the community Mass, especially in the houses of religious.

Yet, the same concession of the council is equally applicable, with the requisite permission, to the chief daily Mass in parish churches and other churches and chapels. In this case, the principal celebrant is joined by a priest or priests who, on a given day, may be free of any pastoral obligation of celebrating Mass individually for a congregation of the faithful. Or, the opportunity may be afforded for concelebration by a priest or priests who are resident in a parish but are without parochial duties. The extension of concelebration is especially applicable in the case of a visiting priest who may be invited to concelebrate as a sign of fraternal welcome into the local community, in accord with a venerable tradition of the Church.

The unity of the Eucharist is enhanced by the single celebration on a particular day for the whole parochial or other community. Pastoral needs, however, regularly dictate that there should be several celebrations of Mass. Ideally, there should be but one concelebration of Mass each day in a church or chapel for the principal Mass of the community. Nevertheless, the bishop or religious superior may permit another concelebrated Mass if the number of concelebrants is large.

All this is concerned with the primary instance of concelebration—the principal Mass on a Sunday or weekday. The constitution also provides for another case of a more specialized nature, namely, for any kind of meetings of priests, whether secular clergy or religious.

This concession, for which again the permission of the bishop or appropriate religious superior is needed, is intended to provide for those cases where—

apart from the ordinary instance of the principal Mass of the day—there is some kind of gathering of priests. This may be for a congress or convention, retreat or study meeting; no restriction is placed upon the kind of meeting or assembly of priests.

It is important, however, that this second case of concelebration, for meetings of the clergy, should not overshadow the first, the concelebration of the principal Mass in a parish church or community chapel. There will be circumstances where, for an exclusively clerical meeting, the concelebrants themselves will be almost the only ones present. But, this should be the exception not the rule if the celebration of Mass is to signify and proclaim the whole Church assembled, with various roles for the different members.

The Meaning of Concelebration

If we look to the motives for this liturgical reform, we find that the rite of concelebration has certainly not been extended merely because it is ancient. Nor has it been extended merely because it can serve as a practical solution to the problems which arise when many priests are gathered for a meeting. It is true that concelebration is the most satisfactory solution to the problem of arranging for the suitable celebration of the Eucharist by a large number of priests when facilities are limited. But, it would be regrettable if either priests or laymen were to view the rite as a mere convenience or as a compromise measure to be adopted only when the reverent celebration of individual Masses is impossible.

Equally regrettable would be the use of the rite of concelebration as a means of adding solemnity to holy Mass. Neither priests nor laity should be given the notion that concelebration is an impressive liturgical display, intended to enhance a special feast or occasion. A number of priests concelebrate at one altar, not for reasons of solemnity, but in order to signify the unity of the Church.

The history of the rite of concelebration leaves unsolved many problems about the ancient form of the rite, and we must even now expect a future refinement and development of the new, revised rite. History, however, does clarify the true meaning of concelebration. In both the East and the West, priests celebrated the Eucharist together with their bishops as a sign of unity.

The Unity of the Priesthood

The council refers to this directly by speaking of concelebration "whereby the unity of the priesthood is appropriately manifested" (SC 57). The priestly ministry as it exists in the Church is a college of individuals sharing in the one priesthood of Christ. When an individual priest offers the sacrifice of the Mass, he does so in virtue of the one priesthood of Christ, who is the chief celebrant, to whom it belongs to consecrate the sacrament of his body and blood. The truth that is contained implicitly when one priest celebrates is made explicit when a group of priests gather to offer the unique sacrifice. The unity of the priesthood is made concrete.

The unity of the priesthood is effectively taught when bishops of various dioceses join together to concelebrate, and when the Holy Father concelebrates with other bishops. In a diocese, the unity of the priesthood is ideally shown when priests gather around their bishop, as the center of unity, to celebrate the Eucharist. By concelebrating with the bishop, just as when they were ordained, priests show their oneness with him in their priestly ministry. When priests concelebrate among themselves, they also manifest this unity of the priesthood.

The council has spoken of the corporate unity of the priestly college with the bishops in various ways. "The very unity of priests' consecration and mission requires their hierarchical communion with the order of bishops. At times, they express this communion in a most excellent manner in liturgical concelebration" (*Decree on the Ministry and Life of Priests*, n. 7).

The Unity of the Church

This unity of the ordained priesthood is clearly manifested in the external rite of concelebration, whether the bishop is the chief celebrant or another takes his place. Yet, concelebration is even more significant as the full sign of the Church itself, the people of God assembled at God's call to hear his Word and to respond in prayer and sacrifice.

In defining the Church, the *Constitution on the Liturgy* quotes the teaching of Saint Cyprian. Liturgical services are "celebrations of the Church, which is the 'sacrament of unity,' namely, a holy people united and ordered under their bishops" (SC 26; St. Cyprian, *On the Unity of the Catholic Church*, 7). The liturgical expression of the Church is explained in the following key sentence of the constitution, a perfect description of the concelebrated Mass:

> . . . The preeminent manifestation of the Church consists in the full active participation of all God's holy people in these liturgical celebrations, especially in the same Eucharist, in a single prayer, at one altar, at which there presides the bishop surrounded by his college of priests and by his ministers (SC 41).

It is essential that both priests and laity have a correct understanding of the pastoral significance of the extension of concelebration. The concelebrated Eucharist should be to the whole people of God a sign of their unity, a sign that helps them to be more aware that "They are the Body of Christ, not many bodies but one body" (St. John Chrysostom, *In Cor. Hom.* XXIV, 2, *PG* LXI, 552).

In what ways can participation in a concelebrated Mass foster the piety of priests and laymen? The concelebrated Mass manifests visibly to both priests and laymen that the Mass is the sacrifice of the Mystical Body of Christ. The mystery of unity and diversity—one Christ in many members—is brought before the eyes of all in this one Mass celebrated by many priests, with the full and active participation of the entire congregation of the faithful. The communal and hierarchical nature of the Church—composed of diverse members: bishops, priests, and ministers, lay men and lay women—is made evident in the concelebrated Mass. There the bishop (or the priest who takes his place) is the primary celebrant, the priests are sacramental concelebrants, and lay men and lay women are co-offerers through the priests who are their pastors.

The eucharistic piety of both priests and laity is, thus, deepened by participation in the concelebration of Mass. The stress is on the community nature of the eucharistic sacrifice, with a role and part for all the members in the sacred celebration which proclaims the Church at prayer. The unity of the body of priests is experienced and expressed. Even more, the unity of the Church as the assembly and communion of worshipers is made evident.

"This kind of celebration," says the document implementing the council's decision, "in which the people take part together, consciously, actively, and as a community, and particularly when the bishop presides, is truly a preeminent manifestation of the Church because of the oneness of the sacrifice and the priesthood, the one giving of thanks around the one altar with the ministers and the holy people" (*Ritus*, decree, March 7, 1965).

8

Communion under Both Kinds

Statement, Bishops' Commission on the Liturgical
Apostolate
July 1966

(See also nos. 29, 37)

This statement is somewhat longer than the one on concelebration, which it closely parallels. Both restored liturgical usages were implemented for the Church at large at the same time by means of a decree of the Roman Congregation of Rites—prepared, as were all such documents of the period, by the Consilium—dated March 7, 1965, effective on Holy Thursday of that year, April 15 (DOL 222, 286).

In the case of concelebration, the Roman document had a substantial discussion of the rationale for the restoration; in the case of communion under both kinds, there was only a brief statement on the need for prior catechesis. This included a rather defensive assertion of the Church's right to make disciplinary change, always conscious of the late medieval and modern prohibition of communion from the cup by the laity and by the clergy other than the presiding celebrant. But, the conclusion was positive: "At the same time the faithful should be encouraged to take part more intensely in a sacred rite in which the sign of the eucharistic meal stands out more explicitly."

Vatican II had also approached the matter with circumspection, remembering past controversies and insisting upon the teaching of the Council of Trent concerning the presence of Christ under one kind only (SC 55). Once the discipline was opened up, however, the restored rite quickly spread, and very soon, in almost all dioceses of the United States, the general permission of the bishop was at least implicitly granted in all the cases then permitted.

In some ways, this statement of the American liturgical commission anticipates the treatment of communion from the cup in the important doctrinal and disciplinary instruction on the Eucharist issued the following year by the Apostolic See (*Eucharisticum mysterium*, May 25, 1967; DOL 179). There, the doctrinal and religious importance of communion under both kinds is stated succinctly:

Holy communion has a more complete form as a sign when it is received under both kinds. For in this manner of reception (without prejudice to the principles laid down by the Council of Trent, that under each element Christ whole and entire and the true sacrament are received), a fuller light shines on the sign of the eucharistic

53

banquet. Moreover, there is a clearer expression of that will by which an everlasting covenant is ratified in the blood of the Lord and of the relationship of the eucharistic banquet to the eschatalogical banquet in the Father's kingdom (see Mt 26:27–29) (EM 32).

The American statement is much more expansive, and it is hardly necessary to summarize it; this is done adequately by the subheads in the text. Over and above the basic teaching that underlies the practice—the more explicit, adequate, and effective sign of sharing in the blood of the Lord—a few particular points should be noted: the ecumenical implications of the restoration; the importance of the cup for lay women and lay men as well as for the ordained ministers; the analogy with the sign of communion "from this sharing of the altar" (rather than from consecrated bread from a previous celebration); the insistence that only communion from the cup is truly expressive of the ritual and religious act of drinking; the sign of the Christian community sharing the one cup at the one table of the Lord—in contrast to very individualistic approaches to holy communion.

With regard to practice, the four so-called modes of receiving the Eucharist are not elaborated upon in the statement, beyond a reference to the cup and to the other, less significative, modes: by means of a spoon; by means of a strawlike tube; by intinction. Neither the spoon nor the tube seems to have been of much interest or attraction in pastoral practice, although they are more expressive of drinking than is intinction as now sometimes practiced in the Western Church. This will later become an issue, in which the preference for communion from the cup will not always be easily maintained. It has been made an issue, although not always a genuine one, by reason of hygiene; it will even be an issue when communion received in the hand is introduced, since intinction by the minister precludes communion in the hand, as it also impinges on the liberty of the individual to receive under the form of bread alone.

The context of the 1966 statement is the list of cases or instances then permitted for communion under both kinds. The *Constitution on the Liturgy* had given only three examples, leaving the enumeration of cases to the Apostolic See, as was done in the decree already mentioned. The several cases referred to were limited at the time, although one of them—in favor of all the lay brothers who took part in the daily concelebrated Mass of a religious community—was indicative of a much broader enumeration in the years ahead. When expanded lists were given in later Roman documents, they included not only specified categories of recipients but others who were present at the liturgy, indeed whole congregations on certain special occasions. Finally, in the instruction *Sacramentali Communione* of June 29, 1970, the Apostolic See, in effect, shifted its responsibility to list cases for communion under both kinds to the conferences of bishops, with a number of cautionary comments (DOL 270).

This account may be completed by mention of the decisions of the National Conference of Catholic Bishops after 1966. These decrees, prepared by the commission, reflect very much the spirit of the statement and the commission's hope for further spread of communion from the cup. In November 1970, the conference took full advantage of the Roman instruction of the previous summer by extending the list of cases, at the discretion of the individual Ordinary, to: (1) all present on any occasion when communion is given under both kinds to persons listed in the concessions made by the Apostolic See, as well as at funeral Masses and Masses for a special family observance; (2) at Masses on days of special religious or civil significance for the people of the United States; (3) at Masses on Holy Thursday and at the Mass of the Easter Vigil; and (4) at weekday Masses. As is evident, these occasions and opportunities are very broad, some of them deliberately overlapping. They effectively eliminated any restriction of communion under both kinds to certain persons at a given eucharistic assembly: if one person besides the presiding celebrant might receive in this manner, all present would be so permitted. From another viewpoint, the 1970 decree recognized and regularized the growing practice in many groups, communities, and parishes. By then, it had become the sense of the Church in the United States that communion from the cup should not be an exceptional privilege. It was to be the accepted rite "in which the sign of the eucharistic meal stands out more explicitly."

In 1970, the commission recommended, but the conference of bishops did not accept, the extension of communion under both kinds to Sunday Masses in general, that is, simply because it is the Lord's day, the first holy day of all (SC 106). Some hesitation was felt about broadening the usage to large congregations, although several of the occasions already agreed upon did envision large numbers and many possible Sunday celebrations.

A few years later, the specific omission of Sundays and holy days as sufficient reason in themselves for communion under both kinds was remedied by the National Conference of Catholic Bishops. In November 1978, the bishops acted favorably upon a report that explained:

At the time [of the 1970 decree] it appeared that the large numbers of communicants at some Sunday Masses might create problems of order or be a source of inconvenience, a possibility to which the Roman instruction [of June 29, 1970] had adverted. (In conceding Communion under both kinds for Holy Thursday and the Easter Vigil, occasions when very large numbers might be present, the NCCB had insisted that the norms of the instruction concerning reverence and good order be observed.)

After the experience of more than eight years with the present enumeration of cases and the experience of more than fourteen years with the practice itself, it seems desirable to reappraise the question and remove even the appearance of a restriction upon Communion under both kinds on Sundays.

Nevertheless, the decision of the conference of bishops was not acceptable to the Apostolic See until 1984, when the Congregation for Divine Worship confirmed the 1978 NCCB decree. At the congregation's request, and with its approval, the secretariat issued a comprehensive booklet with the relevant norms and the basis for catechesis: *This Holy and Living Sacrifice: Directory for the Celebration and Reception of Communion under Both Kinds* (Washington, D.C.: USCC Office of Publishing and Promotion Services, 1985). It was only then that "even the appearance of a restriction upon Communion under both kinds on Sundays"—and, indeed, on any day—disappeared in the dioceses of the United States "if, in the judgment of the local Ordinary, it can be given in an orderly and reverent manner."

The story has been pursued from the initial decisions taken in the aftermath of Vatican II and the formal statement of the Bishops' Commission on the Liturgical Apostolate in 1966 in order to illustrate how the wheel has come full circle. A kind of presumption against communion under both kinds has now been replaced by the opposite presumption, and the Church has returned, in principle and in accepted discipline, to what was the ordinary sign of the sacrament from the very institution of the Eucharist through the first millennium and beyond in the West—a usage that was never abandoned in the Eastern Churches.

The immediate significance of the successive decisions for the dioceses of the United States is that communion under both kinds has become, in principle and in accepted discipline, the rule rather than the exception, the norm rather than the concession, the preference rather than the privilege. The greater significance lies in the doctrine of the fullness of the eucharistic sign of the Body and Blood of the Lord Jesus, as the 1966 statement asserted and proclaimed.

The Second Vatican Council decided after study and debate that communion under both kinds, under the appearance of both bread and wine, should be permitted more widely, as "a more perfect form of participation in the Mass" (cf. SC 55).

This decision may be viewed both as a radical departure from long-standing Roman Catholic custom in the West and as a step toward restoring a tradition followed everywhere for twelve centuries and still observed faithfully by the Orthodox and other Christians.

Yet, it is really the logical outgrowth of a richer understanding of the mystery of the Eucharist. The change in eucharistic practice that was decreed by Pope St. Pius X inevitably led to a more profound appreciation of the Eucharist as the sacrificial banquet of the Christian Church. The same pope took the first step toward the council's decree by approving the reception of communion under both kinds by Latin Catholics participating in the Oriental liturgies (September 14, 1912).

According to the terms of the *Constitution on the Liturgy*, communion under both kinds "may be granted when the bishops think fit, not only to clerics and religious, but also to the laity, in cases to be determined by the Apostolic See . . ." (55). The three examples mentioned by the council (one for the clergy, one for religious, one for the laity) were enlarged by the Holy See in its decree on implementation.

Now, with the bishop's permission, communion under both kinds is possible and, indeed, desirable in the case of the newly baptized, confirmed, ordained, and married; for the deacon and subdeacon of Mass; for newly professed religious; on certain jubilee celebrations of individuals; etc. (*Ritus*, March 7, 1965, n. 1). Whether a general concession is made for all these cases whenever they occur or whether the usage is gradually introduced depends on the pastoral judgment of the individual bishop.

Already the practical consequences of the council's 1963 decision have been realized and welcomed in many places, with the requisite permission of the individual bishop. At wedding Masses, it has become the usual practice, a sacramental seal expressive of the deepest unity of Christian marriage in the Body and Blood of the Lord; in many houses of religious communities it has become the daily sign of the full unity of the priests and brothers.

The reverence with which the people have received communion from the cup and the desire for the restoration of the practice as a sign of the full solemnity of special religious occasions already show the wisdom of the council's action. At present, the custom is limited, as the council decreed, to specific cases enumerated by the Holy See. If, in the future, these cases are enlarged by the Holy See, for example, in favor of small and special congregations of the faithful or in favor of lay persons who exercise a particular ministry at Mass, it is evident that this development too will be welcomed.

Yet, the practice must be accompanied by understanding, by the preparatory instruction or catechesis mentioned in the 1965 document of implementation. This decree sums up the meaning of communion under both kinds in a sentence: ". . . the faithful should be urged to take a more active part in this sacred rite in which the sign of the eucharist banquet shines forth more clearly" (*Ritus*, n. 2).

Reasons for Restoration

This instruction should take into account some of the reasons for the restored practice as well as the full doctrine of the Eucharist.

The first and obvious reason for restoring communion under both kinds to wider use is the desire to observe more exactly the eucharistic celebration narrated in the gospels and the injunction of our Lord: "Unless you eat the flesh of the Son of Man, and drink his blood, you shall not have life in you. He who eats my flesh and drinks my blood has life everlasting and I will raise him up on the last day. For my flesh is food indeed, and my blood is drink indeed. He who eats my flesh, and drinks my blood, abides in me and I in him" (Jn 6:54–57).

In the past, doctrinal disputes required the continuance of a different church usage—communion under the form of bread except for the celebrating priest— largely because of the Church's stress on the sufficiency or adequacy of communion under one kind. The Council of Trent, while recognizing communion under both kinds as the ideal, canonized this point of view: "Under only one species Christ is received whole and entire and a true sacrament is received and therefore, so far as the fruits are concerned, those who receive under only one species are not deprived of any grace necessary to salvation" (Sess. XXX, c. 9).

The word *necessary* is perhaps the key to the historical differences between the sixteenth century and the present time, which now permit this meaningful change in church discipline "for the devotion and for the advantage of the recipients" (*Ritus*, n. 2). In the past, the Church's proper concern was to show that communion under both kinds was not necessary or essential to the life of Christians. And, since it was not necessary, the Church felt justified in restricting the practice to communion under one kind in the Latin liturgy.

Today, with the dangers of misunderstanding long past and in a period of better religious education, our concern is with what is useful, desirable, and spiritually profitable—in this case the more complete expression of the Eucharist as the holy banquet of God and man, the sacred meal of food and drink which seals the covenant of reconciliation.

In the context of our times, seeking more authentic and vivid manifestations of worship, communion under both kinds also remains a matter of ecumenical importance. Its extension in the Latin Church is a recognition of the fidelity of all the Oriental Churches to the gospel tradition. It recognizes too the deep significance communion from the cup has for Anglican, Protestant, and other Churches and Christian communities.

The Lay Role

Finally, again in the context of today's circumstances, communion under both kinds for the newly baptized or newly confirmed adult, the bride and groom at the wedding Mass and at the jubilee of marriage, the lay religious at the Mass of profession and at jubilees, emphasizes the recovery of the role of lay men and lay women in the Church.

For many centuries, the laity of the Latin Church had received communion from the cup as well as under the form of bread—except in unusual circumstances, for example, when infants received communion under the form of wine only or when communion was carried to the sick under the form of bread only. The usage changed, partly because of practical inconvenience when the number of communicants was very large, partly because of a weakening of eucharistic understanding.

In effect, if not in purpose, this resulted in a deprivation, even an exclusion, of the laity, of religious, of the clergy other than the priest celebrant, from communion under both kinds. Today, the partial restoration of the traditional usage removes this apparent distinction. It becomes another symbol of the Christian responsibility and vocation of every member of the Church.

Each time new stress is placed on the Eucharist as the source of the Church's strength (SC 10), it is a reminder that all who take their place at the Lord's table must "express in their lives, and manifest to others, the mystery of Christ and the real nature of the Church" (ibid., 2). Moreover, as the council teaches, with particular application to the mission of lay men and lay women, "the aim and object of apostolic works is that all who are made sons of God by faith and baptism should come together to praise God in the midst of His

Church, to take part in the sacrifice, and to eat the Lord's Supper" (ibid., 10).

The common call of all the laity to a part and place in the mission of God's people is suggested by the recovery of roles in the Church's liturgy and now by the restoration of communion under both kinds on at least some occasions.

The Sacramental Sign

When all this is said, the basic reason for the change is that the reception of the Eucharist under both kinds more fully manifests the sign of the eucharistic meal as instituted by Christ. Communion from the cup does signify more clearly the taking and drinking of the precious Blood of our Lord.

This attempt to show forth and to experience the fuller meaning of the Eucharist has a parallel in the regular reception of communion from hosts consecrated at the same Mass rather than those consecrated at a previous Mass.

In 1947, Pope Pius XII stressed the devotional and theological importance of communion, as the canon of the Mass says, "from this sharing of the altar." The motive was the more adequate expression and experience of the oneness of the eucharistic sacrifice, which was instituted by Christ in the form of a ritual supper, a sacred banquet. The faithful, Pius XII explained in his encyclical letter *Mediator Dei,* should thus "aim that all their actions at the altar manifest more clearly the living unity of the mystical Body" (MD 122).

The Second Vatican Council reiterated this principle in its strong commendation of "that more perfect form of participation in the Mass whereby the faithful, after the priest's Communion, receive the Lord's body from the same sacrifice" (SC 55).

Communion under both kinds proclaims more adequately what the celebration of the Lord's sacrifice in the Church truly is: "a memorial of the Savior's death and resurrection, a sacrament of love, a sign of unity, a bond of charity, a paschal banquet . . ." (ibid., 47). It is the sacrificial meal, which the Lord shares with his people, the fraternal and loving banquet of unity. "The Lord left behind a pledge of hope and strength for life's journey in that sacrament of faith where natural elements refined by man are changed into His glorified Body and Blood, providing a meal of brotherly solidarity and a foretaste of the heavenly banquet" (*Constitution on the Church in the Modern World,* n. 37).

The Eucharist as the food and drink of the pilgrim people of God is most properly experienced when, in addition to the "holy Bread of eternal life" (Roman canon), the worshiper drinks from the cup or chalice, itself an act symbolic of unity and love. Thus, the normal mode of communion under the form of wine is by drinking from the chalice. If this is inconvenient in particular circumstances, the bishop may indicate other ways of receiving the Blood of the Lord—such as receiving the host which has been dipped in the consecrated wine or receiving the consecrated wine from a spoon or through a tube— even though these modes may be less expressive of the eating and drinking of the holy banquet. It is for the bishop, in individual cases, to determine which of the four rites or modes is to be used (*Ritus,* n. 1).

What is new, of course, is the reception of communion under the species or appearance of wine by others than the priest celebrant. This demands a deeper appreciation of the "chalice of everlasting salvation" (Roman canon).

Cup of Everlasting Salvation

In the Eucharist, Christ nourishes his Church with his own Body and Blood, as with two aspects of the one undivided mystery which is Christ. In other words, under the aspect of his precious Blood, his sacred Body is contained as well, and vice versa: each contains the whole and complete Christ.

But, each of these aspects has its own message. The aspect of the precious Blood reveals elements of the mystery of Christ to the believing Christian which are not necessarily revealed by the aspect of his sacred Body, although they are certainly not absent from the latter.

There is no other Christian symbol, with the possible exception of the cross itself, that so insistently calls for commitment as does the sacred cup. Even before the Last Supper, Christ used the cup as the symbol of his sufferings (Mk 10:38; 14:36; Jn 18:11). Before one dares to take the chalice to his lips, he must answer Christ's challenging question to the sons of Zebedee: "Can you drink of the cup of which I drink?" Each reception from it is a renewal of the covenant. This cup is a share in the Blood of Christ (1 Cor 10:16). In a much fuller way than the blood of the Old Covenant (Ex 24:8), this Blood of the new and eternal covenant brings to us the atoning efficacy of the perfect Sacrifice (Heb 8:6). By this Blood of his beloved Son, God was pleased to cancel the debts which no amount of perishable gold and silver ever could (1 Pt 1:19). We who were once far-off strangers have been brought near, actually made members of God's household by this Blood (Eph 2:13). Shed "unto the forgiveness of sins," it is this Blood that makes pure hearts, fitted with holiness for the service of God (Acts 5:9), for the priestly service of the Church (Acts 1:5–6), and for entrance into the holy place in the very presence of God (Heb 10:19).

The aspect of the precious Blood of Christ should help the communicant to understand more vividly that, as blood is the seat of life (Dt 12:23), Christ gives his own life to and for the communicant. And the life of Christ, signified under the aspect of his precious Blood, in its very fluidity reveals to the believer that the power which animated Christ, his Holy Spirit, given in baptism and sealed in confirmation, is once again communicated in the sacred banquet.

Since the aspect of the precious Blood is taken from a common cup, the faithful will begin to realize more concretely the essential community they share in the Church, a community that is familial, brotherly, loving, intimate. Each Christian lives by Christ, the same Christ, by his Spirit, the same Spirit. In Christ, there are no differences among men: "There is neither Jew nor Greek; there is neither slave nor freeman; there is neither male nor female. For you are all one in Christ Jesus" (Gal 3:28).

These are, of course, but a few of the elements of the message which God speaks to his Church under the aspect of the precious Blood. The fullness of this message is his beloved Son, his revealing Word become flesh, dwelling

60

among us sacramentally. But, we may hope that a greater fullness of God's message will be made manifest in his Church through living dialogue with our Risen Lord in the aspect of his precious Blood in that more perfect participation of communion under both kinds. And, this manifestation will enrich and vivify the Christian life; it will inspire in each person that deep sense of community in which can be recognized the individual and personal responsibility which each Christian has for the work of building up the Body of Christ, his Church.

The restoration of communion under both kinds and its extension, on certain sacred moments of Christian life, to the Church's members in general is a disciplinary and pastoral change. Like every revision of liturgical usage, it must be understood by all who take part in the most sacred mystery of the Eucharist.

In holy Mass, we celebrate the Lord's passage from death to life, from passion to glorification, by eating his flesh which was broken for us and drinking his blood which was poured out for us. This command we fulfill when we receive communion under the form of bread only. We fulfill it more evidently and more fruitfully in communion under both kinds. This, in turn, may result in our better realization of the eucharistic sacrifice. "The Church," as the council teaches, "has never failed to come together to celebrate the paschal mystery: reading those things 'which were in the Scriptures concerning him' (Lk 24:27), celebrating the Eucharist in which 'the victory and triumph of His death are again made present' (Council of Trent, Sess. XIII, c. 5), and at the same time giving thanks 'to God for his unspeakable gift' (2 Cor 9:15) in Christ Jesus, 'in praise of his glory' (Eph 1:12), through the power of the Holy Spirit" (SC 8).

61

9

Liturgical Change and Experimentation

Statement, Chairman of the Bishops' Commission on the Liturgical Apostolate November 17, 1966

(See also nos. 11, 36)

The burden of this very short statement is a rebuke to unauthorized experiments and liturgical aberrations. It was issued by Archbishop Paul Hallinan on behalf of the commission—he had just moved from the position of secretary to that of chairman—in the setting of a meeting of the American episcopate. One reason for its inclusion here is to note the meagerness of authorized adaptations of the Roman liturgy by the Church in the United States.

Unquestionably, there were in November 1966 many instances of communities, probably more nonparochial communities than parishes, where the partial liturgical reform had prompted alterations, innovations, creative additions, and abuses in local celebrations of worship—under the umbrella of "liturgical experimentation." Of course, as has been true ever since, the numbers of such aberrations or abuses were small by comparison with the total numbers of parish and other communities in the country. Their numbers were certainly much smaller than the numbers of communities guilty of the opposite all too common abuse: the failure to embrace and fulfill the opportunities of a vernacular liturgy.

This latter problem, still with us and still far more widespread than radical creativity, was to be taken up at length the next year in *Liturgical Renewal*, a statement the commission prepared for the conference of bishops to share with the priests of the country. In 1966, however, the need was to make the point that liturgical adaptation on private authority was the enemy of genuine, hoped for reform and revision—and certainly the enemy of radical liturgical adaptation of the Roman liturgy, once its various rites would be revised and issued by the Roman See.

The matter was further complicated by a misuse of the very term *experiment*—or *experimentation* at the time. As often as not, it referred to innovations and deviations that were not introduced experimentally at all. Some of these became known as "standard deviations," for example, communion in the hand or unauthorized communion from the cup. These had little to do with real experiment in the sense of trial, testing, preliminary evaluation, and the like.

The free introduction of liturgical variants in the period from 1964 to

1969 created pressures upon the American commission, equally from those friendly and from those still unfriendly to liturgical change; they created pressures too on the Roman Consilium of Implementation, which was trying to revise the rites in accord with both the best traditions and contemporary pastoral needs, while avoiding radical change until the Roman liturgical books could be completed. In hindsight, it is curious how difficult it was to urge patience—and, perhaps, curious that so little was made of the radical nature of the Roman reform still under preparation at the time. From another viewpoint, it gives the lie to revisionists of the 1980s who believe that the reformed liturgical rites were suddenly foisted full-blown on the church community.

The mildly negative tone of the statement reflected a strong personal conviction of Archbishop Hallinan as well as of his fellow commission members, themselves anxious to respond to the other bishops concerned over aberrations. What is more important is the promise held out: authorized experiment and profound adaptation.

The chairman spoke from his own experience with the process of amendment of the *Constitution on the Liturgy* when he was a member of the conciliar commission in 1962–1963. He had a similar experience with the complex pattern of exhaustive study and thorough revision of the Roman liturgical books as a member of the Consilium from its establishment in 1964.

The articles on liturgical adaptation in the constitution—including all change and development over and above the basic reform of the Roman liturgy that was decreed by the council—were positive and encouraging. Under the heading "Norms for Adapting the Liturgy to the Culture and Traditions of Peoples" (referred to in the statement as "regional adaptation" to be made by the conferences of bishops with the approval of the Apostolic See), Vatican II had made some clear distinctions.

To begin with, once a liturgical rite had been revised by the Roman See, the national or regional bodies of bishops were free to make the variations and additions to be specified in the Latin books (SC 38–39). These have generally been called lesser or minor adaptations. They were to be listed, sometimes generously, sometimes in only very slight matters, in all the books of ritual issued by papal authority by mandate of Vatican II. In turn, they were to be reviewed and almost always acted upon by the American conference of bishops in the following years. These liturgical opportunities, though often of lesser consequence, were ordinarily grasped by the American episcopate and decreed as liturgical law for the United States.

More important, the constitution opened the way to more profound or radical developments—and it is these which the statement anticipates. Such adaptations go by varied terminology (*inculturation, acculturation, indigenization, accommodation*) that is a good deal less significant than the fact of liturgical development beyond the core Roman rite. They were to require not merely the *review* of the decrees of the conference of bishops by the Apostolic See but its *consent*. And, said the constitution, "the Apostolic See will grant power to this same territorial ecclesiastical authority [the conference of bishops] to permit and direct, as the case requires, the necessary preliminary experiments within certain groups suited for the purpose and for a fixed time" (SC 40).

For one thing, the notion of controlled experiment, followed by the decision whether to admit a rite or usage into the official regional liturgy, was clear enough. For another, there was a firm basis for the expectation of the statement: "The bishops have moved to offer the People of God the opportunity to use . . . approved experiments, and also channels by which permission may be obtained through the bishops for experimentation that will lead to greater participation, not to individual innovations that will divide and deny the people the best of our national efforts." Rightly or wrongly, the American commission was convinced that the process enshrined in the *Constitution on the Liturgy* was not only the means to profound liturgical adaptations but also the best way to head off unauthorized—and often poor—liturgical changes.

A series of efforts to press for sound and substantial liturgical adaptation in the United States can be listed: the establishment of the short-lived Subcommittee on Liturgical Adaptation (March 1967), chaired by the Reverend Charles K. Riepe of Baltimore; review of specific proposals for experiment; designation of centers of research and experiment; development of procedures for liturgical adaptation (approved by the conference of bishops in 1966 and again in 1972); and carefully drawn up guidelines for liturgies with small and specialized groups and with children. (It is ironic that guidelines for liturgies with children, which were not accepted, were less radical than the directory on the subject issued in Rome in 1973.)

By and large, these efforts did not succeed, although they raised the level of consciousness of the bishops, liturgical commissions, and the pastoral-liturgical specialists. The most ambitious proposals, approved by the National Conference of Bishops in November 1966, were the following:

The first concrete plan was to permit experiment in a limited number of parishes and other communities under the direction of academic centers and under the supervision of the Conference of Bishops and the local bishop.

The second proposal was that the Holy See permit the National Conference of Catholic Bishops to designate places to try out liturgical changes without prior examination of the changes by the Holy See.

In effect, this was a petition from the American episcopate that the Roman See delegate to the conference or its commission the broad responsibility for liturgical experiment prior to radical adaptation, as described in article 40 of the *Constitution on the Liturgy*. The positive position taken by the conference of bishops prompted the optimistic facet of the statement. But, the request was never granted by the Apostolic See. As a result, the centers (at such institutions as the University of Notre Dame and Saint John's University, Collegeville) were limited to study and research, without authorization to go beyond the limits of the official and approved liturgy. The commission and its Subcommittee on Liturgical

Adaptation were not able to move much further on radical, cultural, regional, accommodation of the Roman liturgy to the circumstances of the Church in this country.

The subsequent story is of a piece with what has been said, and the expectations of the American commission in 1966 were not fulfilled. Despite substantive liturgical adaptations permitted in the 1960s and early 1970s by the Apostolic See, especially in undeveloped countries, almost all American developments have been within the range of "minor adaptations." The *Roman Missal* of 1970 raised hopes of openness to further change:

> The purpose of this Instruction [the *General Instruction of the Roman Missal*] is to give the general guidelines for planning the eucharistic celebration properly and to set forth the rules for arranging the individual forms of celebration. In accord with the *Constitution on the Liturgy*, each conference of bishops has the power to lay down norms for its own territory that are suited to the traditions and character of peoples, regions, and various communities (no. 6).

The Roman policy since then, however, has more nearly reflected the rather negative statements in an instruction *Liturgicae instaurationes* issued by the Congregation for Divine Worship the same year as the missal (September 5, 1970: DOL 52).

A more recent instance is the request, made by the American conference of bishops at its November 1982 meeting, for the faculty to conduct a controlled and limited three-year experiment with the ecumenical adaptation of the order of readings at the Sunday Eucharist (the *Common Lectionary* of the North American Consultation on Common Texts). The Roman denial of this opportunity to experiment on a very restricted scale, but with a view to future alternatives for some of the Sunday readings, serves as an inhibition to development of regional liturgical changes, in accord with the *Constitution on the Liturgy*, which the 1966 statement of the commission's chairman anticipated.

A strongly negative conclusion would be faulty. Throughout the twenty years since the brief statement was issued, the commission has been consistent and effective in taking advantage of all the potential minor adaptations that are regularly enumerated in the Latin liturgical books. These include both ritual variants and additional texts, the latter generally those prepared by the International Commission on English in the Liturgy.

All the official liturgical books in English illustrate the special decisions made by the National Conference of Catholic Bishops, after study and recommendation by its commission, for the dioceses of the United States. *The Sacramentary*, for example, appends a list of these lesser adaptations to the *General Instruction of the Roman Missal; Ritual Revision: A Status Report* (Washington, D.C.: USCC Office of Publishing and Promotion Services, 1981) also lists these and the adaptations of the rites of the other sacraments and services.

It is the mind of the Liturgy Constitution of Vatican II that liturgical change take place in two ways: (1) revision of the Roman liturgy by the Consilium (the official postconciliar body of bishops and *periti*) and (2) regional adaptation by episcopal conferences with the approval of the Holy See.

Obviously, the constitution intends experimentation in order to achieve the most suitable form of liturgy, in the light of liturgical research and the contemporary needs of the people. Obviously, too, the Church through the council means just what the council said: "Absolutely no one, not even a priest, may add, remove or alter any part of the prescribed rite on his own authority." "Unauthorized experimentation," introduced as innovations by priests or laymen is simply, in the light of Article 22, §3, a contradiction in terms.

The bishops, three years ago, voted in Rome, almost unanimously, to move forward into the liturgical renewal for our people. The main thrust of the intervening years has been the introduction of maximum vernacular and greater participation, and the setting up of groups to plan music, art and architecture, seminary programs and the full participation in the international body working toward a new English translation. Thousands of priests and laymen have devoted their energy and creative skills to prepare for this renewal. Divisive and diversionary movements have appeared, of course, because some fail to understand what liturgical renewal is. To the extent that they have disturbed many Catholic persons, they have slowed down true renewal. To the extent that they have attracted the energy of earnest persons, they have cut down the necessary pastoral education and parish promotion of the liturgy.

The bishops have moved to offer the people of God the opportunity to use both results of the Consilium and approved experiments, and also channels by which permission may be obtained through the bishops for experimentation that will lead to greater participation, not to individual innovations that will divide and deny the people the best of our national efforts.

10

Masses in Homes and Music

Statement, Bishops' Commission on the Liturgical
Apostolate
February 17, 1967

(See also nos. 4, 6, 14, 15, 31)

As the title suggests, the February 1967 statement has a twofold purpose, but its brief treatment of music is largely a repetition of what had been said in the earlier statement *The Use of Music for Special Groups* issued the previous April; here, it is quoted in the context of a particular special group, those gathered for a eucharistic celebration in a family home.

The statement was occasioned by the appearance a few weeks earlier of a formal declaration by the Congregation of Rites (December 29, 1966: DOL 35) and the need to correct reactions and misinterpretations. The Roman document, which appeared in *L'Osservatore Romano* on January 3, 1967, had forcefully repudiated arbitrary liturgical innovations occurring at "family eucharistic meals" in private homes followed by dinner, as these had been publicized in the press. They were described by the declaration as "travesties of worship" with their "novel and improvised rites, vestments, and texts, sometimes with music of an altogether profane and worldly character, unworthy of a sacred service."

It was not until eighteen months later that the new Congregation for Divine Worship issued a more substantive instruction on Masses for special groups, *Actio pastoralis* (May 15, 1969: DOL 275). While still cautionary in tone, and deeply conscious of potential liturgical abuses, this instruction recognizes the evident worth, communal and individual, of special gatherings, whether of sectors of a parish or of groups of the faithful of the same interest or category. It is a thoughtful exploration of sound pastoral possibilities of group liturgies and the application to the form and style of the liturgical elements.

Only in 1973 was a somewhat analogous situation officially recognized in a supplement to the *General Instruction of the Roman Missal*. This is the *Directory for Masses with Children,* again from the Congregation for Divine Worship (November 1, 1973: DOL 276; published in American editions of *The Sacramentary*). The directory is a still more positive and open document, opening up large areas of flexibility and adaptability for the Eucharist with children "in which only some adults take part" and even for the Eucharist with adults "in which children also take part."

Standing by itself, however, and without these later tempering reflections and guidelines, the Roman declaration of December 1966 was entirely negative and harshly expressed. It had no special relevance to the United States, and, indeed, one must always discount the sensationalism in most reports of perceived abuses—as well as attend to the actual number of instances, which may be relatively small. Nonetheless, it struck a sensitive nerve on the American liturgical scene, where in some local churches diocesan bishops and their commissions had been warmly encouraging neighborhood Masses in private homes. The development was not on a very wide scale, given the size of the country, nor was it a development as profound as the base communities of Latin America.

The rationale for such home or family Masses, especially in 1966 and 1967, is easy to understand. In the face of a strong tradition of large congregations at Masses hurriedly and routinely celebrated in many parishes, the eucharistic liturgy in the vernacular, together with the preliminary revisions of the period, needed, at the very least, some breathing space and some opportunity for leisurely and more intimate celebration. This was provided by weekday celebrations, ideally bringing together a few families from a given neighborhood, ideally helping the worshipers to be a leaven in the larger congregation that would assemble for the Sunday Eucharist in the parish church. While there might be irregularities or even abuses, they are not inherent in the place of celebration—and such Masses might be the most carefully prepared and celebrated, with the very greatest religious spirit and spiritual efficacy for the small gathering.

Those who encouraged the neighborhood Masses, both diocesan bishops and parish priests, respected the norm that only the local Ordinary had the right to permit the celebration of Mass outside a "sacred place" (church or oratory). Under the old law, the 1917 *Code of Canon Law,* canon 822 §3 had grudgingly permitted this concession "for a just and reasonable cause, in some extraordinary and individual case." (This norm was later abrogated. The *General Instruction of the Roman Missal* said only: "For the celebration of the Eucharist, the people of God normally assemble in a church or, if there is none, in some other fitting place worthy of so great a mystery." Canon 932 §1 of the 1983 *Code of Canon Law* suppressed the requirement of episcopal or other permission where there is need to celebrate the Eucharist outside a place of worship.) The pastoral need was seen to be more than verified in the circumstances, and the positive values of neighborhood weekday Masses for small congregations—as well as similar liturgies for nonparochial communities—were fully recognized.

Thus, in its statement, the commission had the task of offering every encouragement to the developing practice, while not countenancing violations of ecclesiastical discipline or liturgical law. More important, it wanted to counteract the possibility that a misunderstood declaration from Rome might be an obstacle to good diocesan and parish programs. At the same time, as is evident, the statement insinuates that there were other problems to be corrected, quite aside from any liturgical abuses: eucharistic celebrations narrowly confined to a single family (or, it might be added, confined to an entirely homogeneous, exclusive group) and Sunday celebrations in homes and small groups, to the detriment of the Sunday celebration of the heterogeneous Christian community of a parish.

Some worry over favoritism to particular groups or households is also apparent.

Finally, the occasion was taken to use the context of observations on Masses in homes in order to repeat cautionary but positive words about new musical idioms and compositions: "the newer modes of meaningful music . . . must not be deterred by the regrettable abuses of some."

The joint declaration concerning unauthorized "family eucharistic banquets" issued recently by the Congregation of Rites and the Postconciliar Liturgical Commission (Consilium) has been the subject of misinterpretation. It was not a new decree or new legislation, much less was it a "papal ban" on the use of contemporary music. The confused reporting of this statement is a reminder that the official texts of such documents should be examined carefully and calmly.

1. The warning to observe the present liturgical discipline was directed against abuses, not against the proper celebration of Mass in homes and neighborhood communities with the authorization of the local bishop.

As the chairman of this commission pointed out last November, private innovations in the liturgy disrupt the desired unity and order in the community. They divide rather than unite. They divert us all from true liturgical progress because they are directly contrary to the intent of the council.

2. Diocesan programs for the celebration of Mass on weekdays in private homes or small neighborhood communities are not affected by the warning against abuses.

For a long time, local bishops have permitted Mass outside a church for sufficient reason. They have thus brought consolation to the sick confined to their homes for long periods. Obviously, other serious reasons will prompt the use of such faculties, in particular, diocesan programs for weekday Masses in homes and neighborhoods.

The assembly in small communities for Mass should not ordinarily be restricted to one or two families. The purpose should be to form a small worshiping community in which the genuine sense of community is more readily experienced. In turn, this experience can contribute significantly to growth in awareness of the parish as community, especially when all the faithful participate in the parish Mass on the Lord's day. The parish is the basic unit of the total ecclesial community, and it is in the parish that the Church exists in miniature.

3. It is difficult to give an easy answer to questions concerning music worthy of the liturgy. If free from improper associations, the music of any age can be accommodated to the service of the liturgy. The character of music "is to be considered the more holy in proportion as it is more closely connected with the liturgical action" (SC 112).

We, therefore, repeat our recommendations of last April, calling for "musical compositions in idioms that can be sung by the congregation and, thus, further communal participation:

"Experience has furthermore shown that different groupings of the faithful assembled in worship respond to different styles of musical expression which

69

help to make the liturgy meaningful for them. Thus, the needs of the faithful of a particular cultural background or of a particular age level may often be met by a music that can serve as a congenial, liturgically oriented expression of prayer.

"In this connection, when a service of worship is conducted primarily for gatherings of youth of high school or college age, and not for ordinary parish congregations, the choice of music which is meaningful to persons of this age level should be considered valid and purposeful. The use of this music presupposes:

a) that the music itself can be said to contain genuine merit;

b) that if instruments other than the organ are employed as accompaniment for the singing, they should be played in a manner that is suitable for public worship;

c) that the liturgical texts should be respected. The incorporation of incongruous melodies and texts, adapted from popular ballads, should be avoided."

Finally, both the developing programs of neighborhood Masses and the newer modes of meaningful music, which are the responsibility of the local bishop, must not be deterred by the regrettable abuses of some.

Our concern is to satisfy legitimate desires for needed liturgical change. The condemnation of abuse must never obstruct desirable and necessary programs of liturgical renewal. It must never encourage or give comfort to a negativism which is foreign to the promptings of the Holy Spirit for change in our day.

A positive and open approach is needed. This means taking advantage of the changes already accomplished and making them more deeply effective in vital Christian living.

11

Liturgical Renewal

Pastoral Statement, National Conference of
Catholic Bishops (Prepared by the Bishops'
Committee on the Liturgy)
April 1967

(See also nos. 9, 28, 33, 34, 36)

This lengthy statement of the conference of bishops, adopted at its April 1967 meeting in Chicago, requires less commentary than the two previous statements in this collection. It has greater breadth, but its observations and exhortations are for the most part self-explanatory.

The genesis of the statement was in a suggestion to the commission from its former chairman, Archbishop John F. Dearden of Detroit, who had become the NCCB president in the previous year after chairing the liturgical commission since 1963. He proposed "that questions of liturgical change and experiment be treated in a broad and positive context rather than as a mere correction of abuses. Originally, it was planned to issue the statement in the form of the customary recommendations or guidelines from the committee, but it was then suggested by Archbishop Dearden that, because of the importance of the matter, it should be a statement of the National Conference of Catholic Bishops and should, as an indication of particular concern, be sent before publication to each priest in the United States through the individual bishops." (In February 1967, the commission had been renamed "Bishops' Committee on the Liturgy," without change of its status or responsibilities as the national episcopal liturgical commission.)

This was done, and the committee's draft was readily accepted by the conference of bishops. After distribution to the bishops, and through their offices to the priests of the country, most of the text was published in the June 1967 issue of the committee's *Newsletter*. It was not separately published and perhaps because of this and the original manner of dissemination, which was not universal, it did not receive the attention that was expected. It remains an important landmark because of the timing— after the initial liturgical reforms, especially of the eucharistic rite, and before the broader reforms—and because of the underlying principles. The document sums up very many issues of the time in liturgical renewal and, while it takes its official character from its adoption by the conference of bishops, it has a special significance as reflecting the strongly held position of Archbishop Dearden and of Archbishop Hallinan, who had succeeded him as chairman.

The conviction of the committee itself, shared by most of the American episcopate, was that the answer to liturgical innovations and abuses of one kind or another did not lie in condemnation but in better catechesis, planning, and actual celebration. Perhaps, above all, it was felt that those responsible for celebration, especially the priests who preside over the liturgy, needed to take advantage of all the riches, all the advances, all the opportunities of a eucharistic rite that was only partially revised. To put it differently, there was a need to say with some delicacy that better celebration was the issue of the moment, entirely apart from matters of incomplete liturgical reform and restoration.

In a sense, this was to go back to the preconciliar period when the liturgical movement, small and with little influence, and liturgical promoters, relatively few in number, had urged with wearying consistency that there could be better comprehension, participation, and celebration even without liturgical reform. By 1967, the date of the pastoral statement, the reform was well underway, but once again the greatest potential lay in employing the liturgical forms, elements, and words, as they then existed, to best advantage.

One facet of this liturgical potential depended on a better appreciation of the diverse options already available, as the statement asserts: "Much has been said about liturgical experiment, authorized and unauthorized. What may not be so evident is that a very wide field of diverse liturgical practice is now open, within the limits set by the present discipline and regulations."

Another thesis of the statement echoes what was pointed out in the commentary on the previous statement *Home Masses and Music:* ". . . if we must reprove the innovators, we must even more strongly and positively urge priests—pastors and assistants, secular and religious, old and young—to fulfill our common hopes of renewal. . . . No one should criticize the errors of liturgical innovators without also criticizing the extreme apathy of others." The same words could be repeated in the late 1980s, along with the positive commitment made by the episcopate in the concluding section of the statement.

A final point is suggested by that characterization of the concluding paragraphs. Clearly, a pastoral statement of this kind is designed to teach and exhort in a moving and balanced fashion. But, it also serves to place the author (officially, the National Conference of Catholic Bishops) on record. In effect, it put in the mouths of all the bishops the solid approach to liturgical renewal to which they had, in principle, committed themselves during the Second Vatican Council.

The principal limitation of the statement is hardly a defect. It was too sanguine about the prospects of substantial liturgical adaptation possible in the United States, as had been the simple statement of the previous November, *Liturgical Change and Experimentation.*

The Mass has become a new experience for the people of God, bishops, priests, and laity together. We listen to more of the Scriptures and to homilies that proclaim the wonderful works of God. The priest speaks in the language

72

of the people, and they respond and sing according to their proper role. The liturgy of the Word of God, with the priest presiding, stands out more clearly; the celebration of the Eucharist, with the priest facing the people, has greater meaning.

Communion is received under both kinds on certain occasions, and frequently priests join in the concelebration of Mass. The rites and prayers of the other sacraments will carry the same marks as they are revised: the mystery of Christ brought closer and the good news of man's salvation heard more intimately.

Now our common determination, clergy and laity alike, must be to continue the progress begun by the Second Vatican Council through its *Constitution on the Liturgy*.

This was the purpose of the steps taken at the bishops' meeting last November, when further proposals were submitted to the Holy See. These decisions of the bishops reflect the desires and concerns of the people of this country, who have already shown their devotion to a renewed liturgy.

The approval of alternative biblical readings at weekday Masses will relieve the monotony of repetition and will broaden the biblical knowledge of the worshipers. This temporary measure, for which no new liturgical books are needed, will serve until the postconciliar liturgical Consilium completes its work on the Roman lectionary, as directed by the Vatican Council.

The canon of the Mass may now be spoken aloud or sung. This may seem a small change, but the canon is the eucharistic prayer in which we proclaim the Lord's death until he comes; it is the central affirmation of Christian faith. When the canon is spoken publicly and reverently for all to hear, its significance becomes more evident. If it becomes possible, with the Holy See's permission, to use our own language in the canon, the sacramental sign of the Eucharist will be more readily expressed and understood.

The Beginning of Renewal

In 1963, the council decreed that all the rites of public worship should be reviewed and revised. The first steps have already been taken—to clarify and simplify the Mass, to restore the roles of all who have a part in it, to employ the people's language.

Thus, the council's first liturgical aim, the involvement of the whole worshiping congregation, is being accomplished. We must intensify this process and bring our entire Christian life into the worship of God.

No one can easily measure the present impact of liturgical change upon the activities of the Church, which is God's people. How much more committed are we to the needs of all mankind? How much better do we manifest to others the true meaning of the Church? Self-questioning and self-criticism are good signs, if they make us aware of our sins against others, our failures as Christians, and our need of positive action.

Unquestionably, we are more conscious of the universal claims of Christian faith and love. If the liturgy has been speaking more clearly of these claims, and if it has moved us a step toward the great goals of the council, the renewal may be said to be underway.

73

We experience difficulties, but many of these are the inevitable problems of transition and growth. Old liturgical defects, of which few were aware, are coming to light as we use the vernacular. Gradual and uneven liturgical changes have to be appreciated for what they are, first steps.

Many of the liturgical complaints have obvious solutions: if a hymn is poor, there are many good hymns to be chosen; if a lector is ineffective, he should be better trained and prepared; if the manner of liturgical celebration seems awkward or inept, it should be studied and planned more carefully.

Celebrating the Present Liturgy

Liturgical Education and Understanding

The present need is for better liturgical education and, thus, a more profound understanding of the spirit and purpose of renewal. A deeper knowledge of the Scriptures and a better biblical orientation are essential to this educational process. Priests, preachers, teachers, and indeed each individual worshiper must be truly involved in it.

Diversity in Practice

Liturgical renewal is a continuing responsibility. Fresh viewpoints as well as fresh means of devotion now permitted should be constantly employed. This is clear in the case of the liturgical revisions that are planned or expected. It is true also of the present possibilities opened up by the preliminary revisions and demanded by the nature of the liturgy as explained by the council.

Since the priest has the role of presiding and leading, each priest and, in particular, each pastor is called upon to take advantage of liturgical possibilities now authorized.

Much has been said about liturgical experiment, authorized and unauthorized. What may not be so evident is that a very wide field of diverse liturgical practice is now open, within the limits set by the present discipline and regulations.

Some examples may be mentioned: the various combinations of song and spoken prayer in the liturgy; the freedom in the "prayer of the faithful": the choice of simplicity and solemnity of rite; the possibilities of preparatory commentary and explanation; the free structure and content of bible services; the diversity of styles and texts of sacred song; the involvement of the laity in the roles of lector, commentator, and cantor.

Much of this depends on the leadership of bishops, priests, and lay leaders. Upon them rests the hope of liturgical progress.

Parish differs from parish, occasions and circumstances differ, and no single, rigid pattern of liturgical celebration is now possible or desirable. Almost every priest knows the limits of such diversity and flexibility; not all priests appreciate how wide the opportunities are for planning lively and intelligible celebration.

74

Sometimes, the present liturgy seems to include abstract and irrelevant elements. Although this criticism has been exaggerated, we should try to make the liturgy, especially the eucharistic liturgy, as concrete and contemporary as possible.

There are many means to this goal: the use of introductory comment by a lay or clerical commentator; the selection of texts when there is free choice, especially sacred songs, refrains, and responses; efforts to set the biblical readings in proper context; careful preparation of the prayer of the faithful with application to the immediate situation and congregation; and, of course, a concrete preaching of God's Word. In every case, the goal should be to go from the abstract to the concrete, from the universal to the particular, from the broad message to its application.

Ministry of Preaching

The passages of the *Constitution on the Liturgy* that deal with preaching God's Word should be reexamined and put into effect. They call for a revolution in content and style of preaching. They demand the centering of all preaching on the mystery of Christ, on the paschal mystery of the Lord's death and resurrection, on man's place in the history of salvation. The homily, prescribed on Sundays and holy days, is also warmly encouraged at weekday Masses.

"Liturgical preaching" is often misunderstood as if it were expository or explanatory of liturgical forms and rites. On the contrary, liturgical preaching is preaching that flows from the proclamation of the Scriptures in the assembly. It is in the context of the occasion, the particular liturgical celebration, the facet of the one mystery of Christ expressed in the feast or season.

Equally important—and almost neglected—true liturgical preaching, as an extension of the call of God, is a call to Christian living. It demands concrete and direct response. Those who really hear God's Word spoken by the preacher commit themselves to greater faith and greater love. Indeed, by God's grace and as a necessary part of the liturgy, they commit themselves to greater Christian action in this world.

Channels for Sound Experiment

The liturgical changes introduced so far seek to increase the liturgy's effectiveness. While this general revision goes on, we are equally conscious of the need for adaptation to particular needs and mentalities. The decree of the council, for example, requires that the revised *Roman Ritual*—for baptism, marriage, funerals, etc.—be varied and adapted in national rituals.

This major task of adaptation, entrusted by the council to the national episcopal conferences, is being undertaken by the United States Bishops' Liturgical Commission, with the help of a study committee, including pastoral specialists, lay men, and lay women. The bishops therefore renew the invitation, extended at their meeting last November, for concrete and specific proposals of revised liturgical rites.

Such suggested rites or projects for experiment should include full details and background, texts and alternatives. They should indicate, moreover, the particular community's past liturgical program and its capacity to evaluate and report the experiment. The consent of the diocesan bishop is needed in every case.

Proposals of this kind and all requests for permission to experiment should be addressed to the Bishops' Committee on the Liturgy, 1312 Massachusetts Avenue, N.W., Washington, D.C. 20005, according to the procedure already announced. Proposals that are judged favorably by the National Conference of Catholic Bishops will be submitted to the Holy See for permission to experiment.

Liturgical Innovations

Liturgical experimentation has acquired several meanings. If it means employing the flexibility that is now permitted in the liturgical discipline, it is most desirable at every level. If it means, on the other hand, privately initiated innovations, it must be disapproved. The fathers of the council had no intention whatever of encouraging experiment contrary to liturgical usage and discipline:

"Regulation of the sacred liturgy depends solely on the authority of the Church, that is, on the Apostolic See and, as laws may determine, on the Bishop.

"In virtue of power conceded by law, the regulation of the liturgy within certain defined limits belongs also to various kinds of competent territorial bodies of bishops legitimately established.

"Therefore, absolutely no other person, not even a priest, may add, remove, or change anything in the liturgy on his own authority" (SC 22).

Unauthorized liturgical innovations are not genuine experiments at all. They are diversionary. They turn us away from the tasks already mentioned. They divert us from the educational work of renewal and from realizing the full potential of the present liturgy.

Furthermore, this kind of unauthorized initiative is divisive of the Christian community. It can create fragmented communities that are closed and narrow, ultimately out of communion with their brethren and with their chief liturgist, the bishop. Liturgical norms support and strengthen the unity that must exist in the Body of Christ, without destroying lawful variety and diversity.

A grave fault, however, lies with those who have resisted or neglected the liturgical program of the council, those who have accepted it only externally, those who have simply refused to embrace the renewal. There is no excuse for indifference among the pastors of the flock, and, if we must reprove the innovators, we must even more strongly and positively urge priests—pastors and assistants, secular and religious, old and young—to fulfill our common hopes of renewal.

Renewal—a Positive Program

The liturgical program is a positive effort of the Church. It demands a willing approach, a humble openness to change on the part of all. It demands great insight, so that ritual and external change will not become a new formalism. The liturgy must be a deeply religious experience of clergy and laity. It must express faith and piety and bring us all to a greater awareness of full Christian responsibility.

To this end, we welcome the development of dialogue and communication. Liturgical change must always be done carefully and expertly. Yet, the liturgy is the common work of the entire Christian community. It is encouraging, therefore, that channels of communication are being opened, from parish committees on worship to diocesan pastoral councils. Happily, lay men and lay women are becoming more articulate, and they should be heard. If we must, at times, urge patience and defend order in the community, our words should never be interpreted as hesitation or reluctance concerning liturgical renewal.

The accomplishments of the past few years have been remarkable, as evidenced by the contrast in liturgical practice between 1963 and today. Now the understanding must be deepened, to make us ready for greater growth and change in the liturgical forms, and much more important, in their meaning for us as followers of Jesus. Towards this goal, we pledge our own best efforts, and we urge the cooperation of clergy, religious, and lay people in its accomplishment.

12

A Further Instruction on the Correct Implementation of the *Constitution on the Liturgy*

Commentary (Introduction), Bishops' Committee
on the Liturgy
May 30, 1967

(See also nos. 5, 22, 23)

After Vatican II, the second stage in the gradual revision of the Roman rite of Mass—aside from the introduction of the vernacular, country by country—was introduced by a second instruction comparable to the September 1964 document of implementation. This new instruction goes by the name *Tres abhinc annos,* since it appeared almost three years later, on May 4, 1967, to be effective on June 29 (DOL 39). It was prepared by the Consilium of Implementation and promulgated by the Congregation of Rites. At about the same time, two other Roman instructions appeared, more concerned with guidance and direction on particular aspects of the liturgy than with additional reform or revision as such: the instruction on music *Musicam sacram* (March 5: DOL 508) and the instruction on worship of the Eucharist *Eucharisticum mysterium* (May 25: DOL 179).

The response of the American liturgical committee took the form of a commentary of more than twenty pages of typescript, of which only the introductory paragraphs are printed here. To understand them in context, it is necessary to explain the chief features of the second instruction of implementation, which the commentary explained in detail and at length.

The working plan of the Consilium as it carried out the full-scale revision of the liturgical books mandated by Vatican II (SC 25) was to issue instructions and other statements that might be put into effect without requiring the completion of the respective books: the missal, the sections of the ritual and pontifical, and the breviary. (These books began to appear in their Latin editions in 1968: the ordination rites; and in 1969: the rites of marriage, baptism of children, and funerals, and the Order of Mass.)

In 1964, the Consilium's first instruction, published by the Congregation of Rites, had to cover a variety of rather general questions of implementing the liturgical constitution, from catechesis to commissions, from authority to celebrations of the Word of God. Its ritual revisions of the Eucharist and other services were few, provisional, and tentative. In the Mass, for example, there were simplifications (omissions of initial prayers, last gospel, and duplications by the presiding celebrant), clarifications (prayer over the gifts, doxology of the eucharistic prayer, and embolism of the

Lord's Prayer sung or said aloud), and important reorientations of liturgical placement (the use of the presidential chair throughout the liturgy of the Word and the proclamation of all the readings facing the people).

In the parallel instruction of 1967, such ritual changes in the rite of Mass were carried forward a little—along with other, still preliminary changes in other parts of the liturgy—"because pastoral considerations commend them and they seem to offer no hindrance to the definitive reform of the liturgy yet to come. Further, they seem advantageous for the gradual introduction of that reform and are feasible simply by altering rubrics, not the existing liturgical books." Some reforms were slight: the permission to omit the maniple; the radical reduction of the number of times the celebrant was directed to genuflect, kiss the altar, and make signs of the cross; and a further correction of duplications. Other reforms were more consequential: restriction of the number of the opening collects and other presidential prayers to one; permission to sing or say aloud the part of the eucharistic prayer after the Sanctus—and the concession, at the discretion of the conferences of bishops, of the vernacular for the entire eucharistic prayer; the recommendation of a period of silence or a psalm or canticle of praise during the period after communion, after the completion of the communion song.

These details, which were commented upon exactly by the committee in its lengthy commentary, reflected the careful steps taken toward the overall reform of the Order of Mass and the *Roman Missal* by the Roman See. The committee's description was prefaced by an overall introduction and exhortation—the text reprinted here. It is marked by a desire to make the changes appear reasonable and acceptable—in the context of the *Liturgical Renewal* statement of the conference of bishops printed above—and with a brief recital of the process yet to come.

The reference to the Synod of Bishops, which was to meet in the fall of 1967, is worth noting. The synod participated in and then discussed an early draft of the reformed Order of Mass, the core rite then known as the *Missa normativa*. The American bishops' committee was anxious to spread the word that further developments were in order not only in the Eucharist but also, and even sooner, in some of the other sacraments.

This commentary on the liturgical instruction of May 4, 1967, has been prepared by the Bishops' Committee on the Liturgy. It is not a substitute for the Roman document, because the instruction is clear in its explanations. The purpose of these observations, however, is to distinguish between the simple modifications to be introduced in the Roman liturgy on June 29 of this year and those variations that have been left to the judgment of celebrants, while adding some pastoral comments which may be helpful.

Many of the changes or options are of a ritual or ceremonial character. They thus represent an attempt to simplify the liturgy rather than to introduce major developments. They add greater dignity to the liturgical celebration and afford occasions for a somewhat wider choice of liturgical texts. Some of the suggestions made, such as a period of silence or a song of praise after communion, have obvious pastoral significance, and it will be important to take full advantage of them.

It may be difficult for some celebrants of Mass to adjust to the minute ritual changes of gesture, made chiefly by way of omission. This fact, in itself, is also significant since so many of these gestures, genuflections, and crosses become mechanical and almost involuntary. The radical reduction in such cases is a sharp reminder that any formal ceremonial, no matter how often repeated, should be done deliberately and reverently, with full meaning that is apparent to the praying congregation.

Most of the modifications and choices have been introduced because of the experience of Mass celebrated facing the people, the preferable manner of celebration according to the first instruction implementing the *Constitution on the Liturgy* in 1964 (n. 91). The provisions of the new instruction are, nevertheless, applicable even when Mass is not celebrated in this way.

There is no need to repeat here the introductory words of the May 4 instruction, which should, of course, be read carefully. They indicate clearly the context and purposes of the new provisions, in particular the need to preserve the liturgical discipline of the Roman rite, avoiding arbitrary innovations on private initiative.

One statement in the introduction to the instruction should be pointed out. The modifications are all such that they are "useful in the gradual introduction of the liturgical renewal and . . . can be applied through rubrical directions which do not demand changes in the liturgical books now in use."

In other words, no new liturgical books will be needed for these changes. This point should be made clear to lay men and women as well as to the clergy, since so often a contrary impression is given. At the present time, the only liturgical service books needed for the celebration of Mass are the *Sacramentary* (which contains all the parts proper to the celebrant) and the *Roman Missal* (which contains the parts proper to the reader—whether lector, subdeacon, deacon, or celebrant—and the proper chants), plus a Bible for weekday readings. The instruction makes no change in this—nor will the introduction of the eucharistic prayer or canon in English, expected later this year; the latter will require only a simple insert for the *Sacramentary*.

The expression, "gradual introduction of the liturgical renewal," is an explicit indication of the policy of the Holy See, namely, to introduce liturgical reforms step by step, as experience shows the need and as the work of study and preparation is completed. For many, it is not easy to appreciate the flexible and gradually evolving nature of liturgical rites, but this is one of the lessons to be learned. The responsibility rests, for the most part, upon priests, who must plan and prepare for each celebration of the sacred liturgy.

As has already been announced, some major steps of liturgical reform will be submitted by Pope Paul VI to the Synod of Bishops next fall for discussion and consultation, in accordance with the principle of episcopal collegiality. The implications of the *Constitution on the Liturgy* have not always been grasped, but they demand the total revision of the Roman liturgy (SC 25), parts of which will be considered by the synod, as well as a continuing program of prayer and study, education and preparation, by priests and people (SC 14–19).

This is the place to mention the recent pastoral statement on "Liturgical

Renewal" made by the National Conference of Catholic Bishops. Although prepared beforehand and without reference to the new instruction, the statement is in perfect harmony with it and can serve as an excellent introduction to the few reforms now to be observed. The greater significance of the statement by the conference of bishops lies in the breadth of its appeal. It is intended to call for a fresh effort, especially by priests, to stimulate liturgical participation by planning and preparation.

13

Introduction to the Recording of the Roman Canon in English

International Commission on English in the Liturgy
(Distributed by the Bishops' Committee
on the Liturgy)
October 1967

(See also nos. 1, 2, 5, 16, 32, 35)

For many centuries, the Roman canon or eucharistic prayer, apart from the preface, Sanctus, and concluding words, had been said very quietly or silently so that no one but the deacon at his side could hear the priest's words. About the only exception was the concelebrated Mass of ordination.

In the preconciliar liturgical movement, a long history of prayers and devotions parallel to, or at least simultaneous with the silent praying of, the eucharistic prayer had given way to a limited "praying the Mass with the priest" using popular missals. But this was small progress compared with the new reform: proclamation in English of the principal presidential prayer, the anaphora of the Eucharist. With the concession that the prayer might be said aloud or sung (made in the "second instruction" of May 1967) and with the concession of the vernacular (in the same instruction, although the grant had been made to the United States some months earlier), a major liturgical reform—one not specifically anticipated by Vatican II—was at hand.

Something of the background is needed. Prior to the Second Vatican Council, several conferences of bishops, including that of the United States, secured the consent of the Roman See to the limited introduction of the vernacular into the rites of some of the sacraments—in the form of a *collectio rituum*, a bilingual ritual created as a kind of appendix to the *Roman Ritual* that was in general use throughout the Latin Church. But, the principle seemed to be to require the exclusive use of Latin for anything of major significance, such as the euchological texts said by the minister. Of course, the very opposite principle might have been invoked, namely, it is the most signficant texts that should be in the language understood by the people, so that their affirmation of faith and worship might be given with comprehension and conviction.

To a certain extent, Vatican II continued in the same restrictive line, at least in Chapters I and II of the *Constitution on the Liturgy*, although it placed no real limitation on the ultimate expansion of vernacular use. For the Eucharist, it was clear that the starting point would be a limited concession, with the euchological texts, the presidential prayers, and especially the central eucharistic prayer still in Latin. At first, a similar approach was taken with regard to the other sacraments and services: following the first reworking of Chapter III of the constitution by a sub-committee chaired by Archbishop Hallinan, the fathers of the council agreed that the vernacular could be used throughout the celebration of the sacraments other than the Eucharist, but a notable exception was made. Latin was to be required for the central, operative texts called the sacramental forms. This part of the decree was corrected, however, at the recommendation of about six hundred bishops, and the council as a whole finally decided to permit even the forms of the sacraments in the vernacular. The further extension of the vernacular in the eucharistic rite (already basically determined in Chapter II) was left untouched at that time (1963).

Further concessions were inevitable since the bishops very quickly recognized the pastoral needs of the people and the almost universal welcome to the vernacular at Mass. Thus, the Apostolic See enlarged the concessions for the Mass from the basic one (described in connection with the 1965 American statement, *The Use of the Vernacular*) to the presidential prayers outside the canon, to the preface of the canon, and, finally, to the whole of the eucharistic prayer. In other words, the pre-conciliar pattern or principle, to require the retention of Latin for the most important liturgical texts, was gradually eroded and disappeared in 1967.

The International Advisory Committee on English in the Liturgy had already begun its work on the initial projects of its program, with a public consultation concerning the ordinary parts of the people at Mass, but the Roman canon was its first completed text. After the kind of ICEL con-sultation that became usual (with bishops, liturgical commissions, and specialists in various disciplines, from languages and liturgy to pastoral care), the bishops of the United States readily approved the English text submitted by ICEL. Still, there was a last minute effort to maintain Latin for the institution narrative, despite the spirit of the council and the new concession of the Apostolic See. The announcement by the president of the conference, Archbishop Dearden, deserves quoting; it is dated from Rome, September 27, 1967:

Archbishop John F. Dearden of Detroit, president of the National Conference of Catholic Bishops, announced today that an English translation of the canon of the Mass will be used in the United States beginning Sunday, October 22. The text was almost unanimously approved by the American bishops last June [it had been approved in principle, before final revisions by ICEL, at the meeting of the conference in April] and will be introduced into the Mass with the consent of the Holy See on a temporary basis as the sole permitted text.

In making the announcement, Archbishop Dearden explained that no new books or missals of any kind will be needed to put the change into effect. It will be enough for priests to have a small insert for altar sacramentaries or missals, and these inserts will be distributed before October 22. In the near future, three or four new texts as optional alternatives to the present canon are expected. This development has already been announced by the Holy See, and it makes new liturgical books impractical as well as unnecessary at the present time.

The approved translation is the work of the International Commission on English in the Liturgy, set up three years ago by ten English-language hierarchies. It is the result of massive effort by theological, liturgical, and literary experts and has received formal approbation from nine hierarchies representing over six hundred bishops. . . .

The next day, the chairman of the Bishops' Committee on the Liturgy, Archbishop Hallinan, who had succeeded Archbishop Francis Grimshaw of Birmingham as chairman of ICEL, also issued a statement, praising the translation as "simple and eloquent. Prepared by scholars and literary experts, it cannot be called slavish. Instead it is clear and contemporary." (It is a second edition of this translation of Eucharistic Prayer I, with slight revisions, that is now in use throughout the English-speaking countries.)

Archbishop Hallinan repeated the point already made, that new liturgical books would not be needed. This was a constant preoccupation of the committee: to forestall the objection that new and costly books would be required at each stage of reform and would then quickly become obsolete. The final pastoral point of the press release explains why the committee turned to ICEL for a recording of the Roman canon in English:

This reform places a new responsibility on priests—first, to recite this central prayer of the Mass effectively and deliberately; next, to help people to appreciate the profound meaning of each phrase of the present canon of the Mass. It is only when these texts are in our own language that we can appreciate them in the setting of the eucharistic celebration.

The tape recording of the Roman eucharistic prayer in English was provided by ICEL, with the text spoken by Monsignor Joseph Gallagher of Baltimore. It was distributed by the committee's secretariat to all the dioceses of the United States, with permission and encouragement to reproduce it for all the priests to hear. Since it was not known how widely this had been done, the introductory text printed here was published in the October 1967 issue of the committee's *Newsletter*.

Several parts of this introduction should be pointed out. First is a summary exposition of the meaning of eucharistic prayers, which was an indication of the constant concern for catechesis, in this case, primarily a catechesis of priests. Next, there is an explanation of the principles of translation employed; these principles were applied in the notes to the English translation published separately. They bear reviewing twenty years later when the ICEL texts for the Eucharist are in process of revision. The principles anticipate what would be said at much greater length and in greater detail in the Consilium's instruction on translation of liturgical texts for celebrations with a congregation, *Comme le prévoit* (January 25, 1969: DOL 123).

Finally, there is a direct introduction to the text recited on the recording. It deals with the manner of proclaiming the eucharistic prayer, unhappily a manner of recitation not always observed. And, some of the concerns are with us still: care and deliberation in uttering the words; need for inaudible recitation of the common words by concelebrants so that the presiding celebrant's voice alone is heard; intelligible reading according to the division into sense lines—an important feature of English liturgical texts.

This recording of the newly authorized English translation of the Roman canon of the Mass is intended to assist priests in their preparation for the celebration of Mass with the new text. The translation was made by the International Commission on English in the Liturgy, which was established three years ago by the episcopal conference of ten English-language countries. As the *Constitution on the Liturgy* directs, the formal approbation of the translation for actual liturgical use in the celebration of the Eucharist comes from the episcopal conference of the particular country. The reproduction of this translation in any form requires the written permission of the International Committee on English in the Liturgy, Inc., in accordance with its policy on copyright and procedure.

Although, in practice, the canon will be read by the celebrant from an insert to the *Sacramentary* or missal or from a card or booklet, until he is sufficiently familiar with the text to recite it from memory, the best introduction to this translation is by way of the spoken word. The principal aim of the translators was to provide a version that the priest will be able to speak aloud easily and effectively and that the members of the congregation will be able to listen to and comprehend. Thus, the best introduction to the translation is listening to it.

Much may be said about the translation and the principles on which it is based, but first of all, something should be said about the nature of the canon— as we ordinarily call the eucharist prayer of the Roman liturgy.

The eucharistic prayer begins with the greeting and invitation of the priest at the beginning of the preface; it is a complete misunderstanding of the prayer to think of it as beginning only after the Sanctus. In spite of the varied elements within it, the canon is a single prayer that is completed only with the doxology and amen—and, indeed, it is closely related to the Lord's Prayer, which follows, and which introduces the communion rite.

The eucharistic prayer—like the collect, the prayer over the gifts, etc.— is a presidential prayer, spoken by the celebrant on behalf of the whole worshiping community. Like other presidential prayers, it is, in fact, a prayer of the people, expressing their faith and love and depending upon their response and ratification. This is the sense of the acclamations of the people at the beginning of the preface, the common singing or recitation of the Sanctus by the priest and people together with the ministers and choir, and the climactic

85

amen at the end of the doxology. By its nature, the eucharistic prayer is a public prayer, in fact the most public prayer of the community during the celebration of the Eucharist—a fact disguised until very recently by the practice of reciting this prayer in a quiet tone of voice.

The eucharistic prayer or canon is a prayer of blessing—and that not only in the sense of a consecratory prayer but in the fuller and deeper meaning, indeed the original meaning, of a prayer proclaiming the praise of God and giving thanks. It is not always easy to express this kind of prayer in our language, but the sense is that through this prayer we bless God, that is, we proclaim the wonderful deeds of God, the mystery of creation and redemption, and, in so doing, we give thanks to God and are filled with God's blessing.

Central to the eucharistic prayer are the recital of the narrative of the Lord's supper and the memorial of the paschal mystery: the Lord's passion, resurrection, and ascension. In varying degree, not only the Roman canon but also the many other eucharistic prayers used in Christian liturgies attempt to put into words the meaning of the eucharistic mystery: the sacrifice, the memorial, and the banquet.

The Roman canon has many defects, some of which will become more and more obvious when it is regularly recited in the vernacular. Its weakness is in its complex arrangement as well as in the disproportionate space given to prayers of intercession and prayers of offering, with relatively little of praise and thanks after the Sanctus itself. Its strength is in the fact that it has worn so well, with practically no change since the seventh century, and in its special characteristic: the praise of the mysteries of salvation through the variety of prefaces.

Many people have suggested that, rather than a mere translation of the Roman canon, there should be a radical simplification and revision of its text. Another course of action has been chosen: to retain the Roman canon intact and, at the same time, to develop for the future other eucharistic prayers to be used as alternatives to it. The Roman liturgy is rather unique in having only a single eucharistic prayer, a limitation only partially overcome by the variety of the prefaces. It is now possible to look forward to a number of distinct eucharistic prayers, which will embody the characteristics that have developed in Christian usage and will express with varying emphasis the many facets of the eucharistic celebration.

The present text of the Roman canon is a faithful and integral translation.

As indicated already, the aim was to produce a version that could be used effectively in the public liturgical assembly for the celebration of the Eucharist. This has been done with complete fidelity to the Latin text—in such a way as to reproduce, as far as possible, every meaning and value, particularly biblical and liturgical, in the original.

Close study of the translation will reveal that some words found in the Latin text do not have a counterpart in the English. Such omission was done on principle. It soon became evident to the translators that certain words—especially the multiplication of adjectives—were found in the Latin text not for their meaning but for stylistic reasons, in order to satisfy the demands of Latin prose rhythm, or because of a particular cultural mentality associated with the Latin language at the time of composition. Since contemporary English has nothing corresponding to these characteristics of Latin style, it was a conviction of the translators that attempts to find an English word corresponding to each Latin word would result in mistranslation as well as awkwardness and artificiality.

In the preparation of this translation, all available English translations were examined. It was found that even the best of these, although literary and eloquent in some measure, were too greatly concerned with transferring the Latin words rather than the Latin sense into English. Moreover, and more serious, it was found that these translations, however much they attempted a contemporary style, were suited rather for individual and private reading than for public proclamation in the concrete circumstances of the Eucharist.

The great concern of the translators that the resulting text should be contemporary should not be misunderstood. The language of the translation is not ordinary or colloquial or conversational. Its eloquence derives from its directness and simplicity; there is no reason why dignity and, indeed, solemnity of style should be incompatible with clarity and intelligibility.

At the same time, in some instances it is virtually impossible to interpret the concepts of the Latin canon without resorting to terms of biblical or even technical theological reference, unless lengthy circumlocutions or explanatory phrases are introduced. The eucharistic prayer, however, is not a catechetical lesson, but a living announcement of faith. What is expressed succinctly in the eucharistic prayer should be subject of catechesis of the people.

Several examples of this need for catechesis may be mentioned: the profound meaning of blessing, already indicated; the objective nature of the memorial of the Lord's passion and glorification; the biblical concept of God's glory filling all creation; the mediatorship of Jesus; the meaning of the blood of the new covenant; the theological implications of the doxology of the canon.

The direct purpose of this recording of the canon is to suggest the way in which the priest who presides at the eucharistic celebration should say these words. The words of this and other presidential prayers should be spoken clearly, distinctly, and intelligibly—so that all who are present may hear each word and appreciate its meaning. Obviously, it is necessary that in larger churches and gatherings the very best means of mechanical amplification be employed.

The notion of proclaiming God's Word in the readings from Scripture and in the homily has become familiar through the insistence of the Second Vatican Council upon a new appreciation of preaching and proclamation. The council also noted the intimate relationship between the liturgy of the Word and the eucharistic liturgy: the proclamation of God's Word in the reading and preaching is itself an act of worship, since it is the acknowledgment of God's goodness and greatness. The eucharistic act, worship, and liturgy are, likewise, an announcement of God's deeds and the praise of his goodness and greatness.

This means that the manner of speaking or saying the words of the eucharistic prayer should be not unlike that employed in the homily. The eucharistic prayer is a set formula, but it, too, is an announcement of the mystery: we proclaim the death of the Lord until he comes. This obviously demands reverence and dignity, but it also suggests the avoidance of any artificial or dramatic solemnity. The text is simple, and it should be said with meaning and with the greatest attention; it should be spoken deliberately and carefully, never routinely or hurriedly.

Many of these observations are so evident that they do not bear repetition. Recent experience with the use of the vernacular in the presidential prayers of Mass—and in the biblical readings as well—indicates that these are not always said with care and deliberation as sincerity of worship demands. Since the eucharistic prayer is used regularly, an even greater effort is required of the celebrating priest, who must try to speak the words with a fresh realization of their meaning. Inevitably, some will speak the eucharistic prayer in a formalized and ritualistic way, but this will gravely detract from the genuine and authentic expression of the Eucharist.

A special note should be added concerning concelebration. The individual concelebrants who take a particular part of the canon should, of course, say that part carefully and intelligibly. The original directive given for the concelebrants in the case of the Latin canon should also be noted: "The concelebrants say aloud only those prayers which they have to say either alone or with the principal celebrant. They should recite these as far as possible from memory. They are not to say them so loudly that their voice predominates over the voice of the principal celebrant" (*Ritus*, n. 14).

This directive is even more significant now for the English canon. In those parts of the text that are said by the principal or presiding celebrant in unison with the concelebrants, only the single voice of the presiding celebrant should be heard and it should be clear and distinct; the concelebrants should take the greatest pains not to let their voices predominate or obscure the clear speaking of the text by the principal or presiding celebrant. In every case, the words of the eucharistic prayer should be clearly intelligible to all who are present.

The printed text of the new translation of the Roman canon is arranged in sense-lines so that—in addition to the usual punctuation—there may be an indication of the pauses necessary for intelligible reading. Needless to say, the text of the prayer should not be recited too slowly or too ponderously so that the attention of the congregation wanders, but the greater danger to be avoided is that of a hurried recitation with little concern for meaning or understanding. The introduction of our own language into the eucharistic prayer represents another step of pastoral value in the liturgical reform. It can have greater value if priests proclaim these words with simplicity and strength and with deep conviction of their sense in each gathering of the Christian assembly to celebrate the Eucharist.

14

Development of Effective
Liturgical Music

Statement, Music Advisory Board of the Bishops' Committee on the Liturgy
November 1967

(See also nos. 4, 6, 10, 15, 31)

Early in 1968, the election of a new chairman of the Music Advisory Board was announced: the Reverend J. Paul Byron of the Diocese of Raleigh, succeeding Abbot Rembert Weakland, OSB, who had become abbot primate of the Order of Saint Benedict. At the same time, two statements of the board were released.

The first statement *Copyright Violations* was incorporated, after some textual revision, in a statement of the episcopal committee itself that was published in April 1969. Only the second statement is reprinted here.

A few months prior to the statement on the *Development of Effective Liturgical Music,* the Congregation of Rites had issued an instruction, prepared by the Consilium, on the general subject of the music of Catholic worship. Dated March 5, 1967, the instruction *Musicam sacram* (DOL 508) provided the context for this American statement and, indeed, for the longer and more substantial document *The Place of Music in Eucharistic Celebration,* which was to follow.

Here, the concentration is on pastoral programs of education in church music that needed encouragement. The statement is modest, simply offering pragmatic and sensible suggestions, but it indicates how deeply the music board felt about the slow progress of musical developments in the liturgical renewal. It has to be confessed that the response to these recommendations, as is the case with most such exhortations, was scattered. Only a survey of formal educational programs of the kind would reveal the degree of progress in the intervening years. Unhappily, the most recent scholarly survey, the "Notre Dame Study of Catholic Parish Life," showed continuing and serious dissatisfaction with church music in the parishes of the United States. The findings of this study are being published in a series of *Reports,* which began in December 1984.

In the statement itself, it is possible to detect recurring concerns. Even the open sentence, speaking of "the use of music as an integral part of the liturgy," points to a problem present in contemporary music almost as much as in the past, namely, the failure to integrate music with the liturgical act and rite. A caution that will be raised again is the responsibility of diocesan music commissions to encourage creativity "and not merely regulate and restrict." The members of the music board had long memories of quasi-official blacklists of poor or inappropriate church music; the condemnatory approach had failed and certainly could not contribute to positive and effective development. Finally, there is a hint of a resurgent problem in the 1960s: "visiting performers" or not; the group of singers should not be giving a "performance" at the liturgy, whether in classical polyphony or in folk music.

Perhaps, one rather dubious suggestion should be pointed out. It is the possible placement of an instruction in music "following either the homily or the prayer of the faithful" during the eucharistic celebration itself. It is clear enough today that the liturgy should not be interrupted for an educational program, however sound the purpose, not even for doctrinal, biblical, or liturgical instruction that is didactic in character. (The same might be said of an experimental adaptation of the rite of Mass, which was accepted by the Subcommittee on Liturgical Adaptation in 1969. It was an attempt to combine the eucharistic rite with the catechetical instruction of a parish mission. This did not meet with success.)

Otherwise, however, the programs proposed were sound enough, and the major statement to come would explain, at some length, the authentic place of music in the eucharistic celebration.

---

a. In order that the use of music as an integral part of the liturgy might be better understood and practiced, it is imperative for each archdiocese to formulate a program of music education, directed specifically towards liturgical participation.

b. In those places where such a program has not yet been formulated, the Diocesan Music Commission and/or Liturgical Commission (cf. MS ch. IX) should take the initiative in drawing up a workable plan and in offering assistance to the pastors and parishes of the area. The Commission should actively encourage creativity and not merely regulate and restrict.

c. The basis for the program is an understanding of the value and function of music in life and Christian worship. It is the responsibility of the Music Commission to make available for pastors and parish musicians instructional materials which explain the reasons for the use of music in the liturgy.

d. Some materials that may be recommended are the forthcoming statement on *The Place of Music in the Celebration of the Eucharist;* "Musical-Liturgical Artistry in the Mass," by Daniel A. Kister, SJ (*Worship,* vol. 41, no. 8, pp. 450–464); filmstrips and records on the history of the Mass, obtainable from the Liturgical Commission of the Archdiocese of Chicago (P.O. Box 1979, Chicago, IL 60690).

e. The program envisioned here will aim to educate the faithful of all ages in the area, particularly those who are not in a formal education program, and it should, therefore, extend beyond the school to the entire parish.

f. No single program of education will answer all needs. The following approaches are offered as practical suggestions:

(1) The presentation of a series of in-service workshops for the pastors and their parish musicians in a given area (deanery, vicariate, or the like). The primary object of these workshops would be to involve those present in an

effective experience of worship celebrated with music. This experience should then be discussed and evaluated. Those in charge of the workshop should also be prepared to offer advice and suggestions on how to meet specific problems and to indicate musical materials that are available for use in the liturgy.

Pastors (and their assistants) should be encouraged by the bishops to attend these workshops; the meetings should be announced well in advance, and they should be very carefully organized to meet the known needs of the parishes of the area in which they are held.

(2) Depending upon the number of liturgical musicians available in the area, teams of consultants might be formed, who, at the request of a pastor, would come to a particular parish and would work with the pastor and the parish organizations, and would take part in the liturgical assembly at stated times over a period of several weeks. Besides appraising the situation in each parish, they could offer suggestions and practical guidance for improving the parish musical program and for initiating a program where one has not yet been begun. Their endeavor should be to help the parish develop a program which answers its liturgical needs; they should not appear merely in the role of visiting performers. If the area has a major seminary or a community of religious, those seminarians or religious who show competence in liturgy and/or liturgical music should be called upon to provide assistance in this project. Expenses involved in carrying out such a program should be paid by the parish.

(3) There is a special need for the training of cantors and song leaders, as well as other parish musicians. The Music Commission should take the lead in setting up centers where such training can be imparted. Catholic colleges, universities, and seminaries in the area can provide valuable assistance by making their faculty and/or facilities available.

(4) In parishes having competent musical personnel, a sound working relationship should exist between pastor and musicians and with a common goal. The occasional use of time following either the homily or the prayer of the faithful should be given to the musical director to instruct the parish, and thus impress on the minds of all the importance of music in their worship.

g. Regional or national resource centers should be established wherever feasible, in colleges, seminaries, or other diocesan centers. They should be stocked with useful and contemporary musical materials so that the church musicians of the area may consult them and keep in touch with what is being published.

15

The Place of Music in Eucharistic Celebrations

Statement, Bishops' Committee on the Liturgy
November 1967

(See also nos. 4, 6, 10, 14, 31)

Probably no statement of the Bishops' Committee on the Liturgy has had the impact of this one, either in its original version or as revised and expanded in 1972. It was prepared, like the preceding statement on education and formation in liturgical music, in the wake of the 1967 Roman instruction *Musicam sacram* (DOL 508). Written by the Music Advisory Board, it was formally agreed to by the episcopal committee itself: "The committee has approved the statement, adopted it as its own, and recommends it for consideration by all."

There is no need to summarize the matters extensively treated in the statement, but it can be compared with the other substantial statements of the committee on church music and then evaluated for its own principal characteristics. The other major statements, two in number, are not included in this collection, both because of their length and because they are still in print.

After several years, an extensive review and revision of the present statement was conducted by a committee of the Federation of Diocesan Liturgical Commissions (FDLC), which the Bishops' Committee on the Liturgy had convened, and with which it collaborated in many programs, including the sponsorship of annual meetings of members of diocesan liturgical commissions. (After the first separate meeting of commission members in October 1969, held in Pittsburgh, a charter committee of the new federation approved a constitution for the new body in January 1970.)

The revised text, entitled *Music in Catholic Worship*, was formally approved by the committee as *The Place of Music in Eucharistic Celebrations* had been approved in 1967, and it was published in 1972 (revised in 1983). The following excerpt from the introduction indicates the relationship of the two statements:

The following statement on music in liturgical celebrations is a further development of that [1967] statement and was drawn up after study by the committee on music of the National Federation of Diocesan Liturgical Commissions. Their work was reviewed by the Bishops' Committee on the Liturgy and their advisors. The finished copy is presented to all by the Bishops' Committee on the Liturgy as background and guidelines for the proper role of music within the liturgy. . . .

A few years have elapsed, and the pastoral situation in the United States can be regarded with greater calm and serenity. However, it is urgent that fresh guidelines be given to foster interest with regard to music in the liturgy.

After several years with the 1967 statement, it should now be clear that mere observance of a pattern or rule of sung liturgy will not create a living and authentic celebration of worship in Christian congregations. That is why statements such as this must take the form of recommendation and attempts at guidance. In turn, this demands responsible study and choice by priests and leaders of singing: "a very wide field of diverse liturgical practice is now open, within the limits set by the present discipline and regulations. . . . Not all priests appreciate how wide the opportunities are for planning lively and intelligible celebration" (National Conference of Catholic Bishops, April 1967)—especially in the various combinations of song and spoken prayer in the liturgy (MCW, Intro.).

The reference to "greater calm and serenity" suggests, in part, the less than calm and serene reception received by the 1967 version, at least within parts of an entrenched church music establishment—which, indeed, did not accept even the more irenic approach of the 1972 edition.

The broad problem was that of the pastoral and liturgical dimension of church music. No matter how strongly the necessary and integral role of music is stressed, it still remains second to and servant to the liturgical rite, act, and text. To a certain extent, this problem was later faced in the programs of the new National Association of Pastoral Musicians. That association was established in 1978 as a voluntary and unofficial body—that is, like the older Liturgical Conference (1943) and unlike the federation of official diocesan commissions mentioned above. The new body attempted, with some success, in its meetings and its publication *Pastoral Music,* to marry the sometimes conflicting pastoral and musical interests.

One particular point at issue, in which the efforts of the episcopal committee had been resisted, was not substantive. It was the canonical or juridically binding force of the successive statements. With great care, the committee had insisted in 1967 that the statement eschewed any "set or rigid pattern," merely intending to "offer criteria" in the form of "recommendations and attempts at guidance." The same language was employed, again with great deliberation, in the introduction to the 1972 edition. This was done each time precisely because these statements draw their strength from the reasoned presentation and the force of their exposition. Implicit is a recognition that the creative arts cannot be truly regulated, aside from proscribing abuses and aberrations; much less can they be created by norms and laws.

In this, the liturgical and pastoral specialists who advised the committee in the second version of 1972 could take heart from the statement of Pope Paul VI in a very different context. In the apostolic constitution *Laudis canticum* on the liturgy of the hours (November 1, 1970: DOL 424), the pope made the point that those mandated and obliged by the Church to celebrate the canonical hours of prayer "should not only be drawn to celebrate the hours through obedience to law, but should also feel themselves drawn to them because of the intrinsic excellence of the hours and their pastoral and ascetical value."

An analogy may be drawn, related to one's concept of church law as existing because of the will of a legislator or legislature or, rather, intrinsically sound because of the reasons and purposes of the law itself. In the case of the statements on music, the appeal is to the excellence of the doctrine that they propose and to the quality of the reasons and recommendations.

The tenth anniversary of *Music in Catholic Worship* was observed by the committee not by a rewriting or updating of the earlier texts but by a supplementary statement, *Liturgical Music Today,* which appeared in 1982 and is still available. It is supplementary because it avoids retracing the area covered earlier but, instead, elaborates on matters barely mentioned before: music in the celebration of the sacraments other than the Eucharist and the revised liturgy of the hours. It also treats "a number of unforeseen issues in need of clarification and questions revealing new possibilities for liturgical music."

Since the first of the three substantive statements, reprinted here, is the last text on music to be included in this collection (except for a brief 1980 letter to composers), the question may be asked whether a kind of definitive statement is now possible, twenty years after the first effort. The committee of bishops has spoken frequently and positively over many years about the significance of liturgical music of quality, integrated into the liturgy with a fullness of church participation. As noted earlier, there are limits to the effects of statements—and, certainly, the quality of church music has not yet reached a level of general, popular satisfaction. Yet, statements are supportive, and there is a later parallel in the success of the committee's *Environment and Art in Catholic Worship* (Washington, D.C.: USCC Office of Publishing and Promotion Services, 1978), the first section of which eloquently introduces the general matter of the arts of worship, applicable not only to the visual arts and architecture but, indeed, to music itself.

The 1978 booklet on the arts at the service of the liturgy is not included in this collection, both because of its length and because it remains in print (in the original edition, with illustrations, and also in a bilingual English/Spanish edition, with newly chosen illustrations, issued in 1986). This is the place to mention it for the sake of completeness. It resulted from the fruitful collaboration of the committee with the Federation of Diocesan Liturgical Commissions. Perhaps, even more than the statements on music, it avoids any stress on the normative, at the same time being uncompromising on the quality and the liturgical appropriateness of church furnishing, vesture and vessels, decor and design, and the architectural setting of the celebration.

A distinctive feature of the committee's *Environment and Art* was the publication of supporting volumes in the next couple of years. The first is *The Cathedral: A Reader,* a collection of papers edited collaboratively by the secretariat and the Center for Pastoral Liturgy of The Catholic University of America (Washington, D.C.: USCC Office of Publishing and Promotion Services, 1979). The second, prepared in a similar collaboration, is *The Environment for Worship: A Reader* (Washington, D.C.: USCC Office of Publishing and Promotion Services, 1980). These volumes place in context the deep concern for offering broad guidance in the liturgical arts as a whole, as well as in the case of church music, which has been so often addressed.

To return to *The Place of Music in Eucharistic Celebrations* of 1967, which is the direct occasion of this note of comment, the statement has some characteristics worth studying and comparing with what the committee issued later. Perhaps, the first characteristic is that, while disclaiming all rigidity of norms, the text is somewhat apodictic in setting forth criteria. One instance is the succession of theses in capital letters; another is the repeated declaration, in pointing out the principal elements of some part of the eucharistic rite, "All else is secondary."

This tone is explained almost as an attention-getting device, a desire to say as forcefully as possible what had, in fact, been overlooked by professional church musicians. The goal is clearly harmony rather than discord, and an underlying conviction is that the liturgical and pastoral considerations are not in any way the enemy of the highest quality of music, either in composition or in actual singing (and playing, in the case of instrumental accompaniment)—provided always the overtones of "performance" of artists before an audience can be avoided.

This is the sense of the presentation in a theological or doctrinal context, specifically in the context of Christian faith—a matter not attended to or at least not adequately employed as a basic approach in Roman documents on liturgical or sacred music. It is also the sense of the directness with which the "humanly attractive experience" of celebration is described, in particular that celebration in which the musical arts are fully integrated. In this feature, the statement relies not only on the specifics of official texts but on the fundamental position of the *Constitution on the Liturgy*, which had enumerated a critical series of norms based upon the formative and pastoral nature of the liturgy (SC 33-36).

Still, another telling feature of the statement, which required and received later elaboration, is its practical description of the threefold judgment to be made in the selection of church music: musical, liturgical, pastoral. These interdependent considerations can resolve most of the conflicts between the pastoral and the musical emphases if they are thought out fully and applied. It is one of the statement's major contributions, deserving even greater stress.

No single aspect of the threefold judgment can stand by itself. The music may be a religious masterpiece but may not fit the liturgical elements or the character of the assembly. The music may respect the genre of the liturgical text but be tawdry and demeaning to the celebration. The music may meet the experience of the people gathered for worship but contradict the divine reality of the mystery or its tradition—or weaken the liturgy by musical weakness.

As already noted, the practical application in the initial version of the statement on music was limited to the Eucharist, and the deficiency was made up for partly in the second version and especially in *Liturgical Music Today*. These later statements may seem more sophisticated, and certainly, they addressed a more highly developed liturgical renewal. Overall, however, the force of the first effort was hard to equal, and the very concerns—and even antagonism—it aroused proved its worth.

The following statement was drawn up after study by the Music Advisory Board and was submitted to the Bishops' Committee on the Liturgy. The committee has approved the statement, adopted it as its own, and recommends it for consideration by all.

In particular, the committee draws attention to the principles underlying the use of music in the Eucharist and to the following points:

1. While it is possible to make technical distinctions in the forms of Mass—all the way from the Mass in which nothing is sung to the Mass in which everything is sung—such distinctions are of little significance as such, and any combination of sung and recited parts may be chosen. The important decision is whether, in the particular circumstances of the individual celebration, this or that part may or should be sung. The statement attempts to offer criteria; no set or rigid pattern can be proposed.

2. The preferences and priorities indicated in the text should be studied more seriously. For example, the apparent disproportion between the liturgy of the Word and the eucharistic liturgy can be somewhat ameliorated by enhancing the latter by singing the "Holy Holy Holy" or adding an acclamation after the words of institution, even in Masses in which little or nothing else is sung. The disproportion between the entrance rite and the service of the Word may be reduced by reciting rather than singing the "Lord, Have Mercy" and the "Glory to God."

3. Above all, it should now be clear that mere observance of a pattern or rule of sung liturgy will not create a living and authentic celebration of worship in Christian congregations. That is why statements such as this must take the form of recommendations and attempts at guidance. In turn, this demands responsible study and choice by priests and leaders of singing: "A very wide field of diverse liturgical practice is now open, within the limits set by the present discipline and regulations . . . not all priests appreciate how wide the opportunities are for planning lively and intelligible celebration" (National Conference of Catholic Bishops, April 1967)—especially in the various combinations of song and spoken prayer in the liturgy.

It is planned that further recommendations and guidelines will be published when the texts of the Simple Gradual and other alternatives to the present liturgical chants become available in English.

[The instruction frequently referred to below is *Musicam sacram* (= MS), issued on March 5, 1967, by the Congregation of Rites.]

I. The Theology of Celebration

GOOD CELEBRATIONS FOSTER AND NOURISH FAITH. POOR CELEBRATIONS WEAKEN AND DESTROY FAITH.

We are Christians because through the Christian community we have met Jesus Christ, heard his word of invitation, and responded to him in faith. We assemble together at Mass in order to speak our faith over again in community and, by speaking it, to renew and deepen it. We do not come together to meet Christ as if he were absent from the rest of our lives. We come together to deepen our awareness of, and commitment to, the action of his Spirit in the whole of our lives at every moment. We come together to acknowledge the work of the Spirit in us, to offer thanks, to celebrate.

People in love make signs of love and celebrate their love for the dual purpose of expressing and deepening that love. We too must express in signs our faith in Christ and each other, our love for Christ and for each other, or they will die. We need to celebrate.

We may not feel like celebrating on this or that Sunday, even though we are called by the Church's law to do so. Our faith does not always permeate our feelings. But this is the function of signs in the Church: to give bodily expression to faith, to transform our fragile awareness of Christ's presence in the dark of our daily isolation into a joyful, integral experience of his liberating action in the solidarity of the celebrating community.

From this, it is clear that the manner in which the Church celebrates the liturgy has an effect on the faith of men. Good celebrations foster and nourish faith. Poor celebrations weaken and destroy faith.

II. The Principle of Pastoral Celebration

THE PRIMARY GOAL OF ALL CELEBRATION IS TO MAKE A HUMANLY ATTRACTIVE EXPERIENCE.

A. *Good Signs: Simple and Comprehensible*

To celebrate the liturgy means to do the action, or to perform the sign, in such a way that its full meaning and import shine forth in the most clear and compelling fashion. The signs of sacramental celebration are vehicles of communication and instruments of faith. They must be good signs, simple and comprehensible; they must be humanly attractive. In order to fulfill their purpose, liturgical actions must be genuine celebrations: in themselves, in articulation and proportion, in manner of celebration.

1. *In themselves.* "The rites should be distinguished by a noble simplicity; they should be short, clear, and unencumbered by useless repetitions; they should be within the people's power of comprehension and normally should not require much explanation" (SC 34).

2. *In articulation and proportion.* Each part of the celebration should be clear in itself. (E.g., an entrance rite should clearly demonstrate by the elements that make it up and by the manner in which these are carried out in the celebration just what its purpose is.) Each part should be so articulated with the other parts that there emerges from the celebration the sense of a unified whole. What is of lesser importance should appear so; what is of greater importance should clearly emerge as such. (E.g., the offertory procession, from its manner and length of celebration, should not appear to be of greater importance than the canon.)

3. *In manner of celebration.* Each sacramental action must be invested with the personal care, attention, and enthusiasm of those who carry it out. (E.g., when the celebrant greets the community, he should do so in a way indicating clearly that he knows what he is doing and that he really means to do it.)

B. *Four Criteria: Humanly Attractive Experience, Degree of Solemnity, Nature of Congregation, Available Resources*

The celebration of any liturgical action, then, is to be governed by the need for the action to be clear, convincing, and humanly attractive; the degree of solemnity suitable for the occasion; the nature of the congregation; the resources that are available.

1. Under this principle, there is little distinction to be made between the solemn, sung, and recited Mass. Cf. MS 28: "For the sung Mass (*missa cantata*), different degrees of participation are put forward here for reasons of pastoral usefulness, so that it may become easier to make the celebration of Mass more beautiful by singing according to the capabilities of each congregation."

Cf. also MS 36: "There is no reason why some of the Proper or Ordinary should not be sung in recited Masses. Moreover, some other song can also, on occasion, be sung at the beginning, at the offertory, at the communion, and at the end of Mass. It is not sufficient, however, that these songs be merely 'eucharistic'—they must be in keeping with the parts of the Mass, with the feast, or with the liturgical season."

Cf. also MS 5: "They (pastors of souls) will try to work out how that assignment of different parts to be performed and duties to be fulfilled, which characterizes sung celebrations, may be transferred even to celebrations which are not sung, but at which people are present."

2. Under this principle, the celebrant may speak those parts that he cannot sing effectively. Cf. MS 8: "Whenever, for a liturgical service which is to be celebrated in sung form, one can make a choice between the various people, it is desirable that those who are known to be more proficient in singing be given preference; this is especially the case in more solemn liturgical celebrations and in those which either require more difficult singing or are transmitted by radio or television. If, however, a choice of this kind cannot be made, and the priest or minister does not possess a voice suitable for the proper execution of the singing, he may render without singing one or more of the difficult parts which concern him, reciting them in a loud and distinct voice. However, this must not be done merely for the convenience of the priest or minister."

3. Under this principle, each single song must be understood in terms of its own specific nature and function. Therefore, the customary distinction between the ordinary and proper parts of the Mass with regard to musical settings and distribution of roles is irrelevant. For this reason, the musical settings of the past are usually not helpful models for composing truly contemporary pieces (cf. MS 6).

4. Under this principle, it is clear that all sacramental celebrations are in themselves pastoral. Liturgies of a more elaborate form (e.g., pontifical liturgies, liturgies of special occasions) must not be less pastoral than those of

any parish. The pastoral purpose always governs the use and function of every element of the celebration. Cf. MS 11: "It is to be borne in mind that the true solemnity of liturgical worship depends less on a more ornate form of singing and a more magnificent ceremonial than on its worthy and religious celebration, which takes into account the integrity of the liturgical celebration itself, and the performance of each of its parts according to its own particular nature. To have a more ornate form of singing and a more magnificent ceremonial is at times desirable when there are the resources available to carry them out properly; on the other hand, it would be contrary to the true solemnity of the liturgy if this were to lead to a part of the action being omitted, changed, or improperly performed."

III. The Place of Music in the Celebration

MUSIC, MORE THAN ANY OTHER RESOURCE, MAKES A CELEBRATION OF THE LITURGY AN ATTRACTIVE HUMAN EXPERIENCE.

A. *The Amount of Singing Will Vary According to the Circumstances* (cf. MS 5)

B. *Music Serves the Expression of Faith*

Music in worship is a functional sign. It has a ministerial role (cf. MS 2). It must always serve the expression of faith. It affords a quality of joy and enthusiasm to the community's statement of faith that cannot be gained in any other way. In so doing, it imparts a sense of unity to the congregation.

C. *Three Judgments to Be Made about Music in Worship: Musical, Liturgical, Pastoral*

One of the major concerns of good celebrations is to select suitable music and perform it adequately. Such concern calls for different kinds of judgments:

1. *The musical judgment.* Is the music technically and aesthetically good? This question should be answered by competent musicians. This judgment is basic and primary. The musician has every right to insist that the music used be good music; but when this has been determined, there are still further judgments to be made.

2. *The liturgical judgment.* The nature of the liturgy itself will help to determine what kind of music is called for, what parts are to be preferred for singing, and who is to sing them.

a. *Text requirements.* Thus, we must ask, first of all, Does the music interpret the text correctly and make it more meaningful? Is the form of the text respected? Is this piece of music properly proportioned to the feast for which it is intended and its specific role in the liturgy? (E.g., in the "Holy Holy Holy" the musical setting must not only enhance the meaning of the text, lifting it to a higher expressive level, but also respect its basic character: that of an acclamation by all assembled, which flows immediately from the preface.) In making this liturgical judgment, we must keep in mind the four principal classes of texts:

Readings: Proclamations of God's Word: epistle, gospel; proclamation of faith: creed.

Acclamations: "Holy Holy Holy," Alleluia, Amen.

Psalms and Hymns: The psalms sung between the readings (gradual, tract, etc.), entrance songs, communion songs, closing songs, offertory songs, "Glory to God."

Prayers: Priest's prayers: eucharistic prayer (canon), collect, prayer over the gifts, postcommunion; people's prayers: litanies, "Lord, Have Mercy," "Lamb of God"; responses: "And with your spirit," "Thanks be to God," etc.

b. *Role differentiation.* In addition, the liturgical judgment must take into account the different kinds of people who fulfill specific functions in each of these rites. (E.g., the celebrant, whose function it is to pray in the name of the entire assembly, must be heard and understood by all present—cf. 1 Cor 14:16.) In this regard, special attention should be paid to the role of cantor.

c. *The cantor.* While there is no place in the liturgy for displays of virtuosity for its own sake, an individual singer can effectively lead the assembly and proclaim the Word of God in song, especially in the psalm sung between the readings. Cf. MS 21: "Provision should be made for at least one or two properly trained singers, especially where there is no possibility of setting up even a small choir. The singer will present some simpler musical setting, with the people taking part, and can lead and support the faithful as far as is needed. The presence of such a singer is desirable even in churches which have a choir for those celebrations in which the choir cannot take part but which may fittingly be performed with some solemnity and, therefore, with singing."

3. *The pastoral judgment.* The pastoral judgment must always be present. It is the judgment that must be made in this particular situation, in these concrete circumstances. Does music in the celebration enable those people to express their faith in this place, in this age, in this culture? A musician may say, for instance, that Gregorian Chant is good music. His musical judgment really says nothing about whether and how it is to be used in this celebration. The signs of the celebration must be accepted and received as meaningful. They must, by reason of the materials used, open up to a genuinely human faith experience. This pastoral judgment can be aided by sociological studies of the people who make up the congregation, studies which determine differences in age, culture, and education, as they influence the way in which faith is meaningfully expressed. No set of rubrics or regulations of itself will ever achieve a truly pastoral celebration of the sacramental rites. Such regulations must always be applied with a pastoral concern for the given worshiping community.

4. *There is a further problem.* It is the problem of faith itself. The liturgy, by its nature, normally presupposes a minimum of biblical culture and a fairly solid commitment of living faith. Often enough, these conditions are not present. The assembly or many of its members are still in need of evangelization. The liturgy which is not meant to be a tool of evangelization, is forced into a missionary role. In these conditions, the music problem is complex. On the one hand, music can serve as a bridge to faith, and, therefore, greater liberty in the selection and use of musical materials may be called

100

for. On the other hand, certain songs normally called for in the climate of faith (e.g., psalms and religious songs), lacking such a climate, may create problems rather than solve them.

IV. Application of the Principles of Celebration to the Eucharist

The best places to sing are at the "Holy Holy Holy," the Amen at the conclusion of the eucharistic prayer, the communion song, the responsorial psalm following the lessons.

Other places to sing are entrance and dismissal, "Lord Have Mercy," "Glory to God," Lord's Prayer, offertory song.

The celebration of the Eucharist has two parts: the liturgy of the Word, and the Liturgy of the Eucharist. The liturgy of the Word is generally introduced by an entrance rite, which varies in length and solemnity. A preparatory rite known as the offertory or preparation of the gifts precedes the eucharistic prayer. After the communion there is a brief conclusion known as the dismissal rite.

A. *The Liturgy of the Word*

1. Service of the Word

a. The purpose of the service of the Word is to proclaim the Word of God in the Christian assembly in such a way that the people hear and respond to God's message of love and become involved in the great covenant of love and redemption.

b. The service of the Word, at present, consists of epistle, psalm (gradual, tract), gospel, homily, creed, prayer of the faithful. Of these elements, the proclamation of the Word, response to the Word, and homily are primary. Everything else is secondary.

c. Recommendations for the celebration of the service of the Word:

(1) In the United States, it seems that the hearing of God's Word is a more meaningful and stirring experience when the lessons are read rather than sung.

(2) The psalms which follow the epistle make most sense when they are sung. They should be proclaimed in such a way that their words can be heard and reflected upon. Unlike the other uses of psalmody in the Mass, where the psalm accompanies a procession (e.g., entrance, communion), this psalm is sung for its own sake. The present text can be set more elaborately for a cantor to sing in true cantorial style; it can be set in choral form for the choir; or it may be set so that the people can participate by a brief refrain. It may be desirable that there be a brief period of reflective silence immediately after the reading of the epistle. When the text is not sung, it is more desirable that it be read by an individual or by the lector and listened to by the people rather than recited by all.

(3) Whenever the psalm is proclaimed in song, the "Thanks be to God" should be answered by the server only.

(4) The creed should be spoken in a declamatory fashion. This is usually preferable to singing it.

(5) The prayer of the faithful, if it is used properly, can be a most effective moment for achieving both the personal and communal experience. It can be sung in various forms, be spoken by one person, or be spontaneous. The purpose of the prayer of the faithful is to open the minds of the assembly to the concerns of the Church and the world. The intentions, whether spoken or sung, ought to be stated in a brief and concise manner.

2. The Entrance Rite

The service of the Word is generally introduced by an entrance rite, which varies in length and solemnity.

a. The entrance rite is quite secondary to the proclamation of the Word. It should be celebrated in such a way that it fulfills its purpose and leads quickly to the actual service of the Word.

b. The entrance rite should create an atmosphere of celebration. It serves the function of putting the assembly in the proper frame of mind for listening to the Word of God. It helps the people to become conscious of themselves as a community.

c. The entrance rite consists of entrance song (introit), confession prayers, "Lord, Have Mercy," "Glory to God," prayer. Of these elements, the entrance song and prayer (collect) are primary; the rest is secondary.

d. Recommendations for the celebration of the entrance rite:

(1) The musical setting of the entrance song should help the celebration tone of the entrance rite. There are a number of possibilities: the hymn, unison or choral, or both; psalms in various settings with or without refrain.

(2) The confession prayers: Under the present circumstance, if an entrance song is used, the least objectionable practice is that the celebrant and server recite the prayers quietly and with dispatch while the entrance song is being sung. If an entrance song is not used, the recitation of these prayers by the celebrant and the people can be pastorally effective.

(3) Reciting, rather than singing, the "Lord, Have Mercy" and the "Glory to God" may help achieve a better proportion between the entrance rite and the service of the Word on less solemn occasions such as weekdays. When both of these are sung, from the point of view of sign, they may tend to make the entrance rite top-heavy compared with the proclamation of the Word. When everything that can be sung is sung in the liturgy of the Word, the entire rite should not be out of proportion to the major sign, which is the liturgy of the Eucharist, particularly the eucharistic prayer. The musical setting of the "Lord, Have Mercy" should be simple, because it is a simple litany.

(4) The prayer (collect) may be sung or spoken, whichever is more effective.

B. *The Liturgy of the Eucharist*

1. The Eucharistic Prayer

a. The eucharistic prayer is the praise and thanksgiving pronounced over the bread and wine which are to be shared in the communion meal. It is an acknowledgment of the Church's faith and discipleship transforming the gifts to be eaten into the Body which Jesus gave and the Blood which he poured out for the life of the world, so that the sharing of the meal commits the Christian to sharing in the mission of Jesus. As a statement of the universal Church's faith, it is proclaimed by the president alone. As a statement of the faith of the local assembly, it is affirmed and ratified by all those present through acclamations like the great Amen.

b. Now that the eucharistic prayer is proclaimed in the vernacular, the quality of the celebration will be even more dependent upon the celebrant. From the viewpoint of music, it is not so important that he sing—to sing the eucharistic prayer for many celebrants would be to detract from its effectiveness—as that he proclaim the prayer in such a way as to elicit a spirited response from the assembly.

When in addition to the Roman canon we will have the other expected eucharistic prayers, these may be chosen in its place. In each of these, there is a provision for a short acclamation after the words of institution, by which the assembly expresses its faith in, and gratitude for, the death and resurrection of the Lord.

This acclamation (frequently called an anamnesis), along with the "Holy Holy Holy" and the great Amen, will be much more meaningful and effective when sung. Among the most urgent tasks for composers is that of providing suitable settings for these acclamations. Instrumental preludes to the acclamations are to be avoided.

The great Amen at the end of the eucharistic prayer requires care. It is difficult to make an enthusiastic acclamation out of this single two-syllable word. Composers should feel free to repeat it several times or to explicate its many meanings when setting it to music.

c. Preparatory Rite (offertory):

(1) The purpose of the rite is to prepare bread and wine for the sacrifice. The secondary character of the rite determines the manner of celebration.

(2) The rite consists of the bringing of the gifts with accompanying music, the prayers said by the celebrant as he prepares the gifts, the "Brethren, pray," and the prayer over the gifts (secret prayer). Of these elements, the bringing of the gifts, the placing of the gifts on the altar, and the prayer over the gifts are primary. All else is secondary.

(3) Recommendations for celebrating:

(a) Bringing the gifts in procession is a most effective sign. The hosts that are distributed at Mass should be consecrated at that Mass, to give meaning and significance to the sign of the rite. The procession of gifts can vary in solemnity with the occasion. Ordinarily, it should be done rather simply. To elaborate the rite too much is to distort the proportionate value of the rite.

(b) The prayer over the gifts is sung or spoken, whatever is more effective.

(c) The celebrant's role and all prayers except the prayer over the gifts are secondary in the rite.

(d) The procession can be accompanied by song. Song is not always necessary or desirable. Organ or instrumental music is also fitting at this time. When song is used, it is to be noted that the song need not speak of bread and wine or of offering. The proper function of this song is to accompany and celebrate the communal aspects of the procession. The text, therefore, can be any appropriate song of praise or of rejoicing in keeping with the season. Such songs are even more desirable. The song need not accompany the entire preparation rite. In fact, it is good to give the assembly a period of quiet before demanding, at the preface, their full attention to the eucharistic prayer.

2. Communion Rite

a. The celebration of this part of the Eucharist must show forth in signs that the first fruit of the Eucharist is the unity of the Body of Christ, Christians loving Christ through loving one another.

b. Of the parts that comprise the communion rite, the most important are the Lord's Prayer, the communion procession accompanied by song, the postcommunion prayer. All else is secondary: "Lamb of God," priest's prayers, etc.

c. Recommendations for celebration:

(1) The principle of good celebration requires that the Lord's Prayer be done in the most effective manner possible. At times, the pastoral judgment may dictate that it be sung by all, at other times that it be spoken.

(2) The "Lamb of God" can be sung or spoken according to circumstances. If it is sung, the settings should be in keeping with the litany character of the prayer. Its purpose is to accompany an action: the breaking of the Bread. According to no. 34 of *Musicam Sacram*, the "Lamb of God" may be repeated as often as necessary, especially during concelebrations.

(3) The communion song should foster an experience of unity. For this reason, the following points touching its nature and the manner of carrying out are essential:

—It is to be sung during the actual distribution of communion.

—It should not become wearisome. If the communion time is of any length, variety should be sought (e.g., instrumental interlude, period of silence, choir song, etc.).

—The ideal communion song is the short refrain sung by the people alternated with cantor or choir. The song can be learned easily and quickly. The people are not burdened with books, papers, etc. For the same reason, the metric hymn is the least effective communion song.

—The communion song can be any song that is fitting for the feast or the season; it can speak of the community aspects of the Eucharist. Most benediction hymns, by reason of their concentration on adoration, are not suitable.

—A new provision provides a period of silence and/or song before the postcommunion prayer. If song is used at this point, it may well serve in place of a final hymn.

d. The Dismissal Rite:

(1) The purpose of the dismissal rite is to bring the Eucharist to an orderly conclusion. The dismissal rite consists of the greeting, the blessing, the dismissal, followed by the closing hymn.

(2) The dismissal rite should be so performed that greeting, blessing, and dismissal form one continuous action.

(3) It is important to sing a closing hymn of fitting nature. The celebrant remains at the altar, singing with the people, for some portion of the hymn. On occasion, an instrumental recessional may be equally effective.

16

Latin in the Liturgy

Statement, Bishops' Committee on the Liturgy 1968

(See also nos. 1, 2, 5, 13, 32, 35)

This document, which was never published in the *Newsletter* of the Bishops' Committee on the Liturgy or elsewhere, was submitted to the bishops of the country for their information, guidance, and use. It has its genesis in some limited opposition to the use of the vernacular in the liturgy and also in a certain misunderstanding. Read in the light of the 1964 position of the committee (*Liturgical Constitution and the Vernacular in the United States* and *Use of the Vernacular*), this statement suggests that an important if small minority—never more than ten or fifteen percent of the Catholic faithful—might have been overlooked.

To appreciate the situation, it is necessary to explore a little pastoral history, somewhat oversimplified, and then the disciplinary steps taken to introduce the vernacular.

From the 1940s (and before) through the early 1960s, promoters of pastoral-liturgical renewal in the United States had moved, soundly and strongly, in the direction of a fully participated Latin liturgy—with emphasis on liturgical catechesis, communal song and spoken word, and broader ritual involvement. All this was without much hope of a vernacular liturgy or of a liturgy with reformed structures, improved selection of prayers and readings, and the like.

In the mid-1960s, the decisions concerning the liturgy in the vernacular, first by Vatican II, then by the conference of bishops, gradually but rapidly led to a fully vernacular liturgy, with minimal ritual changes but with an expectation of thorough reform and subsequent regional adaptation. Throughout the United States, the vernacular liturgy had become almost universal in parochial celebrations of the Eucharist and, of course, in the other sacraments and rites. All this left uncertain and disaffected those small numbers of people who had resisted the change and of people who had not expected the change and were dissatisfied when it occurred.

Little has been done to identify the reasons for this failure to accept, whether wholly or partially, a restoration undertaken for the most evident pastoral reasons. And, the matter is only complicated by uncertainty as to the desiderata of those disaffected by this aspect of the change: a desire to preserve the music written for the Latin; a preference for silent celebration to permit freer rein for individual piety; a will to maintain elements of continuity with the past; a simple nostalgia; a psychological resistance to change; only a partial acceptance of the vernacular, for example, for the readings. The question, moreover, is and was closely related to, but distinguishable from, the desire to retain the 1570 eucharistic rite of Saint Pius V (presumably with the modifications of subsequent popes up to and including Saint Pius X and/or John XXIII).

This last issue has gone by the misnomer of Tridentine Mass advocacy, because the Council of Trent did entrust the Roman See with the preparation of the *Roman Missal* and *Breviary*. It is a misnomer, however, because the reform of Pope Pius V in 1570 (when the first *Roman Missal,* quasi-universal in the West, was promulgated) did not make substantive changes in the Order of Mass. Only in 1984 did the issue of the "Tridentine Mass" become of major concern, when—despite the small numbers of advocates and despite an almost unanimous denial of any real problem by the Catholic episcopate—Pope John Paul II permitted bishops to allow very limited use of the preconciliar missal of Pope John XXIII.

Because the numbers of advocates of a return to a preconciliar rite are very small indeed, this has been less of a pastoral problem, albeit a serious anomaly and a symbol of rejection of Vatican II. It has served to separate those who reject the present Roman Order of Mass as heretical and invalid, those who accept its legitimacy but question it on every other ground, those who for whatever reason are uncomfortable with liturgical change or ecclesial growth, and those who simply prefer the retention of the Latin language. It is only to the last group that the present document was addressed, on the assumption that the conciliar teaching on the communal nature of the liturgy and the proper participation of the whole people of God in it had been "received" by the Church.

To go back to the beginning of this commentary on the statement, such individuals and groups in the Catholic community who are devoted to Latin usage are in a theoretical position not unlike the liturgical promoters and pastors of preconciliar days: It may be assumed that they are able, if they use Latin and have the will to follow Vatican II and the liturgical reform, to celebrate the revised rite with all the signs of participation by word, song, gesture, action, silence, and interior devotion that the reformed liturgy of its nature demands—language alone excepted.

As one reads the statement, it may seem that the above is really a debater's assumption. Experience with celebrations in which Latin is used suggests that the assumption is not true. Typical of such Masses is celebration with elaborate choral music in Latin, with the congregation in silent attendance, or celebration of recited Masses with few signs of active, communal participation.

A word needs to be said about misunderstandings, in response to which the statement takes on a certain defensive tone. It was clear and certain that Vatican II made concessions of the vernacular but did not impose them. It was clear and certain that the National Conference of Catholic Bishops, beginning in April 1964, made these concessions available in the United States but did not impose them. The common view of these decisions, however, was far different.

In 1964, and, indeed, in each successive expansion of permitted vernacular in the Mass (the rest of the liturgy seems not to have been at issue), the individual diocesan bishop was faced with a pastoral question. While the Catholic people might be favorable to the liturgical vernacular (later surveys showed this to be an overwhelming preference of the people), many priests exercising the pastoral office were not prepared for and not desirous of the change. The vernacular was unsettling to priests who were in a tradition of silent Masses, hurried Masses, routine Masses. In many dioceses, therefore, the date for the initial concession of the vernacular became also, by episcopal decree, the date for a required use of the vernacular in regularly scheduled Masses with congregations of the people.

Thus, what was a concession became overnight a requirement. The permitted English replaced the Latin, which became only tolerated or—according to the widespread misconception—proscribed. At this late date, or even when the statement on "Latin in the Liturgy" was written, it is hard to say how the misunderstanding arose. From a pastoral viewpoint, however, it is certain that a mere permission to use the vernacular in a given diocese would have resulted in the most diverse practices—and, in days before parish councils and worship committees, would have deprived a very large percentage of the Catholic people of the fruits of the council's first decision. Such fears and, most likely, the bishops' desire for uniform practice within dioceses more than explain the diocesan decisions.

In turn, the committee developed the statement, which is somewhat defensive in its explanation of the diocesan situation but very clear in relation to the pastoral, liturgical, and spiritual needs of the Christian people. The commission tried to set straight some of the neglected and basic principles of action: The reform of the liturgical celebrations, both as to congregational participation and as to the ritual and other changes (including those to come), could not be compromised, whatever the language of celebration. If the Eucharist is celebrated in Latin, well and good, but every other element of liturgical renewal has to be respected and supported.

The evident viewpoint of the commission was one of sympathy for those still desirous of the use of Latin. Even in the recital of possible reasons for this desire, however, it tried to explain and educate, with the realization that the numbers of such disaffected members of the Catholic community would surely diminish in the future. Anecdotal evidence is enough to suggest that, after a period of time, even people strongly nostalgic for the Latin would not relish abandoning the vernacular, especially throughout a given liturgical service.

A more important contribution of the statement is the reasoned recommendation that, indeed, Latin should be used on occasion (certainly without any special concession or permission) in some limited parts of the liturgy. On the other hand, Latin is neither appropriate nor desirable for the euchological texts spoken by the priest for all to hear and affirm with their response, which should be conscious and faith-filled. The same holds equally for the readings and, at least in large measure, for the variable parts. But, the common sung parts, the so-called ordinary chants, may well be in Latin on occasion, once the people can understand their meaning. This suggested policy has some limited application to choral music, but surely to the chants of Kyrie, Sanctus, Agnus Dei, for which the simple melodies are highly suitable.

In turning in this direction, the commission took advantage of the 1967 instruction *Musicam sacram,* already mentioned. In no. 50 of that document, the Congregation of Rites had stated rather cryptically: "In view of local conditions, the pastoral good of the faithful, and the idiom of each language, parish priests (pastors) are to decide whether selections from the musical repertoire composed for Latin texts should be used not only for liturgies in Latin but also for those in the vernacular" (DOL 508). The norm of the instruction can best be interpreted as presupposing a liturgy either in Latin or in the vernacular and then proposing the possibility of introducing one or more Latin chants into the otherwise vernacular celebration (or, as may be equally evident, vernacular song in the otherwise Latin celebration).

The commission properly sought to correct the either-or mindset and, positively and significantly, to encourage Latin chants in eucharistic celebrations with vernacular prayers and readings. Given the strong positions taken by some specialists in Gregorian chant against its use to accompany vernacular texts, this may be, even in the 1980s, the best or only hope that the simple chant melodies may have a deserved place in the vernacular liturgy.

In more recent years, the issue has been complicated, in a way that the committee could not anticipate, by the concession, albeit limited, of the use of the preconciliar eucharistic rite mentioned above. Those who legitimately and reasonably seek a degree of Latin in the liturgy, specifically for the sung texts accompanied by the treasury of past liturgical music, should not be confused with those who are alienated by the conciliar and postconciliar reform.

The introduction of the English language into our liturgy on a wide scale, beginning in 1964 as a result of the decision of the Second Vatican Council, has had a transforming effect. From every pastoral point of view, it was desirable that obscurity give way to intelligibility, remoteness to immediate awareness—even for the minority who had previously understood the liturgy at second hand, through translations, and for the much smaller number who understood Latin.

Nevertheless, if we prescind from broader questions, there remains the plea frequently heard that the Latin liturgy should not disappear, particularly that Mass should sometimes be celebrated in Latin. Here, only the desire of some lay men and women is referred to; in these matters, the preferences of the clergy, who are the servants and ministers, must be secondary. That the request comes from a relatively small number does not matter. Similarly, whether the request arises in a deep appreciation of the cultural and spiritual values of the Latin texts used in the liturgy or simply in a desire for signs of stability and strength in times of radical change, it should not be lightly rejected by bishops with their liturgical commissions or by pastors with their parish councils or committees on worship.

The purpose of this statement is to suggest how this concern for some continued use of Latin, especially in the celebration of Mass, can be reasonably handled, without injury to the overwhelming majority who now benefit from the English liturgy and without affront to the principles of liturgical participation or involvement which all should accept.

1. First, it must be stressed that neither the Second Vatican Council nor the National Conference of Catholic Bishops nor the Bishops' Committee on the Liturgy has, at any time, prohibited or reprobated the use of Latin in the Roman liturgy. The decisions of the council and of the conference in this matter have been expressed exclusively as concessions or permissions; the concessions of the conference are applicable in every liturgical celebration with the people in all the dioceses of the United States.

At the same time, very many bishops, properly exercising their pastoral authority and in consultation with their liturgical commissions, have required that public liturgical celebrations employ the vernacular for the sake of the people. Such decisions, which go beyond the concession of the vernacular, should be respected.

2. The Second Vatican Council, in dealing with the vernacular, stated that "the use of the Latin language is to be preserved in the Latin rites" (SC 36 §1), that is, in the Roman and other rites of the Western or Latin Church. Without any knowledge of future developments, the council could hardly specify how the liturgical use of Latin should be thus preserved.

One possibility was that two distinct forms of the Roman liturgy, one Latin, one vernacular, should exist side by side—whether the Latin liturgy would be celebrated regularly in some Masses or in some communities, especially more highly cultivated congregations or restricted communities or religious institutes. The fact, however, is that the pastoral reasons for the vernacular apply to the most limited communities as well as to average congregations.

Another possibility of preserving the Latin, as a matter of principle, was and is the insistence upon that language as the basis and exemplar of vernaculars, with the latter employed in practice, the former remaining as a prototype. Perhaps, the rule in effect up to the present time that the Latin originals be included in the official liturgical books illustrates this possibility. Even such an attenuated "preservation" of the Latin as prototype will inevitably have less meaning as the liturgy is more broadly adapted in accord with the *Constitution on the Liturgy* (37–40, 63).

The following statement from the instruction of January 25, 1969, on the translation of liturgical texts (n. 43) is pertinent:

Texts translated from another language are clearly not sufficient for the celebration of a fully renewed liturgy. The creation of new texts will be necessary. But translation of texts transmitted through the tradition of the Church is the best school and discipline for the creation of new texts so that any new forms adopted should in some way grow organically from forms already in existence (SC 23).

3. In the case of the Mass, the council made a practical decision, looking to the gradual introduction of the vernacular and the limited preservation of the Latin. It specified limits to the vernacular, within the authority of the episcopal conferences, but immediately opened the way to further or complete

use of the vernacular if, in the period after the council, the Holy See should consent (SC 54).

The conciliar decision represented a compromise between extremes. The council did not anticipate that almost all episcopal conferences would permit the vernacular to be used to the full extent of their authority (that is, in all the nonpresidential texts of the Eucharist and throughout the other sacraments and rites) or that the Holy See would quickly accede to the extension of the vernacular, wherever the episcopal conferences judged it desirable, in the presidential prayers of Mass—in the collects and parallel prayers, in the preface, and in the eucharistic prayer.

This action by the Holy See and by the episcopal conferences, in their respective spheres, should be understood as legitimate progress, perhaps more rapid than expected, beyond the explicit terms of the *Constitution on the Liturgy,* but in complete harmony with it. There have been and will be many other examples of this kind of development; one is the progress of communion under both kinds from special or individual cases which were immediately envisioned by the council to entire groups, such as participants in retreats or meetings of pastoral commissions.

4. Again treating the Mass, the council directed "that steps should be taken so that the faithful may also be able to say or to sing together in Latin those parts of the ordinary of the Mass which pertain to them" (SC 54). This is another means of preserving the Latin of the Roman liturgy, at least in some measure. In accord with this, the Bishops' Committee on the Liturgy, in 1964, recommended to the bishops and to publishers and editors that the Latin responses and ordinary chants of Mass should be included in hymnals, service books, and missals of a permanent character which are published for congregational use.

Several reasons can be given for the council's directive: to afford some greater continuity through the alternative use of Latin in the simpler, invariable, and more easily understood texts of Mass; to encourage singing of the traditional chants in Latin by the people, at least where this tradition has existed; in particular, to provide a common liturgical language when different language groups would come together, for example, at international shrines or congresses.

This last consideration underlies the following statement from the instruction *On Music in the Liturgy* (March 5, 1967), prepared to implement the conciliar constitution: "Where the vernacular has been introduced into the celebration of Mass, local ordinaries will judge whether it may be opportune to preserve one or more Masses celebrated in Latin—especially sung Masses—in certain churches, above all in large cities, where many come together with faithful of different languages" (MS 48). In many circumstances the needs of migrants or tourists or even international communities may be better served by providing liturgical services in the various vernaculars, but this does not deny the advantages of a broad knowledge of the Latin responses and ordinary chants for the sake of international and interlingual assemblies.

5. A prominent motive for retaining or restoring a knowledge of the simpler Latin texts of Mass is the chant and other musical settings to which they may be sung by congregations. Again, the same instruction expresses the council's intention: "Pastors, having taken into consideration pastoral usefulness and

the character of their own language, should see whether parts of the heritage of sacred music, written in previous centuries for Latin texts, could also be conveniently used, not only in liturgical celebrations in Latin, but also in such celebrations in the vernacular. There is nothing to prevent different parts in one and the same celebration being sung in different languages" (MS 51).

This very limited statement must, of course, be further qualified. Apart from the chant settings themselves, a large quantity of music for the celebration of Mass, although of the highest musical excellence, was composed without sufficient understanding of the liturgical context—for example, in ignorance of the popular and acclamatory nature of the Sanctus as an integral part of the eucharistic prayer. Thus, in the choice of music, irrespective of the question of language, liturgical and pastoral as well as musical judgments must be made. In this connection, the statement prepared by the Music Advisory Board and adopted by the Bishops' Committee on the Liturgy should be consulted (see *The Place of Music in Eucharistic Celebrations*).

It remains important, however, to insist upon the possibility of integrating one or other Latin text into a eucharistic celebration otherwise in the vernacular, if the musical setting is itself appropriate. Pastoral considerations give an immediate preference to the vernacular, but they do not exclude all Latin texts, particularly when the music will strengthen or enhance the celebration.

6. None of these observations resolves the questions raised by those who seek to have the Mass celebrated frequently or regularly in Latin for particular groups of the people. The concrete judgment must be made by the bishop with his liturgical commission and by the pastor with his parish council or committee on worship, but some guiding principles may be suggested:

a) While it is most desirable to make provision for the needs or desires of even the smallest number, pastoral considerations demand that the community at large not be deprived of the advantage of vernacular celebration. Thus, for example, if the Latin celebration cannot conveniently be provided for the limited group (that is, as an addition to the regular celebration of Mass for a given parish), it should be limited to a few occasions or to one or other Mass in a large church or parish, where the needs of the larger community are otherwise cared for.

b) Where there is substantial demand for the celebration of Mass in Latin, the possibility, mentioned above, of employing Latin for certain parts of Mass, especially sung texts, should be explored.

c) Even when Mass is celebrated in Latin, it is always possible and desirable that the principal variable parts, the readings from Scripture and the eucharistic prayer or canon, should be in English.

d) When Mass is celebrated in Latin, it is of the greatest importance that there be no diminution of liturgical participation through responses by the people, common recitation of prayers, and congregational singing. The use of Latin in the liturgical celebration should never be construed as the occasion to employ a form of Mass contrary to the principles of the *Constitution on the Liturgy*, especially Chapter I. For example, even if the eucharistic prayer is said in Latin, it should be proclaimed aloud or sung, as the rubrical revisions permit, so that the public and community nature of this central prayer is not neglected.

No one should judge harshly those who prefer elements of the older usage, in particular the use of Latin. In some instances, this desire may be esthetic, because of dissatisfaction with the language or music of the renewed liturgy; in other cases, it may be a simple matter of fear of change and preference for what is stable and certain. Since so often liturgical changes have been introduced without sufficient explanation and preparation, or without a real sense of living, personal, and authentic celebration, we should hesitate to be critical. As time goes on, it becomes more difficult for most people to appreciate the values once ascribed to a liturgy celebrated exclusively in Latin, but this need not prevent our having a genuine concern for those who can profit from the traditional Latin.

17

Ordination Rites: Introductory Notes

Introduction, Bishops' Committee on the Liturgy
April 1969

(See also no. 19)

The first of the Roman liturgical books to be published in the comprehensive revision decreed by Vatican II (SC 25) was the *Ordination of a Deacon, Presbyter, and Bishop,* by decree of August 15, 1968. The rites, which constituted a major section of what had been Part I of the old *Roman Pontifical,* were preceded by the text of an apostolic constitution of Paul VI, *Pontificalis Romani recognitio,* dated June 18 of the same year (DOL 324). In this document, the pope provided for a new form for the ordination of bishops in the Latin Church and determined the central formulary, requisite for validity, within each of the forms or consecratory prayers for the three sacramental orders. The revision of the rites themselves followed the mandate of Chapter I of the *Constitution on the Liturgy* and reflected the theological and ecclesial direction of Vatican II concerning admission into each of the collegial orders of the Church. This is evident not only in the liturgical texts and signs but also in the model or exemplary instructions on which the bishop is to base his own words before the individual ordination.

This first definitive volume of the reform in Latin set the pattern for those to follow, even in its title. The ordination rites were the first part of *The Roman Pontifical Revised by Decree of the Second Vatican Ecumenical Council and Published by Authority of Pope Paul VI.* A similar style was to be followed for the successive parts of the pontifical, ritual, and missal. The rites for ordination, however, lacked the extensive *praenotanda* or introduction that characterizes other revised liturgical books.

To make up, in part, for this lack, the Bishops' Committee on the Liturgy prepared introductory notes, included in its *Newsletter* for April 1969. The purpose of the text was "to assist in the pastoral planning of the services and in their study." It appeared together with the provisional English translations prepared by ICEL and approved for the dioceses of the United States. The text is given in the present collection because it does not appear in the English-language edition, *The Roman Pontifical I* (Washington, D.C., 1978), which was later published for all the countries participating in ICEL and which included, among other rites, the definitive liturgical translation for ordinations.

A primary concern in the American introductory notes is that the entire eucharistic celebration, within which the ordination takes place, should be fully participated in by the whole people, with their communal sharing expressed especially in song. In other words, the committee foresaw the possibility that in the celebration of ordinations, especially in the case of episcopal and presbyteral ordinations, the presence of highly trained choirs of seminarians and priests might well work to the exclusion of congregational singing.

For the most part, the comments offered by the committee highlight ritual or other elements of ordinations which have special doctrinal significance, particularly as these differed in important ways from the usual, received understanding. There are several examples: insistence on the presentation of the candidates to the bishop as coming from the local church; treatment of the place of ordination of bishops in order to counteract a common preference of ordination in the bishop-elect's own church of origin rather than in the one he will serve (with a parallel in the case of the other orders). Other observations are more directly pastoral: correction of the practice of reading the written instruction before ordination verbatim instead of making it in some fashion an unfolding of the Word of God in the context of the sacrament of orders; the introduction of a meaningful sign of popular assent to the ordination (with a hesitant mention of applause, in the unexpressed hope that this sign, appropriate in our culture, would be adopted); a kind of deepening or correction of the way in which concelebration was understood, so that it would be the sign of the presbyterium around the bishop and—on the occasion of episcopal ordination—the bishops of other local churches joining in admitting the elect into the order and communion of bishops.

At the time this introduction was written, neither the *General Instruction of the Roman Missal,* issued in 1969 in connection with the promulgation of the revised Order of Mass, nor, of course, the elaborate *Ceremonial of Bishops* (1984) was available. The committee did draw attention, however, to a useful Roman instruction, *Pontificalis ritus,* on the simplification of pontifical rites and insignia. This had been prepared by the Consilium and issued by the Congregation of Rites on June 21, 1968 (DOL 550). It resolved most questions of any moment for the adaptation of the first stages of reform to liturgies that were presided over by the bishop—and in fact answered, in principle or by analogy, all questions that might arise out of the more definitive reform still to come.

The introduction reprinted here did not, probably could not, anticipate all the actual applications or practices in the celebration of ordinations. Many of these, including some rubrical details, were taken up again much later in the November 1983 issue of the committee's *Newsletter.* Many of the aberrations may be summed up as a species of clericalization of the rite, in which the participation of the people can be overwhelmed by the numbers of participating ordained ministers, some of them taking over the liturgical ministries of the nonordained. Others are a kind of restored complexity of the simplified rite: addition of a second (or third) homily/instruction; reintroduction of a binding of hands after anointing; disproportionate and lengthy exchange of the sign of peace; retention of two "co-consecrating" bishops at the side of the ordaining bishop in place of the assisting deacons; elaboration of the vesting of the newly ordained; addition of songs and chants with the result of lengthening the clear and simple rite of the *Roman Pontifical.*

One development could hardly be anticipated in 1969, namely, the numbers of permanent deacons and the sacramental and ecclesial importance of maintaining in the rite the unity of the one order of deacons, whether they be ordained for stable and permanent service in that order or ordained in anticipation of later admission to the order of presbyters.

Mass of Ordination

Since the ordinations take place as a part of the celebration Mass, at the end of the liturgy of the Word, it is important that plans for the ministers, music, participation of the people, etc. be developed as carefully for the Mass itself as for the special rites. For example, hymns or other sacred songs should be provided for people to sing, especially the Sanctus and the responsorial chants between the readings (see below). In the case of the proper chants, the antiphons of the Simple Gradual may be used with the appropriate psalm verses or, as approved for the United States by the National Conference of Catholic Bishops and confirmed by the Apostolic See, other versions of antiphons and psalms in accord with the principles of the Simple Gradual. With regard to music provided for the entrance procession and for the communion, these periods are often lengthy at ordinations, and a variety of music may be arranged, including instrumental and choral music in addition to congregational singing.

Attention is drawn to the provisions of the recent *Instruction on the Simplification of Pontifical Rites and Insignia,* for example, that deacons may properly serve as assistant deacons, that the deacon and subdeacon of the Mass should in fact be of those orders, etc. If the rite of ordination is celebrated as a low Mass with song, that is, without the assistant priest and assistant deacons, the ordaining bishop should always be assisted by a deacon throughout the rite and throughout the Mass, and the readings before the gospel should be read by a (lay) lector. If there are a number of deacons present, it is proper to distribute the different diaconal ministries among them.

Place of Ordination

Deacons and priests should ordinarily be ordained in the local church or diocese where they will serve. Only in this way will the consent of the people to the ordination become meaningful (see below). If it is necessary for the ordination to take place in another diocese, the presentation of the candidates may be suitably made by a priest representing the particular diocese where they will exercise the ministry.

It is even more important, in the case of episcopal ordination, that a bishop be ordained in his own church, rather than in another diocese, if he is not named from the local presbyterium. The rite is explicit that the local church presents the priest for ordination to the episcopate; the priests who accompany the bishop-elect represent the local presbyterium. Although the principle is not the same for the ordination of a titular bishop, he too should be ordained in the diocese where he will exercise the pastoral ministry, for example, as an auxiliary bishop.

Ordination of Bishops

The principal preliminary observation concerning episcopal ordination is that the bishop-elect should be seen to be presented by representatives of his church—by priests who represent the order of priests and ministers and the people—and that he should be ordained, that is, admitted into the order or college of bishops, by all the bishops who are present.

The *Constitution on the Liturgy* encouraged the practice that all the bishops present should lay hands on the bishop-elect, and this decision has been incorporated in the revised rite. The consecrating bishops do not come forward merely for the imposition of hands; they participate throughout, and it is also desirable that they concelebrate the eucharistic liturgy.

Instructions (Homily)

In each ordination there is to be an instruction at the very beginning, that is, after the gospel and the presentation of the candidates. This instruction, by the ordaining bishop, is addressed to the candidates and to the people. It takes the place of the homily, which is to be omitted at its proper place in ordination Masses.

It is, however, possible and desirable to relate the instruction to the reading of the Word of God which has just been completed, particularly if the readings have been chosen with this in mind (see above). In addition, the words of the bishop should be concerned with the ministry of deacons or priests or bishops according to the occasion.

The rite provides a model or example of such an instruction for each of the ordination rites. Apart from the relation to a particular reading or readings from the Word of God, which would have to be supplied for the occasion, these instructions suggest the content that is appropriate. They are largely based upon scriptural texts and upon the documents of the Second Vatican Council, especially the *Dogmatic Constitution on the Church,* n. 19–21, 23, 26–27 (bishops), n. 28 (priests), n. 29 (deacons); *Constitution on the Liturgy; Decree on the Pastoral Office of Bishops in the Church,* especially n. 6, 15; *Decree on the Ministry and Life of Priests.* These may be consulted as sources for the preparation of the instruction.

It is not intended that the model instruction should be read verbatim, as was generally done in the case of the ordination instructions of the *Roman Pontifical,* although the ordaining bishop may choose to use these texts. No additional sermon should be given and any specific reference to individual candidates for orders, whether for diaconate, priesthood, or episcopate, may be briefly incorporated in the words addressed to the people by the ordaining bishop.

When a bishop is ordained, it is appropriate that he speak to the people briefly before the final blessing and dismissal, especially if he is a diocesan bishop entering upon his ministry in that particular church.

Assent of the People

In each rite, provision is made for the expression of the formal assent or consent of the people to the choice of the candidate. This is done either by the congregation saying "Thanks be to God" at the appointed time or by some other sign of assent. The latter manifestation, which has not yet been developed in most places, may take various forms: standing, singing of an acclamation, applause, etc. Because of its significance, and because it replaces the consultation of the people found in the *Roman Pontifical* (the period of silence after the inquiry by the ordaining prelate), its intent should be explained to the people, so that they may fully participate in this token or sign of their role in the choice of their shepherds and ministers.

Chants during the Ordination Rites

In the various rites, indications are given of the proper moments for the singing of psalms with antiphons, responsories, hymns, etc. It should be noted that the psalm verses with antiphons are always indicated as accompaniments; if the respective rite is quickly completed, there is no need to continue the singing of additional verses.

More important, in all these instances the texts for singing may be replaced by other song, hymns, chants, responsorial singing, psalms, etc., provided these are suitable to the occasion and the part of the rite. This applies also to the *Veni, Creator Spiritus* and the *Te Deum laudamus*.

Rubrical Directions

There is no need to repeat in this introduction the explicit rubrical indications in the individual rites. These should, however, be carefully studied, since major simplifications of ritual have been introduced. For example, the vesting of deacons and priests is done by assisting priests; the enthronement of the newly ordained bishop has been suppressed, etc.

Concelebration

When a bishop is ordained, it is desirable that all the ordaining bishops—that is, all the bishops present—concelebrate the eucharistic liturgy together with the new bishop and his presbyterium. If all the priests of the diocese cannot concelebrate with the new bishop, at least a representative number, such as the presbyteral senate or council, should concelebrate.

The principal ordaining bishop may properly take the second place during the eucharistic liturgy so that the new diocesan bishop is the chief celebrant.

The latter occupies the bishop's seat and the Eucharist is thus celebrated in a way expressive of the full participation of the local church, priests and ministers and faithful, under the presidency of the new bishop (cf. SC 41). This rule is not applicable in the case of titular bishops or when a diocesan bishop cannot be ordained in his own diocese.

When priests or deacons are ordained, it is suitable that the members of the local presbyterium concelebrate with the bishop. If there are new priests, they take the first places next to the bishop and the concelebration in the eucharistic liturgy is a further sign of their incorporation in the presbyteral order, as members of the college of priests surrounding the bishop. If there are new deacons, the concelebration of the presbyterium or its representatives is a sign that the diaconal ministry is to be exercised in collaboration with the bishop and the priests.

Offering of Gifts

The ritual offering of candles and, in the case of episcopal ordination, of bread and wine has been changed, so that the bringing forward of gifts is properly done by representatives of the people of the local church. When priests are ordained the bread and wine used in the ordination rite for the ritual *traditio* should be that for the eucharistic sacrifice.

Diaconate

The revised rite for the ordination of deacons is used for all deacons, both permanent deacons and those who wish later to be ordained priests, since no distinction of sacramental order is to be made. The text of the consecratory prayer, which had been interpreted as applying to deacons who would later become priests, has been excised in the revised rite.

Priesthood

In this translation, the words *priest* and *priesthood* have ordinarily been used to translate both *presbyter* and *sacerdos, presbyteratus* and *sacerdotium*, except where the Latin text clearly differentiated or where the context seemed to demand the distinct reference to the presbyteral order. In such instances, it appeared necessary to employ *presbyter* and *presbyterate* although the words are not so commonly used.

18

Copyright Violations

Statement, Bishops' Committee on the Liturgy
April 1969

(See also no. 24)

In the spring of 1969, in connection with the plenary session of the National Conference of Catholic Bishops, the committee met in Houston. At the recommendation of its Music Advisory Board, it adopted a formal statement on copyright violations in the field of church music. The first three paragraphs simply quote a 1967 statement of the board itself, somewhat rephrased; the text then brings the recurring issue up-to-date.

Compensation and other forms of remuneration for those professionally and artistically engaged in liturgical worship remain a troubling concern. The salaries of organists and choir directors had also been addressed on earlier occasions. Here, it is the authors, composers, and publishers whose plight is considered. Within the field, perhaps the common practice of compensating composers and authors with flat fees for transfer of copyright to publishers rather than with royalties should have been raised, but the immediate issue was clear violations of natural rights and statutory copyright by parishes and other communities.

In the years since 1969, the problem (and the injustice) has been a little mitigated, with publishers offering various licensing arrangements to permit local photocopying of music for a fixed charge. But, it is still common to find leaflets prepared for special local celebrations or for regular Sunday Masses and even parish or community hymn booklets in which copyright material is included without permission or payment to the owners. It remains beyond the responsibility or the capacity of the Bishops' Committee on the Liturgy to police such occurrences, but the exhortations remain equally necessary.

One point made in the statement is that, in the case of church music and, indeed, in the entire field of liturgical publishing, the profit or non-profit status of the publisher is not relevant. The nonprofit publisher competes in the same market and may already have an additional advantage over the commercial house because of exemption from taxation. It is for this reason that the International Commission on English in the Liturgy does not discriminate among publishers in any way: ICEL liturgical texts are made available on a nonexclusive basis to all publishers who are authorized by the respective conference of bishops. Nonprofit publishing firms are required to pay the same royalties and other fees, which support the ICEL programs and, in turn, protect the literary and liturgical integrity of the texts, as well as the limited quantity of music commissioned by ICEL. Once again, however, it is still common to see such material reproduced without permission.

At its April 1969 meeting in Houston, the Bishops' Committee on the Liturgy, acting at the request of its Music Advisory Board, approved and published the following statement on copyright violations:

> The Church is in constant need of new and artistic creations for its worship, particularly in the field of music. To encourage composers and authors in the creation of such works it is necessary at this time to speak about indiscriminate and unauthorized use of copyright materials.
>
> The practice of private reproduction by photocopiers and other devices substantially diminishes the legitimate royalties due composers and authors for their works. In addition, the loss to publishers of legitimate profits limits their ability to produce materials of quality and diversity. Ultimately, these deprivations will seriously harm music and worship in the United States.
>
> Those engaged in parish music programs and those responsible for parochial music budgets are reminded that it is immoral and illegal to reproduce by any means either the text or music or both of copyrighted materials without the written permission of the copyright owner. The fact that these duplicated materials are not for sale but for private use only within a parish church or school does not alter the legal or moral situation of the practice.

The Music Advisory Board prepared an earlier statement (published in the December 1967 issue of the *Newsletter* of the Bishops' Committee on the Liturgy) on copyright violations.

This practice, however, not only continues but has increased in parishes throughout the country. Apart from the legal and moral implications of this matter, the harmful impact on liturgical renewal is serious. Authors, composers, and publishers lack incentive to employ their talents and efforts in the field of church music because of meager and inadequate financial remuneration. In the meantime, criticism of present vernacular hymns and other sacred songs mounts, and the demand for new and artistic creations increases.

At a meeting of the Music Advisory Board with music publishers in November 1968, the publishers stressed that they have virtually no recourse against illegal copyright procedures since the initial cost of introducing a suit into court is prohibitive.

It is the considered judgment of publishers and the Music Advisory Board that only through a statement on these illegal procedures and a definite policy established by individual bishops in their own dioceses will these copyright violations be both exposed and corrected.

19

Minor Orders

Commentary, Bishops' Committee on the Liturgy Secretariat
November 1969

(See also no. 17)

From its first issue in 1965, the *Newsletter* of the Bishops' Committee on the Liturgy has contained substantial quantities of commentary, responses to questions, and various kinds of explanations and interpretations, all ordinarily prepared by the secretariat. Only rarely have such comments been inserted at the direction of the committee itself. The present commentary is an exceptional case in which the committee, at its September 1969 meeting, decided to publish a text of the secretariat.

It came at a time when there was much uncertainty concerning the status, in the discipline of the Latin Church, of the subdiaconate, minor orders, and tonsure. Already, it was clear that, at the very least, a line had been sharply drawn between the sacramental orders (the threefold ministry of bishops, presbyters, and deacons) and what had been the major order of subdiaconate, the four minor or lesser orders, and the rite of tonsure by which laymen were made clerics. The sharp distinction was, again at the very least, the teaching of Chapter III of the *Dogmatic Constitution on the Church (Lumen Gentium)*, especially nos. 28-29. In 1968, Pope Paul VI had followed that teaching very carefully in the reform of the ordination rites for bishops, presbyters, and deacons, authorized by the apostolic constitution *Pontificalis Romani recognitio* of June 18, 1968 (DOL 324).

Only three years after this 1969 commentary by the secretariat would the questions raised in it be officially resolved. The order of subdeacons, the minor orders of porters, exorcists, readers, and acolytes, and tonsure itself were simply suppressed; admission into the canonical state of clergy or ordained ministers was effected exclusively by ordination to the order of deacons; a rite of admission to candidacy for ordination as deacons and priests was established, without any effect on canonical or other status in the Church. At the same time, two lay ministries were created, employing the same names and functions as the obsolete orders of readers and acolytes. The reforms came about by force of two apostolic letters issued *motu proprio* by Pope Paul VI on August 15, 1972: *Ad pascendum* on the diaconate (DOL 319) and *Ministeria quaedam* (DOL 340) on the new lay ministries—which were reserved to laymen, but with the proviso that other lay ministries might be created by conferences of bishops.

If anything, these later developments and the publication, also in 1972,

121

of new rites of institution of lay ministers and admission to candidacy for orders make more interesting the commentary issued by the committee in 1969. Its speculation is long outdated, but its very uncertainty about the several possibilities only illustrates the significance of the final decisions.

The commentary also reflects the distinction of competence among the dicasteries or agencies of the Roman Curia involved in these matters. On the other hand, the Consilium, which had responsibility for the preparation of liturgical books to be promulgated by the Congregation of Rites, could only propose disciplinary changes affecting the subdiaconate and minor orders to the Congregation for the Discipline of the Sacraments or the Congregation for the Clergy. The same complex distinctions prevailed after the Consilium was succeeded, in effect, by the new Congregation for Divine Worship in 1969, with other congregations retaining competence in the development of changed disciplines. When the several interests were finally reconciled, the papal documents of 1972 were prepared to effect the changes described above.

In relation to each of the three sections of the commentary, some mention can be made of the ultimate disposition and the current practice and liturgy of the Church.

First, there is a point already made by the committee in the introductory notes to the revised ordination rites: the order of deacons is one, embracing both permanent and transitional deacons. Then, among the several possibilities for the old institute of tonsure, both the suppression of the rite and effect of tonsure and the creation of a new rite of admission to candidacy were adopted by the Apostolic See. After the admission to candidacy for ordination, however, the individual remains a layman.

Second, the discussion on the minor orders in the commentary keeps open, as the Consilium had kept open at the time, the possibility of retaining a minor order of readers. This was under consideration partly out of respect for the Eastern and Western traditions. In the event, all the minor orders and the subdiaconate were simply suppressed as obsolete.

The commentary anticipates the requirement that, before admission to the order of deacons by the sacramental rite, laymen should first have been instituted in each of the two lay ministries, the norm of the apostolic letter *Ad pascendum*. This requirement, in turn, created an anomaly, which is adverted to in the commentary, that the suppressed minor orders might appear to survive as a quasi-clerical rite in the Church. Thus, the commentary says: ". . . if a service of appointment or designation is created for readers in general, it would be appropriate for seminarians to receive it—if they had not received it before they presented themselves as candidates for the permanent or ordained ministry." This was the sense and intent of the decrees of the National Conference of Catholic Bishops in November 1972, decrees enacted in the light of the changed discipline:

No one instituted as a reader may be instituted as an acolyte, and no one instituted as an acolyte may be instituted as a reader until he has actually exercised the first ministry for a period of at least six months; the Ordinary may dispense from this norm in particular cases, but only if this can be done without detriment to the distinction of the two ministries and the authenticity of their exercise.

Candidates for the transitional or permanent diaconate who are obliged to be instituted in the ministries of reader and acolyte (if they have not already been so instituted) shall actually exercise the ministry of reader or acolyte for a period of at least six months before institution in the other ministry. They shall actually exercise the second ministry for a period of at least six months before ordination to the diaconate; the Ordinary may dispense from this norm in particular cases, but only if this can be done without detriment to the distinction of the two ministries and the authenticity of their exercise.

From all this, it is evident that in 1972 some of the difficulties insinuated in the 1969 commentary had arisen, especially the likelihood that the ministries might become artificial formalities rather than authentic lay ministries in the church community. There was strong concern lest, as required ministries before admission to the order of deacons, the lay ministries might reassume the character of minor orders or steps to ordination or, indeed, that an artificial sequence might be canonized: first, admission to candidacy; next, institution as readers; finally, institution as acolytes. Such a development would run counter to the pattern of the *Roman Pontifical* in the pertinent rites that appeared in November 1972. The Latin pontifical and its English counterpart, *The Roman Pontifical I*, were careful to locate the institution of lay ministers (sometimes called conferral, investitutre, or installation) ahead of, and separate from, admission to candidacy for ordination.

As is well known now, liturgical institution in the lay ministries has been rarely celebrated in the dioceses of the United States, chiefly because of the reservation to laymen, and the rites are celebrated almost exclusively in seminaries. Inevitably, this has given the two ministries a false appearance of minor orders revived or of steps or stages on the way to diaconal ordination, to "the detriment of . . . the authenticity of their exercise." Nor has the establishment of new lay ministries of catechists or teachers of religion and of music, both open to women, been achieved as proposed by the Bishops' Committee on Pastoral Research and Practices and agreed upon by the National Conference of Catholic Bishops in November 1973.

Third, the commentary takes up the subdiaconate and correctly envisions a possible unification of the functions of subdeacons and acolytes. This did come to pass through the papal documents already mentioned, and ultimately, the sections of the *General Instruction of the Roman Missal* about subdeacons were eliminated.

The resolution of another issue mentioned in the commentary, the commitment of ordained ministers to a life of celibacy, was referred to in the papal letter *Ad pascendum*. Pope Paul VI required "a declaration drawn up and signed in the candidates' own hand, by which they testify that they are about to receive the order freely and of their own accord." With reference to the liturgical rite spoken of in the commentary, the papal letter went on:

The special consecration to celibacy observed for the sake of the kingdom of heaven and its obligation for candidates to the priesthood and for unmarried candidates to the diaconate are in truth connected with the diaconate. The public commitment to celibacy before God and the Church is to be celebrated, even by religious, in a special rite, which is to precede ordination to the diaconate.

In the published ritual, a part of the *Roman Pontifical,* the rite of commitment to celibacy was made a part of the ordination of deacons itself, although not affecting married candidates for the order.

Ordinarily, the lay ministries of readers and acolytes have not been recognized and sanctioned by the liturgical rites of institution in the United States, and it has been necessary to substitute for them popular services of commissioning for readers, acolytes, catechists, and others. Nonetheless, the developments considered in the commentary reprinted here have clarified roles and offices in the Church. They have certai.,ly enhanced the tradition of the threefold sacramental orders, as described in *Lumen Gentium* 28: "Thus, the divinely established ecclesiastical ministry is exercised in different orders by those who already from antiquity are called bishops, presbyters, and deacons." In doctrine and in practice, the other "orders" have been suppressed. At least in principle and in liturgical rite, the meaning of lay ministries of persons who are instituted by the Church and supported by its suffrages is clearer.

Many questions have been raised about the present status and future role of tonsure, minor orders, and subdiaconate in the Church. None of these is mentioned in the first published section of the revised *Roman Pontifical,* for the ordination of deacons, priests, and bishops (1968).

At its meeting in September, the Bishops' Committee on the Liturgy decided to have a brief summary prepared for the *Newsletter* simply to give the state of the question.

First, it is customary to distinguish the liturgical celebration of the several orders, sacramental or not, from the canonical aspects, such as admission to or advancement in the clergy. The two aspects are, of course, very closely related, but any liturgical revision is complicated by uncertainties over canonical changes affecting the clergy or the "clerical state."

In the case of the diaconate, the liturgical revision was on surer ground, since the constitution *Lumen Gentium* of Vatican II had described the office of deacons both doctrinally and very practically (LG 29). When the council enumerated the functions of deacons in general, it was obviously influenced by its desire to restore the diaconate, where needed, to a position of stability and permanence rather than of simply preparation for the next higher order of priests or presbyters.

This purpose is somewhat reflected in the restored liturgical service for the ordination of deacons. The rite is intended for the ordination of all deacons, permanent or temporary, since it is the same sacrament and the same grade of holy orders, but any apparent reference to diaconate as a mere step toward higher orders was eliminated. Thus, the liturgical celebration corresponds to the actual situation in the Church.

In the papal document that implemented the conciliar decision to restore the diaconate (*Sacrum Diaconatus Ordinem,* June 18, 1967), there is a single reference to the other orders: "With regard to . . . the orders which precede the diaconate, the discipline now in effect shall be maintained until revised by the Holy See" (no. 36).

Tonsure

As a liturgical rite, tonsure includes the cutting of the new cleric's hair and the ritual presentation of the surplice. The former has long been obsolete in most of the world where the tonsure is not worn. It is possible that the latter could be rethought in relation to the more general question of clerical garb and liturgical vesture.

There are several possibilities in the case of tonsure: (1) the rite could be simply suppressed, together with its canonical consequence of admission into the clergy; (2) the rite could be revised and updated like other services, in accord with the decrees of Vatican II, while retaining the notion of a "lower clergy" to be entered upon the reception of "tonsure"—the determination of the stable or temporary (i.e., preparatory) character of the office or function is a distinct question; or (3) a new rite could be created to signify initial commitment to the ministry, without necessarily implying admission into the clerical state. Even in the past, when it was usual for seminarians to wear clerical garb before becoming clerics, there was often some informal rite of this last kind. Whether it should be in the nature of welcome to the candidate or his profession of intent or both requires study.

Minor Orders

The chief difficulties raised about the four minor orders are two: (1) the functions or offices themselves lack authenticity in the Church: they are either not exercised or usually exercised by the unordained; (2) the liturgical rites are partly obsolete, and the texts for the bishop's instructions to the candidates are not appropriate nowadays. To a limited extent, the latter difficulty can be overcome if the bishop employs the printed instruction or address merely as an exemplar, as is explained in the new ordination rites for diaconate, priesthood, and episcopate. This does not help resolve the question that exorcists and porters never exercise their office or that acolytes and readers have probably exercised those functions long before ordination to the respective minor orders.

Among the proposed solutions is the simple suppression of the four orders which, like the subdiaconate, can be properly viewed as extensions or even as subdivisions of the functions of the order of deacons or ministers. This would correspond to the reality of the situation in which the significant functions of reading the word in the liturgical assembly (office of lector) and of

125

lesser service at the altar (office of acolyte) are performed by the unordained. If this course were to be taken, a new question would arise, whether it is desirable that readers and, perhaps, servers should be liturgically commissioned or deputed in the presence of the community, apart from any concept of clerical status. In the case of lectors, this is often done already, and this suggests a very natural ritual need.

This brief summary cannot list all the possibilities, but distinguishing the various functions of liturgical ministry from the office of the "minor" clergy could open up clearer expressions of the functions themselves. Thus, if rites were created for the public designation and acceptance of a person to serve in the liturgical celebration (as in other aspects of the Church's mission), these would have to be attuned to such functions as reader, server, cantor or leader of song, minister of communion in the absence of a deacon (a rite already used in places where the practice is permitted).

The above possibilities would divorce the several liturgical ministries from any direct relationship to the clerical state in the Church or preparation for holy orders. Another approach, however, would be the retention of one or other minor order as a step toward holy orders. Because of its real significance, this might be done, for example, in the case of the order of acolyte or server; in this case, the liturgical ordination demands revision. But there is a further difficulty, in that the liturgical function of the acolyte is not clearly distinct from that of the subdeacon. At times, the roles of the two in the celebration seem almost interchangeable. Thus, the new basic Order of Mass includes a deacon but no subdeacon; the missal's general instruction treats the presence or absence of the latter more as a matter of solemnity, and the functions of servers or acolytes may be distributed and redistributed at will.

A clearer suggestion is that only one of the four minor orders, the office of lector or reader, be retained in the present canonical and liturgical sense—whether as part of the clergy or as a preparatory stage looking to the higher orders. This has the advantage of respecting (1) the most venerable tradition of the so-called minor orders, (2) the rediscovered sense of proclaiming the Word of God as an integral part of the liturgy, and (3) the general usage of the Eastern Churches, which have otherwise had great diversity in the acceptance of the several minor orders.

Should some such solution be worked out, the present usage of laymen (and lay women, if only with limitations) serving as readers has to be respected and enhanced. If the office of lector remains one of the orders, it would be important that only those candidates or seminarians would receive it who had not been previously designated or commissioned liturgically as readers in the Church. In other words, if a service of appointment or designation is created for readers in general, it would be appropriate for seminarians to receive it— if they had not received it before they presented themselves as candidates for the permanent or ordained ministry.

The Council of Trent (sess. 23, on reform, ch. 17) attempted to restore the minor orders to authentic use, permitting the exercise of the orders by married clerics, in much the same way as the Second Vatican Council restored the permanent diaconate. The decree of Trent was not effectively implemented, nor is it likely that the minor orders as such—including the reservation of the functions to the ordained clergy—could be restored today. The principal questions to be explored are the desirability of improved liturgical rites for either ordination or other designation of persons for such functions, the even greater diversity of ministries both stable and temporary at the present time, and the relationship of these to preparation of candidates for the higher orders.

Subdiaconate

Although the Western usage is to consider the subdiaconate a major order, this is by no means accepted in the Eastern Churches, and *Lumen Gentium* (ch. 3, esp. nos. 28 and 29) tends to draw the line between the orders of bishops, presbyters, and deacons, which are carefully treated, and the other orders, which are not discussed. The same point of view is evident in the liturgical reforms. As mentioned above, the first published section of the *Roman Pontifical* relates and coordinates the three orders of deacons, priests or presbyters, and bishops, but omits the subdiaconate and minor orders for the present. The new missal retains the functions of subdeacon but reduces the significance of the liturgical office.

Even if the subdiaconate may be considered a minor order in the future, the rite of ordination needs revision in the light of a somewhat clearer notion of the subdeacon's function as a secondary server or minister—one among several servers, but the first among the servers not ordained to the sacramental diaconate. Or, along similar lines, there could be a kind of union of the orders of acolyte and subdeacon, perhaps with special reference to service as minister of communion in the absence of a deacon (see above).

From this point of view, the subdiaconate can be considered also as a major step of candidates for the ordained ministry of deacons or priests, and it is possible that this kind of emphasis could be found in a revised rite.

A related question is whether the public commitment of the cleric to celibacy in the Latin Church should be a part of the liturgical ordination of subdeacons or of deacons. At the present time, there is an implicit commitment even in tonsure (except for those who intend to be married deacons) because even tonsure has been considered a step always directed toward the major order of priests. Religious do not make any commitment to celibacy in the subdiaconate ordination because they have already made public profession of the vow. In recent years (since 1930), candidates for the subdiaconate have made a written, canonical commitment to celibacy, asserting their freedom and willingness, prior to the public ordination and in very formal terms ("This I promise, this I vow, this I swear . . ."). And, most recently, even the slight reference to celibacy in the subdiaconate ordination has become inappropriate for candidates for the married diaconate.

All this needs clarification in the liturgical celebration of the several orders. One possibility would be to make the public commitment to celibacy an entirely distinct liturgical service, at a time appropriate in the period of probation or candidature, unless it is preferred to place the emphasis upon the written expression of this dedication rather than upon the liturgical rite. Another possibility, which would make a sharp distinction, is to transfer the present rite expressive of celibacy—or any newly designed rite—from the subdiaconate to the diaconate. Then, in harmony with the present discipline, (namely, to allow married men to become deacons, to maintain an order of permanent unmarried deacons as well, and to prohibit married deacons to advance to the order of priests), unmarried candidates for the diaconate would give public witness before the community to their intention to remain celibate, while married candidates would not.

The above indications are little more than a checklist of possible developments now in need of study. In the *Constitution on the Liturgy,* the council decreed that the ordination rites should be revised in ceremonial and texts (SC 76), including tonsure, minor orders, and subdiaconate, together with all the other liturgical services (SC 25). Pope Paul VI has already indicated his intention (in the *motu proprio* referred to above, *Sacrum Diaconatus Ordinem*) to revise the canonical dispositions affecting these orders. Further possibilities are open; the above enumeration may serve as a starting point for study.

20

General Intercessions

Guidelines (Introduction), Bishops' Committee on the Liturgy
1969

(See also no. 30)

Only the introductory paragraphs and the brief observations on the name, "general intercessions," are reprinted here from the longer guidelines, prepared by the committee in 1969 and sent to the bishops and diocesan liturgical commissions for their guidance. This section was published in the September-October 1970 issue of the committee's *Newsletter*. The substance of the document, however, was redone and incorporated in a 1979 statement with the same title, which is also included in this present collection.

The immediate background is, of course, the formal decision taken by the Second Vatican Council, in Chapter II of the *Constitution on the Liturgy*:

> Especially on Sundays and holy days of obligation there is to be restored, after the gospel and homily, "the universal prayer" or "the prayer of the faithful." By this prayer, in which the people are to take part, intercession shall be made for holy Church, for the civil authorities, for those oppressed by various needs, for all people, and for the salvation of the entire world (SC 53).

Invoking 1 Timothy 2:1-2 for the antiquity of such priestly prayer of the Church, if not for the diversity of its forms, Vatican II engaged in a genuine restoration, one that very readily became an accepted part of the liturgy of the Word at eucharistic celebrations. This was achieved with relatively little structural reform or alteration, although the sequence of the profession of faith or creed and this intercessory element of the liturgy was not completely resolved. The question was whether the prayer should follow the homily directly or be added only after the profession of the faith. The constitution seems to say one thing, without excluding the other; regularly, the succeeding revisions have interposed the creed, if proclaimed, between homily and intercessions—although the marriage ritual maintained the other sequence: gospel, homily, intercessions, profession of faith.

The guidelines of 1969 incorporate the summary explanation of the nature of the intercessory prayer from the *General Instruction of the Roman Missal*. This had been preceded as early as the first instruction of implementation in 1964 with a similar statement and a norm, under the heading, "Universal Prayer or Prayer of the Faithful":

> In places where the universal prayer or prayer of the faithful is already the custom, it shall take place before the offertory, after the *Oremus,* and, for the time being, with formularies in use in individual regions. The celebrant is to lead the prayer at either his chair, the altar, the lectern, or the edge of the sanctuary.
>
> A deacon, cantor, or other suitable minister may sing the intentions or intercessions. The celebrant takes the introductions and concluding prayer, this being ordinarily the *Deus, refugium nostrum et virtus (Missale Romanum, Orationes diversae,* no. 20) or another prayer more suited to particular needs.
>
> In places where the universal prayer or prayer of the faithful is not the custom, the competent territorial authority may decree its use in the manner indicated above and with formularies approved by that authority for the time being (no. 56: DOL 23).

Already in 1964, the ritual pattern had been agreed upon: first, an introduction or invitation addressed to the congregation by the presiding celebrant (one element widely misunderstood and often converted into a preliminary prayer or intercession addressed to God); then, the intentions sung or said by a minister (preferably the deacon or cantor) with the people making their response; and, finally, the concluding prayer (in collect form) sung or said by the priest with the people responding Amen.

In the United States, such a universal or common prayer did not really exist before the council, except in the attenuated form of prayers for the dead recited after the gospel and before the homily. The new pattern was learned easily enough, and the Bishop's Committee on the Liturgy and the conference of bishops did not attempt to impose any rigid formularies, preferring to leave this to diocesan and parish initiatives.

An important (but neglected) document from the Apostolic See was issued in 1965 as a manuscript and then published in a second edition in 1966. It was entitled *The Universal Prayer or Prayer of the Faithful* (DOL 239). This is a valuable tract, including a practical directory, sample texts, and an appended history of the prayer.

As for the content of the prayer, the basic statement of the *General Instruction of the Roman Missal* (DOL 208) deserves quotation:

> In the general intercessions or prayer of the faithful, the people, exercising their priestly function, intercede for all humanity. It is appropriate that this prayer be included in all Masses celebrated with a congregation, so that petitions will be offered for the Church, for civil authorities, for those oppressed by various needs, for all people, and for the salvation of the world.

That problems arose in the first years of the reform, especially by way of particularizing the prayers or composing the intercessions too loosely, is suggested by the hesitant but reasonable tone of a later Roman instruction *Liturgicae instaurationes* (September 5, 1970: DOL 52):

> The general intercessions in addition to the intentions for the Church, the world, and those in need may properly include one pertinent to the local community. . . . Intentions for the general intercessions are to be prepared and written out beforehand and in a form consistent with the genre of the prayer. The reading of the intentions may be assigned to one or more of those present at the liturgy.

This instruction suggests how, from 1964 to 1970, the intercessory prayer developed so that, rather than a formulary demanding official approbation of the conference of bishops, it was taken for granted that it would consist of original texts carefully prepared before the liturgy. The texts in the *Roman Missal* of 1970, and, indeed, those found in the other rites of the revised liturgy, thus became models and examples rather than fixed formularies.

A fuller but compatible exposition was offered in the introduction to the 1981 edition of the *Lectionary for Mass:*

> Enlightened by God's word and in a sense responding to it, the assembly of the faithful prays in the general intercessions as a rule for the needs of the universal Church and the local community, for the salvation of the world and those oppressed by any burden, and for special categories of people.

In this more recent document, too, there are signs of greater flexibility, but also the effort to retain the general character of the prayer and the structured roles of priest, minister, and people.

This is the broad context in which the 1969 guidelines from the American committee should be viewed. The first section reprinted here advances a continuing thesis: If problems of private liturgical initiatives exist, the ministers of the Church should seize on a part of the liturgy that remains "open and relatively free—as a legitimate outlet for the desire to make the liturgical celebration concrete, authentic, and relevant."

The other brief section of the guidelines that is reprinted points out a troubling matter. Among all the possible names for the intercessory prayer, the one quickly adopted (from the tradition and from the *Constitution on the Liturgy*) was "prayer of the faithful," a term still found in some of the liturgical books, at least as an alternative. Yet, it was just as quickly found to be misleading, as if the (lay) faithful were largely confined to these petitionary prayers rather than having a part in the petitions of the presidential prayers, including the intercessions found in all the eucharistic prayers.

Partly because of this, terms such as *oratio communis* and *oratio universalis* are preferred in Latin. They have the advantage of counteracting, if reflected upon, the tendency to devote the petitions largely to the local congregation or community or to narrow interests and concerns. After lengthy discussion, the International Commission on English in the Liturgy chose "general intercessions" as the preferred title. On the one hand, it stresses the breadth of the communal petitions of the priestly people assembled for the Eucharist. On the other hand, the use of "intercessions" indicates that it is indeed intercessory in character (rather than didactic or an expression of praise and thanksgiving).

As already mentioned, the committee was to return to this old but new, and truly significant, part of the restored Order of Mass in a statement issued under the same title in 1979. That statement is given in full later in this collection.

The general prayer or prayer of the faithful, restored to the Roman liturgy by the Second Vatican Council, has been accepted readily and profitably in very many places. The purpose of these guidelines is to encourage the universal use of this prayer in the United States and to suggest its significance in liturgical renewal.

The needs for which we pray change rapidly. In a world that changes and develops so quickly, this is evident from the common and universal concerns of man. It is equally true of the particular problems and responsibilities of the individual worshiping community.

Therefore, a certain freedom, spontaneity, and adaptability are of the essence of the prayer of the faithful. In a period when it is hard to restrain the temptation to private liturgical initiatives, happily the prayer of the faithful remains open and relatively free—as a legitimate outlet for the desire to make the liturgical celebration concrete, authentic, and relevant. In a period of hesitation and questioning, this prayer is also a profession of faithful dependence upon God; it is the humble plea of each person in the assembled community of Christians.

Nothing in these recommendations is intended to introduce a static or rigid format for the prayer of the faithful. But the structure described, which reflects the best usage that is now widespread, can make the prayer consistent with the rest of the Mass of which it is an integral part. Just as the homily, once considered a disproportionate interruption, has recovered its integral role in the Mass, so the prayer of the faithful—the final element of the service of the Word—should by its form and length harmonize with the other parts of the Eucharist, which must be understood as one single act of worship (SC 56).

These guidelines say nothing about the history of the prayer of the faithful and do not repeat all that is said in the instruction issued on this matter by the postconciliar liturgical Consilium several years ago.

The following statement from the *Institutio Generalis* of the revised *Ordo Missae* (April 6, 1969) sums up that document:

In the general prayer or prayer of the faithful, the people exercise their priestly function by praying for all mankind. It is desirable that this kind of prayer be ordinarily included in Masses celebrated with a congregation, so that petitions may be offered for holy Church, for civil authorities, for those in need, and for all men and the salvation of the entire world [cf. SC 53] (no. 45).

In restoring the prayer of the faithful the Church has drawn from its treasure something very old, which is at the same time remarkably suited to the present. It is a prayer simple and moving, communal in spirit, committed to the needs of the whole world. Much good can come of it if much is made of it.

Name

Although the term, "prayer of the faithful," has quickly become the accepted name for the intercessory prayer at the end of the liturgy of the Word, its significance can better be seen in various other terms used for it. In fact, it should be clear that it is not *the* prayer of the faithful in the sense of the principal prayer of petition said by the people: this is the Lord's Prayer, used at Mass as the table prayer of the sacrificial banquet.

The prayer of the faithful is sometimes called the "common prayer" because—apart from the Lord's Prayer and the eucharistic prayer or canon itself—it does serve as the chief expression of the common needs of God's people assembled.

The prayer of the faithful is known technically as the "general prayer (intercessions)" or the "universal prayer," to suggest that, however concrete and particular it may be, it should always go beyond the concerns of the local eucharistic community to the needs of the whole Church, of all the Churches, and indeed of all mankind and the world.

If some hesitation must be expressed about the recent development of the prayer of the faithful, it is on the score of particularism. Important as this form of prayer is to the individual assembly as the expression of the needs its members experience, the more crucial aspect is the universality and catholicity which are expressed through petitions for the whole of God's people. The Church is truly and fully present in each eucharistic community, but the latter is only part of the whole Church, and the prayer of the faithful is a sign of communion of the particular assembly with others and with the whole Church.

The traditional English name for the prayer of the faithful is the "bidding prayers." This expression refers to the litanical or similar forms of the prayer, with successive invitations, invocations, or intercessions, a form which lends itself readily and easily to congregational participation.

Much more can be learned of the background of this prayer, so long absent from the Roman Mass, from its history. Its restoration to the Mass is not for historical or archeological reasons, however, but to fill a genuine need and to correct an omission of long standing.

133

21

Place of Women in the Liturgy

Statement, Bishops' Committee on the Liturgy
February 14, 1971

(See also no. 35)

This brief statement, prepared for the information and use of the members of the National Conference of Catholic Bishops during a meeting of the episcopal committee, barely touches upon the broad questions of liturgical participation by women, much less upon the total role of women in the Church. It is an attempt to mitigate the perceived harshness of certain Roman norms on the subject, while not departing from the general discipline of the Church.

Perhaps, it is noteworthy that the first conciliar document, the *Constitution on the Liturgy,* showed a certain awareness of a question that would be posed increasingly to the church community and its hierarchical ministers. Dealing with the sacrament of marriage, the Second Vatican Council directed that the ancient wedding blessing of the Roman liturgy be corrected "to remind both spouses of their equal obligation [*officia aequalia*] to remain faithful to each other" and that the blessing never be omitted (SC 78).

As the official liturgical reform proceeded in the 1960s and 1970s, some of the disabilities and discriminations against women, arising from cultural traditions as much as anything, were removed. Sometimes, this took place broadly and without hesitation: the recognition of mixed choirs and choirs of women or the potential deputation of lay persons, including women, to conduct funeral rites in the absence of an ordained minister. Sometimes, this took place grudgingly: the selection of women as special ministers of the Eucharist "in cases of necessity, that is, whenever another fit person cannot be found"; the exclusion of women from the liturgical institution of lay ministries among acolytes and readers. (In another connection, it has been pointed out how the 1972 reservation of the lay ministries to men made institution in such ministries almost unfeasible in the United States, except in the special case of candidates for orders.)

Much of the hesitation in Roman documents can be explained, if not justified, by hierarchial concern over the ordination of women. Almost the opposite position might have been taken: the distinctive character of the threefold sacramental orders, which have traditionally not been open to women, might even have been enhanced by openness to every other kind of special liturgical ministry of women—including the liturgical ministry of women at the altar. The received tradition, moreover, had already clearly recognized the presidency of women over ecclesial prayer, specifically at the canonical hours celebrated in religious institutes. And, at least in the Western Church, women are understood to be the equal ministers of the sacrament of marriage itself to their spouses. When the designation of women as eucharistic ministers was permitted in the United States as early as 1969 (DOL 262–264), it was inevitable that the question of women as servers at the altar, a far less important responsibility, would be pressed.

The immediate background of the 1971 statement of the bishops' committee was twofold: first, the *General Instruction of the Roman Missal* that originally appeared with the revised Order of Mass in 1969; second, a Roman instruction of 1970, which has already been mentioned in reference to the statement *General Intercessions*.

The missal's *General Instruction* combined openness with restriction. Its first versions, in 1969 and 1970, were written in a way that gave offense: "The conference of bishops may grant that when there is no man present capable of carrying out the reader's function, a suitable woman, standing outside the sanctuary, may proclaim the readings before the gospel." This was later slightly altered to read:

At the discretion of the rector of the church, women may be appointed to ministries [below those reserved to deacons] that are performed outside the sanctuary.

The conference of bishops may permit qualified women to proclaim the readings before the gospel and to announce the intentions of the general intercessions. The conference may also more precisely designate a suitable place for a woman to proclaim the Word of God in the liturgical assembly (no. 70 of the 1975 edition: DOL 208).

For the United States, there was little question of any exclusion of women from the ministry of reading. Discussions of the area proper for such reading (within the sanctuary, chancel, or presbyterium in which the pulpit or lectern would be ordinarily located) did continue in some places. More serious, however, was the question of women as servers, that is, women or young girls who take the liturgical role of acolytes—apart from service permitted them as eucharistic ministers.

The second Roman document, and the immediate occasion of the statement reprinted here, was the instruction *Liturgicae instaurationes* issued by the new Congregation for Divine Worship on September 5, 1970 (DOL 52). This is generally called the "Third Instruction" of implementation although, unlike its predecessors in 1964 and 1967, it contained no new elements of reform to put the *Constitution on the Liturgy* into effect. No. 7 of the instruction reads:

In conformity with the norms traditional in the Church, women (single, married, religious), whether in churches, homes, convents, schools, or institutions for women, are barred from serving the priest at the altar.

According to the norms established for these matters, however, women are allowed to:

135

a. proclaim the readings, except the gospel. They are to make sure that, with the help of modern sound equipment, they can be comfortably heard by all. The conferences of bishops are to give specific directions on the place best suited for women to read the Word of God in the liturgical assembly.

b. announce the intentions in the general intercessions;

c. lead the liturgical assembly in singing and play the organ or other instruments;

d. read the commentary assisting the people toward a better understanding of the rite;

e. attend to other functions, customarily filled by women in other settings, as a service to the congregation, for example, ushering, organizing processions, taking up the collection, etc.

Read in the light of this Roman instruction, the statement of the Bishops' Committee on the Liturgy has several purposes; it avoids commenting on the patronizing tone of the document. One purpose is a partial rebuttal to the argumentation on the basis of "traditional norms," which are certainly of purely ecclesiastical discipline; this is the reason for the mention of *Gaudium et spes* and the text from Galatians. Another purpose is to narrow the prohibition or restriction of women to "service at the altar itself," with a slightly more nuanced or insistent limitation, namely, to only the immediate area of the altar. There is, thus, an unspoken implication that other services in the sanctuary or outside it remain open to women: servers who carry cross and candles, for example, and servers at the chair are deliberately not mentioned.

No. 2 of the statement from the committee is in reaction to the style of certain Roman documents, which may speak of special qualifications demanded of women ministers but which are equally applicable to men. Nos. 3 and 4 are intended to eliminate once and for all the artificial concerns—aside from "service at the altar itself"—over position and placement when women serve as liturgical ministers.

As is more than evident, the 1971 statement did not resolve more profound questions about the liturgical ministry of women. It attempted, however, within the literal limits of official discipline, to encourage the special participation of women. Fifteen years later, the disabilities referred to above remain in the 1983 *Code of Canon Law* (c. 230 §1 on the reservation of the lay ministries of readers and acolytes to men; c. 230 §2 extending the functions of readers, commentators, cantors, and others to both women and men—the exclusion of any mention of the functions of acolytes or altar servers, a matter left to the liturgical law.)

Another distinct question was not taken up by the Bishops' Committee on the Liturgy in 1971. This is the use of so-called exclusive language in liturgical texts, especially language excluding or, at least, not referring to women in a context that demands their inclusion. Much later, this would be at issue in a statement on an "inclusive" version of the Grail Psalter (1985). In the interval, it would be dealt with directly and forcefully by the National Conference of Catholic Bishops, not by issuing statements but by approving liturgical texts consciously designed to avoid exclusive language.

It is certain that in the liturgical celebration, as in other facets of the Church's life, there should be no discrimination or apparent discrimination against women. The teaching of the Second Vatican Council accepts this principle: "With respect to the fundamental rights of the person, every type of discrimination, whether social or cultural, whether based on sex, race, color, social condition, language, or religion, is to be overcome and eradicated, as contrary to God's intent" (GS 29).

The basic or radical equality of the baptized members of Christ takes priority over, and is more significant than, distinctions of order and ministry: "All of you who have been baptized into Christ have clothed yourselves with him. There does not exist among you Jew or Greek, slave or freeman, male or female. All are one in Christ Jesus" (Gal 3:27–28).

Nevertheless, both doctrine and tradition place certain limitations upon women in the exercise of the sacramental and liturgical ministry. It is not the purpose of this statement to argue or resolve doctrinal questions, but rather to define legitimate liturgical usage.

The Third Instruction issued on September 5, 1970, by the Congregation for Divine Worship offers a simple principle for practice: that women may exercise liturgical offices with the exception of "serving the priest at the altar." There are, of course, even exceptions to this norm, for example, when a woman is given the faculty to distribute Holy Communion, but the principle can be the basis of the following guidelines:

1. With the exception of service at the altar itself, women may be admitted to the exercise of other liturgical ministries. In practice, the designation of women to serve in such ministries as reader, cantor, leader of singing, commentator, director of liturgical participation, etc., is left to the judgment of the pastor or the priest who presides over the celebration, in the light of the culture and mentality of the congregation.

2. Worthiness of life and character and other qualifications are required in women who exercise liturgical ministries in the same way as for men who exercise the same ministries.

3. Women who read one or other biblical reading during the liturgy of the Word (other than the gospel, which is reserved to a deacon or priest) should do so from the lectern or ambo where the other readings are proclaimed: the reservation of a single place for all the biblical readings is more significant than the person of the reader, whether ordained or lay, whether woman or man (cf. GIRM 272).

4. Other ministries performed by women, such as leading the singing or otherwise directing the congregation, should be done either within or outside the sanctuary area, depending on circumstances or convenience.

22

Publication of *The Sacramentary*

Statement, Bishops' Committee on the Liturgy
June 1974

(See also nos. 5, 12, 23)

The sacramentary volume of the *Roman Missal* in Latin appeared in 1970; the corresponding volume in English was completed by ICEL in 1973 and approved, for the dioceses of the United States, by the conference of bishops in November of that year. The Bishops' Committee on the Liturgy issued two statements. One was directed to publishers in particular and to the Church in general; the second took the form of a foreword to the new liturgical book, *The Sacramentary*.

In the period following the council, the introduction of the vernacular liturgical books for the sacraments and rites other than the Eucharist was relatively simple and straightforward. After the promulgation of a Latin edition, whether of the rite of marriage or of baptism of children or of funerals, as soon as the ICEL version was ready, it was approved by the conference of bishops, published by the respective publishing houses, and made effective on a determined date. In the case of the Mass, however, the gradual introduction of the vernacular and the sheer quantity of the texts of the presidential prayers in *The Sacramentary* created a complex pattern.

In 1964, a missal was issued that included the parts of the people, the readings, and the proper chants in both Latin and English, along with the presidential prayers in Latin only. In 1966, the *English-Latin Sacramentary* appeared, including for interim use the presidential prayers in English from the *Maryknoll Missal*. Next, this was supplemented by an insert for the ministerial books to include the eucharistic prayers in English, according to the new concession. Finally, after the *Roman Missal* in Latin appeared, another temporary volume, employing a provisional draft of the ICEL translations, was issued in paper, *Sacramentary for Sundays and Other Occasions* (1972). (This temporary volume had its own distinctive importance, not only in providing new texts for trial use but also in introducing the alternative solemn blessings and prayer over the people at the end of Mass.)

Thus, at the end of this series of provisional publications, the completed *Sacramentary* of 1974—even though its translations were admittedly imperfect and subject to further revision—was the climax of a lengthy development and a major achievement in the liturgical renewal.

The first of the two statements of 1974 grew out of a meeting the episcopal committee had with representatives of publishing firms. Some publishers were prepared to issue official liturgical or ministerial books;

some were engaged in the preparation of popular materials for general use. At the meeting on June 3, the publishers were given the opportunity to discuss proposed embargoes on certain publications, which the committee sought in order to assure a proper reception to the massive addition to the English language euchology of presidential prayers at the Eucharist. Similar efforts were made in relation to other sacraments and services as they were ready for publication, and various detailed guidelines were published in virtue of the responsibility entrusted to the committee by the conference of bishops as far back as April 1964. (The most recent of these are the "Guidelines for the Publication of Liturgical Books" published in the June/July 1985 issue of the committee's *Newsletter*.)

At the request of the publishers, the accompanying statement was drawn up. It is a reasoned exposition concerned with the schedule of publication related to the new texts of Mass: *The Sacramentary* itself, the ministerial book, to be issued promptly in time for use on the First Sunday of Advent 1974; the publication of full popular missals for study purposes only on that date; and the (possible) inclusion of the new texts in missalettes and other participation aids only at the beginning of the following June. The precise scheduling is no longer significant; the theory and the expectations are significant.

The schedule reflects a compromise, since the inclusion of the presidential prayers in missalettes was itself of dubious value; it was a practice the committee could not prohibit. The availability of the new prayer texts for study and reflection was most desirable, but the practice of "following the Mass with the priest" by means of printed text, which had been very appropriate before the introduction of the vernacular, could now be only an inhibition to authentic celebration and community participation.

The statement also uses the occasion to spell out the importance of a worthy sacramentary from which the presiding celebrant sings or says the prayers (rather than from a missalette, a practice that had become widespread)—and to point out the rich diversity of prayer texts in the new liturgical book. Its breadth and diversity should not be undermined by presbyteral use of small booklets, leaflets, and the like, without the full choices and alternatives. It is a problem that remains in the 1980s.

In this whole matter, the committee had to face not only the resistance of the publishing firms, with their understandable concern for the profitability of missalettes and the like, but also a general misunderstanding among ordained ministers. The committee might have preferred a longer embargo on the inclusion of the new presidential prayers in the popular participation aids. It chose a reasonable and balanced compromise, in the hope of raising the level of comprehension and of worthy, authentic eucharistic celebration.

In November 1973, the National Conference of Catholic Bishops gave official approbation to *The Sacramentary*, a collection of the prayers said by the priest who presides over the celebration of Mass. For the most part, these prayers are translated from the *Roman Missal* of 1970, which was revised by decree of the Second Vatican Council and published by authority of Pope Paul VI. The collection also contains original English prayers, which may be used at the beginning of Mass as alternatives or substitutes for the opening prayer. In addition, there are optional introductions to some prayers, which the priest may use to begin the brief period of silent prayer by the congregation.

With the formal confirmation of the Roman Congregation for Divine Worship, *The Sacramentary* will be published in July 1974 in several authorized editions. By decision of the National Conference of Catholic Bishops, priests in the United States may begin using *The Sacramentary* at once. Thus, its prayers may be employed instead of the texts in the *English-Latin Sacramentary* (1966) and the provisional *Sacramentary for Sunday* (1972).

By decision of the Bishops' Committee on the Liturgy and the president of the National Conference of Catholic Bishops, the official effective date for *The Sacramentary* is the First Sunday of Advent, December 1, 1974. On that date, the new collection of prayers will replace those now in use in all dioceses of the United States for the eucharistic celebration.

It is important to understand that *The Sacramentary* does not alter the present Order of Mass, which was introduced in 1970. The wealth of new prayer texts—nearly two thousand in number—will enrich the celebration with variety and depth of meaning, but without disturbing the now familiar Order of Mass. These prayers are called "presidential prayers" by the *Roman Missal* because they are spoken by the priest alone in the name of the entire assembled congregation over which he presides. The new texts include opening prayers (at the end of the introductory rites), prayers over the gifts (to complete the preparation of the bread and wine), and prayers after communion (to conclude the communion rite), as well as a much larger number of prefaces of the eucharistic prayer.

Only two small but important changes will be noticed in the Order of Mass, and these have already been introduced in many places. (1) On Sundays, the penitential rite at the beginning of Mass may be omitted and replaced by the blessing and sprinkling of water, as a sign of baptismal renewal and commitment. (2) The concluding blessing may be enlarged slightly, to include either a brief prayer over the people or short verses to which the congregation responds Amen.

Popular publications, which are directly intended for congregational participation at Mass, are not so directly or immediately affected by the new collection of prayers to be said by the priest. Whether these participation aids take the forms of cards, leaflets, booklets, or books, their purpose is to provide the song and texts proper to the congregation.

The Bishops' Committee on the Liturgy has been seriously concerned that such publications, which are of great importance for congregations, are also being used by priests instead of the complete and official sacramentaries. This practice, while superficially convenient, severely restricts the priest to the limited contents of the people's participation aid. In effect, it can frustrate large parts of the liturgical reform decided upon by the Second Vatican Council and carried out in the liturgical books of Pope Paul VI.

In the hope of restoring primacy to the official and complete *Sacramentary*, the bishops' committee determined that this volume should be in actual use throughout the country over a substantial period of time before releasing the prayer texts for publication in congregational participation aids. The setting of a schedule of release was confirmed by the National Conference of Catholic Bishops at its November 1973 meeting.

In effect, this means that the new presidential prayers will not appear in any of the participation aids for the next few months, specifically until issues dated for use on June 1, 1975. This will not affect or limit congregational participation; music and texts for popular use have already been released. But the decision to delay the inclusion of the new prayers of the celebrating priest in popular participation materials is based on several important reasons:

1. *The Sacramentary* is designed as a book worthy and appropriate to its contents and use. It is the public prayerbook of the eucharistic celebration, from which the priest who presides leads the liturgical assembly in prayer to God. Now it should be restored to regular use as a worthy sign of the priest's role and office. Practically, this means that a period of actual use of the new books is needed, without the alternative of booklet substitutes and the like.

2. Just as important is the effective provision of *all* the approved texts of prayer for the use of the priest who presides. No card, leaflet, or booklet can provide for the priest the diversity of prayer texts for all occasions that is found in *The Sacramentary*. Often, there are wide options given to the priest, and these must not be denied because they cannot all be included in congregational participation aids. From Pentecost to Advent, for example, the priest is free on almost every weekday to choose among the prayer formularies of the thirty-four Sundays in ordinary time, not to mention a large quantity of Mass formularies for votive and other occasions. Even on Sundays, there are the possibilities of ritual Masses and the like.

To remove any inhibition on the freedom of priests to make such choices of prayers, as authorized, and to accommodate to particular circumstances, the effective use of *The Sacramentary* must be assured—even by the omission of presidential prayers from popular aids for a six-month period.

3. A basic principle of liturgical reform determined upon by the Second Vatican Council is the distribution of roles among the members of the worshiping assembly: bishop or priest presiding, deacon or other ministers, readers, singers, and the entire body of believers. "In liturgical celebrations each person, minister or layman, who has an office to perform, should do all of, but only, those parts which pertain to his office by the nature of the rite and the principles of liturgy" (SC 28).

This important lesson can be learned in many ways, and the distinction of the books for the eucharistic celebration is an important way. There are three categories of these books:

1. The various kinds of materials for congregational singing and saying of liturgical texts, including cards, leaflets, booklets, hymnals, popular missals, etc. The principal elements in these materials are the people's part in the Order of Mass (although most of this is known by heart), the responsorial psalm and alleluia, and the songs—for which there is very wide freedom and flexibility of choice.

2. The *Lectionary for Mass*, the book of readings which is comparable in size and appearance to the sacramentaries. It should be worthy of its content, which is the Word of God. This is the book for those who read to the assembly,

and it is an official volume for the use of the (lay) readers of the first two readings and for the deacon (or a priest or even the presiding priest, since a deacon or a second priest is often not available) who reads the gospel.

3. *The Sacramentary* or book of presidential prayers.

It is the expectation of the Bishops' Committee on the Liturgy that the next few months will be employed to recover a sense of these distinctions, to restore the use of worthy liturgical books for priests and readers, and to open up the prayer treasury of *The Sacramentary*.

During this period, when the new official presidential prayers will not be available for printing in publication aids, the Bishops' Committee on the Liturgy suggests that publishers increase the variety of song material in their publications. They may use the occasion to indicate, by appropriate commentary, the nature of the presidential prayers in the context of the Mass.

It is the desire of the bishops' committee to encourage knowledge of the new presidential prayers in *The Sacramentary* and to make them available for people to study and reflect upon in preparation for Mass. Therefore, full popular missals may contain these texts beginning December 1, 1974. Prior to June 1, 1975, however, complete missals of this kind may not be designed for congregational participation, for example, by the inclusion of songs, lest they improperly compete with the periodical booklets which do have the practice of including presidential prayers but must omit the new texts until the later date.

23

The Sacramentary

Foreword, Bishops' Committee on the Liturgy
1974; revised 1985

(See also nos. 5, 12, 22)

Despite its considerable length, this document of the Bishops' Committee on the Liturgy requires little commentary. It was prepared for the first completed English version of the Roman sacramentary, prepared by ICEL and then approved by the American conference of bishops in November 1973, with Roman confirmation dated February 4, 1974. *The Sacramentary* was published in four editions in the United States and came at the end of a lengthy and gradual development, as described in connection with the preceding statement, *Publication of the Sacramentary.*

Other liturgical books, such as the *Rite of Funerals,* had their own explanatory notes proper to the United States, but, of course, the sacramentary for the Eucharist was of much greater importance. The foreword was published in all the editions; the text reprinted here was somewhat revised in 1985 to bring it up-to-date in the new edition of *The Sacramentary,* which was published in conformity with the second edition of the *Roman Missal* (1975).

As is apparent, the foreword was not intended as a commentary on the reformed rite of eucharistic celebration, not even on all the special features of the volume. It does, however, introduce some of the unfamiliar elements of the rite. There is deliberate emphasis upon certain matters: the Sunday renewal of baptism as an appropriate and desirable substitute for the penitential rite at the beginning of Mass; the period of real and prayerful silence after "Let us pray" or other invitations to prayer; some structural elements—important ones such as the several presidential prayers; secondary ones such as the entrance and communion antiphons, which are texts only incidentally included in a presidential liturgical book.

As a desideratum of presbyteral orientation, the foreword begins with a brief exposition of the nature of a sacramentary, even though the term had been used in the United States for several years to indicate the presidential book for the Eucharist. Under "Format" and "Music," an attempt is made to explain how the volume itself was edited and arranged. Moreover, there is a brief explanation of the principles of translation. This explanation relies on quotations from the Roman instruction of 1969 (DOL 123). That document had supported faithful but free versions and urged the avoidance of slavishness or mechanical translating.

Finally, the text offers a few guidelines to some liturgical developments that might well have been overlooked by priests and others, such as the

Directory for Masses with Children (included in *The Sacramentary* for the United States as an appendix to the *General Instruction*) and various specific items of information on homilies, eucharistic ministers, and the like.

In the late 1980s and into the 1990s, the ICEL program moves toward a completely revised translation of *The Sacramentary* and an enlargement of the book with original prayers. The project will move from this kind of limited foreword to substantial pastoral notes. Like the notes already provided in the second editions of liturgical books such as *Pastoral Care of the Sick: Rites of Anointing and Viaticum* and *Order of Christian Funerals,* these will go far beyond the brief commentary that has introduced American editions of *The Sacramentary* from 1974 to the present.

The purpose of this foreword is to draw attention to particular features of this sacramentary and to make it clearer and easier to use for the priest who presides over the eucharistic celebration. The foreword has some few parts applicable only in the dioceses of the United States.

For the most part, this volume is a translation, approved by the National Conference of Catholic Bishops and confirmed by the Apostolic See, of the *Missale Romanum* of 1969 with the variations introduced into the second edition of 1975. The missal was revised by decree of the Second Vatican Council and promulgated by Pope Paul VI. In addition to the translation of liturgical texts and other materials, however, this edition in English includes other texts, with the same approbation as the translations, and follows a somewhat different format.

It is important, first of all, to call attention to the *General Instruction of the Roman Missal,* which is translated below. The present foreword in no way replaces the *General Instruction,* which deserves careful study, in part for its doctrinal and liturgical explanation of the structure, elements, and ministries in the celebration. Without a thorough knowledge of the *General Instruction,* it is impossible for the priest to understand the conciliar reform or to take the principal role in planning the celebration with the other ministers and all who have special responsibilities for it.

Nature of *The Sacramentary*

A sacramentary is a collection of presidential prayers for the celebration of the Eucharist. Such books have been in use from about the fifth century, but in the Middle Ages they were combined with other service books, lectionaries, and collections of chants. The complete missal of the modern period was thus much more than a sacramentary, and it reflected the development by which the priest ordinarily took not only his own part in the eucharistic celebration but also the parts of the assembly, singers, readers, and even the deacon.

The Second Vatican Council restored the basic rule that each member of the worshiping community, whether ordained minister or lay person, should perform all of those parts, but only those parts, which pertain to his or her office by the nature of the rite and the principles of liturgy. This conciliar decision is reflected in the distinct sacramentary, a volume which is limited, with some slight exceptions, to the parts of the rite of Mass which pertain to the priest. *The Sacramentary*, as a volume of presidential prayers, thus reflects a basic element of the liturgical reform: the distinction between the part of the priest and the parts of other members of the assembly, just as in the past the complete missal was a symbol of the absorption of the roles of others by the celebrant.

The Sacramentary does not contain Scripture readings, responsorial psalms, or verses for the gospel acclamation. These are found in the *Lectionary for Mass*. Entrance and communion antiphons have been included for the convenience of the priest, who may use them on occasion. Their use is explained below.

When there are no readers for the first and second readings and when no deacon or other priest is present to proclaim the gospel, the priest uses the *Lectionary for Mass* and, where it is available, *The Book of the Gospels* at the pulpit or lectern. Otherwise, *The Sacramentary* is the single book of the priest who presides: he reads from it at the chair (for the opening prayer of Mass, for the prayer after communion, and for the solemn form of concluding blessing) as well as at the altar. The priest needs no other book, except when he joins the people in the singing from a hymnal or booklet.

Partly because of its long tradition of use in the Church, the sacramentary as a book has symbolic meanings similar to that of the lectionary from which the Word of God is proclaimed. It represents the office of presidency in the prayer of the liturgical assembly—both in the prayers of petition and in the central eucharistic prayer of praise, thanksgiving, and memorial. Since these prayers articulate the action of the Church in celebrating the sacrifice of the Lord, even the book of prayer is an important sign. For this reason, it is expected to be of sufficiently worthy proportions and artistic design to create respect and reverence for its contents.

Format for Sunday Masses

A distinctive feature of this edition of *The Sacramentary* is the double-page spread given for each Sunday Mass and for some feasts of greater importance. This arrangement is intended to stress the importance of the Sunday celebration of the Eucharist, the reform of which was the primary conciliar concern. The actual format is designed to make the relationship of structure and parts completely clear, so that the priest will see immediately the two parts of the eucharistic celebration: the liturgy of the Word (only referred to, but with an indication of the section of the *Lectionary for Mass*, for convenience) and the liturgy of the Eucharist. The introductory rites and the concluding rite have been placed in proper subordination.

Translation of Latin Texts

In accord with directions from the Apostolic See, the translations of Latin texts, prepared by the International Commission on English in the Liturgy, are faithful but not literal. They preserve the intent and substance of the original, but avoid the translation of words in favor of the translation of ideas. This principle is explained at length in the instruction on the subject issued by the Consilium for the Implementation of the *Constitution on the Liturgy* (January 25, 1969):

A faithful translation cannot be judged on the basis of individual words: the total context of this specific act of communication must be kept in mind, as well as the literary form proper to the respective language (no. 6).

The translator must always keep in mind that the "unit of meaning" is not the individual word but the whole passage. The translator must therefore be careful that the translation is not so analytical that it exaggerates the importance of particular phrases while it obscures or weakens the meaning of the whole (no. 12).

The prayer of the Church is always the prayer of some actual community, assembled here and now. It is not sufficient that a formula handed down from some other time or region be translated verbatim, even if accurately, for liturgical use. The formula translated must become the genuine prayer of the assembly and in it each of its members should be able to find and express himself or herself (no. 20).

The prayers (opening prayer, prayer over the gifts, prayer after communion, and prayer over the people) from the ancient Roman tradition are succinct and abstract. In translation they may need to be rendered somewhat more freely while conserving the original ideas. This can be done by moderately amplifying them, or, if necessary, paraphrasing expressions in order to concretize them for the celebration and needs of today. In every case pompous and superfluous language should be avoided (no. 34).

Liturgies with Children

Because the directory was prepared as a supplement to the *General Instruction of the Roman Missal*, this edition of *The Sacramentary* includes the *Directory for Masses with Children*, issued by the Congregation for Divine Worship on November 1, 1973. It appears below, after the *General Instruction*.

The directory offers guidelines for the eucharistic celebration with assemblies of preadolescents. It is for liturgies with those baptized children who "have yet to be fully initiated through the sacraments of confirmation and eucharist as well as for children who have only recently been admitted to holy communion" (no. 1). It may also be adapted for liturgies with assemblies of the physically or mentally retarded (no. 6). And, it contains recommended adaptations not only for Masses at which the assembly consists principally of children (Chapter III) but also for Masses with adult congregations in which a number of children participate (Chapter II).

146

Music

The following music for the ministerial chants has been included in this edition of *The Sacramentary:*

(a) the chants of the prefaces of the eucharistic prayer have been included for every text, in a setting based on the plain chant; in addition the settings already in use in the United States have been appended from *The Order of Mass* (1969);

(b) in the Order of Mass, both the chants of the priest and the chants of the priest and the people together (such as the *Sanctus* and the Lord's Prayer);

(c) in the appendix, alternate settings of the Lord's Prayer and additional chants proper to the priest, including the body of the four eucharistic prayers;

(d) seasonal ministerial chants, such as the Easter proclamation of the deacon.

The chant adaptation was prepared by the International Commission on English in the Liturgy. The various appended settings of the Lord's Prayer, prefaces of the eucharistic prayer, etc., are taken from earlier liturgical books approved by the National Conference of Catholic Bishops.

Sunday Renewal of Baptism

As an alternative to the penitential rite at all Sunday Masses, the blessing and sprinkling of the people with holy water may be substituted. This revised rite of sprinkling is no longer restricted to the principal Mass or to parish churches but may be used "at all Sunday Masses, even those anticipated on Saturday evening, in all churches and oratories."

To make this point clear, the rite is printed in the Order of Mass as an alternative to the penitential rite. The latter is simply omitted when holy water is blessed and sprinkled. The prayer of blessing of the water, which follows the priest's initial greeting, and the selection of songs to accompany the sprinkling indicate the purpose of the rite: to express the paschal character of Sunday and to be a memorial of baptism.

The directions for this brief rite are given in the Order of Mass and in Appendix I of *The Sacramentary*. After the rite of sprinkling, the Order of Mass continues with the *Gloria* or the opening prayer.

Opening Prayer

The collect, sometimes called the prayer of the assembly, has now been given the name "opening prayer" because it is the first prayer of the eucharistic celebration and because it completes the opening or introductory rite. In the *Roman Missal*, this prayer is not directly related to the biblical readings which follow. Instead, it is a general prayer, related to the occasion or celebration, which concludes the entrance rite and serves to introduce the whole Eucharist.

The *General Instruction of the Roman Missal* says:

The priest invites the people to pray and together with him they observe a brief silence so that they may realize they are in God's presence and may call their petitions to mind. The priest then says the opening prayer, which custom has named the "collect." This expresses the theme of the celebration and the priest's words address a petition to God the Father through Christ in the Holy Spirit.

The people make the prayer their own and give their assent by the acclamation, *Amen.*

In the Mass only one opening prayer is said; this rule applies also to the prayer over the gifts and the prayer after communion (no. 32).

In this edition, an optional invitatory (explained below) has been given for the opening prayers on Sundays and certain feasts. It is placed within square brackets to indicate that its use is at the discretion of the priest.

The text of the opening prayer—after the invitatory and the period of silence—has been arranged in sense lines to help the priest to pray it in an audible, deliberate and intelligible manner. The texts of the other prayers have been similarly arranged. The use of the sense lines also avoids the necessity of pointing the text of prayers for occasions when they are sung. Melodies for singing the opening prayer are given in Appendix III.

Alternative Opening Prayers

The prayers of the *Roman Missal* have been translated in a style which, for the most part, retains the succinct character of the original Latin. The translations do not ordinarily employ the development or expansion mentioned in the instruction on liturgical translations (above). In the case of the opening prayer on Sundays and some major feasts, however, an alternative text is printed for use at the discretion of the priest.

The alternative opening prayers are not direct or faithful translations of the corresponding Latin text. They follow its theme or are inspired by it, but they are generally more concrete and expansive. The addition of such texts was promoted by the practice in other Roman liturgical books of offering alternatives and by the following statement in the 1969 instruction on translation:

Texts translated from another language are clearly not sufficient for the celebration of a fully renewed liturgy. The creation of new texts will be necessary. But translation of texts transmitted through the tradition of the Church is the best school and discipline for the creation of new texts so "that any new forms adopted should in some way grow organically from forms already in existence (SC 23)" (no. 43).

Thus, on those occasions when two opening prayers appear side by side, the one on the left is a faithful but not necessarily literal translation of the corresponding Latin prayer, the one on the right is an alternative prayer suggested by the Latin text and in harmony with its theme. Either text may be chosen by the priest.

Conclusion to Prayers

Because the revised rite concludes the presidential prayers in different ways (a lengthy conclusion to the opening prayer or collect, a briefer conclusion to most other prayers), this edition gives the complete conclusion in every case. Very often, the precise formulations of the conclusions are almost interchangeable. Their use is explained in no. 32 of the *General Instruction*, although in English it is sometimes possible to weave the formal conclusion into the last clause of the body of the prayer.

In most instances the distinct conclusion begins either "We ask this . . ." or "Grant this . . ." The purpose of the variation is that the mediation and intercession of Jesus expressed simply in Latin by the preposition *per* bears at least two meanings: (1) that the prayer of petition is addressed to the Father through Jesus in the Holy Spirit and (2) that the action of the Father comes through Jesus in the Holy Spirit. In the lengthy conclusion, the concept expressed in Latin by the words *"in unitate Spiritus Sancti, Deus"* is conveyed more directly in English, "with you [Father] and the Holy Spirit, one God . . ."

In the light of several years of experience with provisional texts, a slight variation has been introduced into the very last words of the conclusions to prayers, namely, "in the name of Jesus the Lord" in addition to "through Christ our Lord" and "for ever and ever." Several variants to express the biblical concept of prayer in Jesus' name are in common use.

The one chosen ("in the name of Jesus the Lord") is very close to the already accepted text, "through Christ our Lord," so that it should be easy for the priest to elicit the response of the people, *Amen.*

Invitatories and Introductions

For the opening prayer, the priest first invites the people to pray, either with the simple "Let us pray" or with the expanded alternative invitatory found in *The Sacramentary,* or in his own words.

This invitatory or invitation to pray is a kind of *monitio* which the priest or other minister may employ to introduce or conclude—in very few words—different parts of Mass (see GIRM 11). In this edition of *The Sacramentary,* it is expanded so that in the period of silence which follows the people may form their petitions. The period of silence will be richer and demand sufficient time so that the people can actually pray. Silence then becomes a real and meaningful part of the celebration (see GIRM 23). The brief, optional expansion of the invitatory structures the silence and helps people to be aware of the petitionary character of the opening prayer. If the priest uses his own words, the invitatory can be more concrete and effective.

The use of adapted introductory comments or invitatories has been explained in the following statement of the Congregation for Divine Worship (circular letter, April 27, 1973):

> Introductions are ways of leading the faithful to a more thorough grasp of the meaning of the sacred rites or certain of their parts and to an inner participation in them. Particularly important are the introductions that

the *General Instruction* assigns to be prepared and spoken by the priest: the comments introducing the faithful to the day's Mass before the celebration, to the liturgy of the word before the readings, and to the eucharistic prayer before the preface; the comments concluding the whole rite before the dismissal. Prominence should also be given to those introductions that the Order of Mass provides for certain rites, for example, the introductions to the penitential rite and the Lord's Prayer. By their very nature such introductions do not require that they be given verbatim in the form they have in the Missal; consequently it may well be helpful, at least in certain cases, to adapt them to the actual situation of a community. But the way any of these introductions is presented must respect the character proper to each and not turn into a sermon or homily. There must be a concern for brevity and the avoidance of a wordiness that would bore the participants (no. 14).

Other Recommendations

The circular letter of the Congregation for Divine Worship from which the above quotation is taken also speaks of accommodating the homily, general intercessions, and other elements of the eucharistic celebration to the particular congregation:

The homily must also be mentioned. It is "a part of the liturgy" by which the word of God proclaimed in the liturgical assembly is explained to help the community present. It is given in a way that is suited to the community's capacity and way of life and what is relevant to the circumstances of the celebration.

Finally much is to be made of the general intercessions, which in a sense are the community's response to the word of God proclaimed and received. To ensure its effectiveness care must be taken that the intentions made on behalf of the whole world's needs are suited to the gathered assembly; this means that there be a certain flexibility proportioned to the nature of this prayer in the preparation of the intentions.

For the celebration to belong to the community and to be vital requires more than choosing texts. The one presiding and others with a special role in the celebration must have a precise sense of the different styles of verbal communication that are involved in the readings, homily, introductions, and the like (nos. 15–17).

Silence

"Silence should be observed at the designated times as part of the celebration. Its function depends on the time it occurs in each part of the celebration. Thus, at the penitential rite and again after the invitation to pray, all recollect themselves; at the conclusion of a reading or the homily, all meditate briefly on what has been heard; after communion, all praise God in silent prayer" (GIRM 23).

In order to facilitate the use of silence, rubrical directions for silent prayer have been indicated in this edition. These silent periods for prayer ordinarily should not be too lengthy. A more lengthy pause for reflection may take place at the penitential rite and after the readings or homily.

The proper use of periods of silent prayer and reflection will help to render the celebration less mechanical and impersonal and lend a more prayerful spirit to the liturgical rite. Just as there should be no celebration without song, so too there should be no celebration without periods for silent prayer and reflection.

Prayer over the Gifts

The prayer over the gifts in style is similar to the opening prayer but with a brief concluding formula. It completes the preparation of the gifts: the people's presentation of the bread and wine and their preparation on the altar.

The prayer over the gifts has its own invitatory ("Pray, brethren . . ."). For clarity, this invitatory has been directly indicated in the Mass formularies. No optional expansion of the invitation to pray has been provided, as was done in the case of the opening prayer.

If song or other music has accompanied the preparation of the gifts, as the *General Instruction* (no. 50) and the Order of Mass (no. 17) prefer, it will be appropriate to pause for a period of silence after the invitation and response, before the text of the prayer over the gifts is said.

If, as is also appropriate, the preparation of the gifts has taken place in silence, there will be no need for an additional period of silence before the priest says the prayer over the gifts.

After the prayer over the gifts, the priest should pause briefly before beginning the eucharistic prayer with the greeting "The Lord be with you."

Prayer after Communion

"After communion, the priest and people may spend some time in silent prayer. If desired, a hymn, psalm, or other song of praise may be sung by the entire assembly" (GIRM 56j; see also no. 23). After this period of prayer in silence and/or song, the priest prays for the effects of the mystery just celebrated (cf. GIRM 56k).

No expanded invitatory is printed for the prayer after communion; in most cases "Let us pray" will suffice.

If the assembly has joined in a song, hymn, or psalm of praise after communion, there should be the usual period of silence—sufficiently protracted for recollection and reflection—after the invitation "Let us pray" (GIRM 23; Order of Mass, no. 33).

151

Concluding Rite

The Order of Mass has a simple concluding rite:

(a) From his chair or at the altar, the priest or another minister may make brief announcements, if any.

(b) The priest gives the formal liturgical greeting, "The Lord be with you," and the people respond.

(c) The priest gives the blessing, and

(d) the deacon gives the liturgical dismissal—or, in the absence of a deacon, this is done by the priest.

A directive in the Order of Mass mentions a substitute for the usual style of blessing: "On certain days or occasions another more solemn form of blessing or prayer over the people may be used as the rubrics direct" (Order of Mass, no. 113).

The Sacramentary gives extensive texts for these substitutes for the usual blessing and thus makes it possible to enrich and somewhat enlarge the concluding rite. All these solemn blessings and prayers over the people are printed together, to allow complete freedom of choice. In addition, the individual Mass formularies for Sundays in the principal seasons and on other occasions give a suggested example so that the pattern may become clear.

Either the solemn blessing or the prayer over the people may be chosen. During Lent, in keeping with ancient tradition, the prayer over the people is principally used. Some of the texts of the blessings and prayers are very general; others are specified for particular seasons or occasions.

The textual differences are these: the solemn blessings are usually divided into three parts or verses to each of which the people answer "Amen"; the prayer over the people is in the style of a collect, to which the people also respond "Amen."

Since the prayer over the people has a conclusion like other presidential prayers (" . . . through Christ our Lord" or "in the name of Jesus the Lord"), the people will respond readily. Special attention is needed in the case of the solemn blessings, since the people will be unfamiliar with the style and the text. The priest should try to invite and encourage response by the inflection of his voice. In the absence of a fixed formula for concluding each of the verses, the tone or stress of the priest's voice must indicate the moment for common response.

Rite of Blessing and Dismissal

The rite for the conclusion of Mass, when the option of a special blessing or prayer over the people is chosen, is as follows:

(1) After the usual greeting by the priest ("The Lord be with you"), the deacon gives the invitation: "Bow your heads and pray for God's blessing." He may also use similar words. In the absence of a deacon, the priest gives the invitation.

(2) The priest then extends his hands over the people while he sings or says the solemn blessing or prayer over the people.

This gesture of stretching his hands over the people is a form of the

152

imposition of hands over the whole community. It should be done carefully so that it truly signifies the priest's role as he invokes God's power and strength on the assembly. (The book should be held for the priest by a server or minister, unless he goes to the altar for the concluding rite.)

(3) In either case—solemn blessing or prayer over the people—the priest concludes with the trinitarian formula and the usual gesture of blessing with the sign of the cross.

Finally, the deacon (or the priest, in the absence of a deacon) gives the dismissal "which sends each member (of the assembly) back to doing good works, while praising and blessing the Lord" (GIRM 57). The recession begins as soon as the assembly has received this formal dismissal. It may be accompanied by a recessional song or other music.

Entrance Antiphon

Although *The Sacramentary* is a book of presidential prayers sung or spoken by the priest, for the sake of completeness, this edition does contain the brief sung antiphons for the entrance and communion processions. These are printed in smaller type in order to indicate that they are not ordinarily said by the priest and indeed are not parts of a sacramentary.

The *General Instruction* takes for granted that there will be singing at the entrance of the priest and other ministers (and during the communion rite; see nos. 26, 56, 83, 119), certainly in the Sunday celebration of the eucharist. When the antiphons are set to music, they may be used for this purpose (i.e., as refrains to psalms). Ordinarily, however, it is expected that full use will be made of the decision to employ appropriate substitutes sung by the assembly with a cantor or choir. For the United States, the National Conference of Catholic Bishops has given the criteria for texts to be sung as entrance songs. (See *Appendix to the General Instruction,* no. 26, below).

Only in the absence of song is the entrance antiphon used as a spoken or recited text. Since these antiphons are too abrupt for communal recitation, it is preferable when there is no singing that the priest, the deacon, or another minister adapt the antiphon and incorporate it in the introduction to the Mass of the day. After the initial greeting, "the priest, deacon, or other suitable minister may very briefly introduce the Mass of the day" (Order of Mass, no. 3). The adaptation of the text of the entrance antiphon for this purpose is suggested by the Congregation for Divine Worship (*Instruction on Particular Calendars and Offices,* June 24, 1970, no. 40a).

Communion Antiphon

The communion antiphon, although it is not ordinarily to be said by the priest, has also been included for completeness. The Order of Mass (no. 108) and the *General Instruction* call for singing during the communion of the priest and people, to "express outwardly the communicants' union in spirit by means of the unity of their voices, to give evidence of joy of heart, and to make the procession to receive Christ's body more fully an act of community" (GIRM 56i). The National Conference of Catholic Bishops has provided criteria for texts to be used (see *Appendix to the General Instruction,* no. 56i, below). For use of the communion antiphon if there is no singing, the directives given in no. 56i of the *General Instruction* are to be followed.

Name of the Bishop

By decree of the Congregation for Divine Worship, October 8, 1972, not only the diocesan bishop but an Ordinary equivalent in law to a diocesan bishop must be named in the eucharistic prayer. This includes a diocesan bishop transferred to another diocese as long as he administers the former diocese; an apostolic administrator, *sede plena* or *sede vacante,* whether permanent or temporary, if he is a bishop and actually exercises the entire governance of the diocese, especially in spiritual matters; a vicar or prefect apostolic; and a prelate or abbot *nullius.* However, it does not include a diocesan administrator *sede vacante.*

In addition, coadjutor and auxiliary bishops who assist the diocesan bishop in the governance of the diocese and other bishops may be named after the Ordinary. If there are several bishops, they may be mentioned as a group ("and his assistant bishops") without adding their names.

In the case of a priest celebrating the Eucharist outside his own diocese but with a congregation from his diocese, he names his own bishop and then the local bishop ("N., the bishop of this Church of N.").

The diocesan bishop may mention his coadjutor or auxiliary bishops and, when outside his own diocese, both the local bishop and himself.

Communion More than Once a Day

Canon 917 of the 1983 *Code of Canon Law* states that, apart from the reception of Viaticum, "a person who has received the Most Holy Eucharist may receive it again on the same day only during the celebration of the Eucharist in which the person participates." The Pontifical Commission for the Authoritative Interpretation of the Code of Canon Law decreed that this canon is to be interpreted as referring only to a *second* Mass, not *as often,* as a person participates in the Eucharist on a given day (*AAS* 76 [1984] 746–747).

Ministers of Communion

On June 21, 1973, the section of the Roman Ritual entitled *De Sacra Communione et de Cultu Mysterii Eucharistici extra Missam* was published. It contains the following paragraphs about the minister of communion, which are applicable to the celebration of Mass:

It is, first of all, the office of the priest and the deacon to minister holy communion to the faithful who ask to receive it. It is most fitting, therefore, that they give a suitable part of their time to this ministry of their order, depending on the needs of the faithful.

It is the office of an acolyte who has been properly instituted to give communion as a special minister when the priest and deacon are absent or impeded by sickness, old age, or pastoral ministry or when the number of the faithful at the holy table is so great that the Mass or other service may be unreasonably protracted.

The local Ordinary may give other special ministers the faculty to give holy communion whenever it seems necessary for the pastoral benefit of the faithful and a priest, deacon, or acolyte is not available (no. 17).

In cases of necessity, a priest may even designate a member of a particular worshiping assembly to assist in giving communion for a single occasion. The special form for this designation is given in Appendix V.

Manner of Ministering Communion

The Roman Ritual (*De Sacra Communione et de Cultu Mysterii Eucharistici extra Missam*) gives the following norm concerning the manner of administration of Holy Communion:

In giving communion the custom of placing the particle of consecrated bread on the tongue of the communicant is to be maintained because it is based on a tradition of several centuries.

Conferences of bishops, however, may decree, their actions having been confirmed by the Apostolic See, that communion may also be given in their territories by placing the consecrated bread in the hands of the faithful, provided there is no danger of irreverence or false opinions about the Eucharist entering the minds of the faithful.

The faithful should be instructed that Jesus Christ is Lord and Savior and that, present in the sacrament, he must be given the same worship and adoration which is to be given to God.

In either case, communion must be given by the competent minister, who shows the particle of consecrated bread to the communicant and gives it to him or her, saying, "The body of Christ," to which the communicant replies "Amen" (no. 21).

The faculty of distributing communion in the hand was conceded by the Sacred Congregation for the Sacraments and Divine Worship to the National Conference of Catholic Bishops on June 17, 1977. For norms pertaining to this practice, see *Appendix to the General Instruction for Dioceses of the United States of America,* no. 240, below.

Eucharistic Fast

The Roman Ritual (*De Sacra Communione et de Cultu Mysterii extra Missam,* with the revisions decreed in 1983) gives the present discipline of the eucharistic fast:

155

Communicants are not to receive the sacrament unless they have fasted for at least one hour from foods and beverages, with the exception only of water and medicine.

The elderly and those suffering from any kind of infirmity, as well as those who take care of such persons, may receive the Eucharist even if they have taken something within the hour before communion (no. 24).

Eucharistic Prayers for Masses with Children and for Masses of Reconciliation

Appendix VI contains the Eucharistic Prayers for Masses with Children and the Eucharistic Prayers for Masses of Reconciliation. While these prayers have been approved by the Apostolic See for an indeterminate period of time, the Latin texts of the prayers are still designated as *ad experimentum*. Hence, they may not be included in the same place as the other four Eucharistic Prayers in *The Sacramentary* and have been included in this appendix.

Blessing of Oils

An appendix to *The Sacramentary* contains, for convenience, the English text of the rites for the blessing of oils and consecration of the chrism, for use on Holy Thursday or on another day chosen by the bishop.

Appendix of Latin Texts

A special Latin appendix is included in this edition by direction of the Congregation for Divine Worship. It contains the *Ordo Missae* in Latin (including the four eucharistic prayers and a number of prefaces) and a selection of formularies for Mass in Latin.

This appendix is intended for the use of visiting priests who may not be familiar with the language of the country. For the ordinary celebration of Mass in Latin, in whole or in part, the *Missale Romanum* and *Lectionarium* should be used.

Additional Appendices VII, VIII, IX, X

The 1985 reprinting of *The Sacramentary* includes appendices containing the additional presidential prayers approved since 1974. These prayers are from the 1975 *editio typica altera* of the *Roman Missal, Pastoral Care of the Sick: Rites of Anointing and Viaticum,* and *The Dedication of a Church and an Altar.* The *Blessing of a Chalice and Paten* Mass is also included in an appendix for use on those occasions when these vessels are blessed at Mass. The last appendix contains additional presidential prayers from the 1975 edition of the *Missale Romanum* in provisional translation approved for interim use, as well as the "Bicentennial Mass" of 1976 with the new title "Independence Day and Other Civic Observances."

24

Liturgical Publishers

Letter, President of the National Conference of
Catholic Bishops
December 12, 1975

(See also no. 18)

Brief as it is, in the form of a letter, and coming from the NCCB president
rather than from the episcopal committee, the text reprinted here has
special importance. It deals with a possibility that would arise later in
the case of *A Book of Prayers,* namely, variant versions of liturgical texts
on the grounds that these are being published for devotional purposes
only.

Archbishop Joseph L. Bernardin of Cincinnati, who had served as auxiliary to Archbishop Hallinan of Atlanta and later as general secretary of
the conference of bishops, succeeded Cardinal John Krol as president of
the conference in November 1975. His December letter was addressed
to publishers of liturgical materials, whether in the form of liturgical books
for ministerial use or in the style of participation aids or devotional publications. The letter was intended both to clarify and to strengthen the
positions that had been taken by the Bishops' Committee on the Liturgy.

The letter deals with such issues by quoting a Roman response, but
the answer was already clear and certainly logical. While the approval
of devotional books and, indeed, participation materials is within the
competence of the diocesan bishop or other local Ordinary—this is true
even today in accord with canon 826 §3 of the 1983 *Code of Canon
Law*—only the official versions of such texts may be used. These, in turn,
are those texts that have been approved for exclusive use in all the dioceses
of the United States by the conference of bishops, with confirmation of
that action by the Apostolic See.

One problematic instance that arose later (and was not the object of
any public statement from the episcopal committee) was the well-inten-
tioned preparation of an abbreviated version of the liturgy of the hours.
This had been prepared as a kind of successor to the highly successful
preconciliar publication, *A Short Breviary.* The latter was a remarkable
contribution to the liturgical renewal by the monks of Saint John's Abbey,
Collegeville, Minnesota. It was used as an office-book for the celebration
of the hours of ecclesial prayer by many orders and congregations of lay
religious as well as by individuals.

The new project, along somewhat similar lines, created a problem for
the committee. On the one hand, the *Constitution on the Liturgy* had not
only recommended such adaptations of the breviary but had formally

recognized them as the liturgical prayer of the Church: "They too perform the public prayer of the Church who, in virtue of their constitutions, recite any little office [parvum Officium], provided this has been drawn up after the pattern of the divine office and duly approved" (SC 98). On the other hand, this particular project employed a translation of the psalter, presidential prayers, nonbiblical readings, and intercessions different from those canonically approved by the National Conference of Catholic Bishops. The book also failed by omission, especially by neglecting the new and highly successful "psalm prayers" of the approved liturgy of the hours.

It is relatively easy, certainly in principle, to deal with the substitution of new or old translations of liturgical texts for those officially adopted, whether this is innocently or purposefully done. The second question, of new and original liturgical texts, is more difficult. The creative development of these texts, even on the legitimate grounds of study and reflection, almost inevitably leads to their actual liturgical use.

Archbishop Bernardin's letter attempted to maintain the strict ecclesiastical discipline, particularly in the case of presidential prayers. If original texts of such prayers are for study or other relatively private uses, no issue arises; if they are put into actual liturgical use (i.e., replacing the official texts), the formalities of official approbation are expected.

Normally, the Episcopal Conference addresses the publishers of liturgical texts through the Secretariat of the Bishops' Committee on the Liturgy. However, in the past two years, there have been certain difficulties in this regard. For this reason, it seems useful to enunciate again the policy of the bishops regarding translations and original texts.

1. All publications containing rites or excerpts of the rites of the Church are to use only the translation approved by the National Conference of Catholic Bishops and confirmed by the Holy See. Even books of a private nature that contain excerpts from the rites of the Church must contain the official translation. A recent letter from Cardinal Knox, Prefect of the Sacred Congregation for the Sacraments and Divine Worship, makes this clear: "Private books of prayer cannot be published without the consent of the Ordinary, who in turn cannot authorize a translation other than that approved by the Episcopal Conference." From this, it is evident that no publishing house may provide its own translation of the rites of the Church.

2. New texts that are not translations but are composed in English require the approval of the Episcopal Conference and confirmation from the Holy See. Thus, it is not possible for a publishing house to compose and publish presidential prayers, eucharistic prayers, etc. Such innovations only serve to confuse people and to cause harm to liturgical renewal. Suggestions for new texts, of course, may be submitted to the Bishops' Committee on the Liturgy for their consideration.

I am confident that our publishers, who have been so helpful to the Church's liturgical life, will comply with the directives of the Holy See and the norms of the Episcopal Conference regarding translations of new rites and new compositions.

159

25

The Sign of Peace

Statement, Bishops' Committee on the Liturgy
November 1976

This statement, much in the pattern of earlier statements such as *Communion under Both Kinds* of a decade earlier, was partly occasioned by a misunderstanding. Yet, it is very positive in its fresh orientation of an ancient ritual gesture recovered from tradition in the postconciliar reform of the rite of Mass. The gesture, whether "the handclasp of fellowship" given to Paul and Barnabas (Gal 2:9) or a stylized ritual handshake, has a profound meaning in Christian liturgy.

By and large, the extension of the sign of peace to the entire celebrating assembly was a welcome feature of the new Order of Mass. Young and old alike seemed to share in the Christian warmth of the exchange of Christ's peace, a sign of Christian charity and reconciliation. Overlooked, however, was an explicit element of the reform. It was no longer to be a sign or kiss of peace taken from the altar that is Christ by the presiding celebrant and extended from him to the deacon, then shared by the deacon with the subdeacon, who, in turn, extended the greeting from one to the other through the sanctuary—and, if the almost obsolete rite of the old missal were followed, through the assembly with each lay person kissing the pax-brede or instrument of peace. Instead, it was to be an exchange, an embrace or handclasp or handshake shared with one's immediate neighbors in the congregation.

Perhaps, because of past clerical usage or memories, the extension of the sign, after its restoration in 1969, in practice was frequently carried out in a manner foreign to the new Order of Mass. It often became a matter of the priest and deacon or other priests going through the entire assembly, offering as it were a greeting from the clergy to the laity. Apart from the disproportionate length of the rite, the intent that each member of the assembly (including the presiding celebrant) should extend a greeting of peace and Christian love to those around him or her was lost sight of.

What had happened was this. The enlargement of the gesture's scope had been achieved, and all could once again participate, but the clerical feature had been maintained: no one could share the sign of peace until the presiding priest had moved throughout the congregation. This was an extreme instance of the misunderstanding, but sometimes a pattern of each member of the congregation greeting all the other members—or as many as possible—was introduced.

The statement speaks well to the problem: Neither the people nor the ministers need try to exhaust the sign by attempting to give the greeting personally to everyone in the congregation or even to a great number of those present. The sign remains just that—"a sign of peace that should exist among all those who celebrate the sacrament of unity."

Thus, the statement was a mild corrective of practices in which the sign of peace became a protracted interruption of the communion rite, disproportionate and even boisterous. At the same time and much more important, it was made in a context of doctrinal and historical exposition, liturgical and social exhortation.

The statement does not speak to an opposite misunderstanding of the new rite: the failure of cantors or choir or even the presiding celebrant to wait a few moments until the assembly has completed the exchange of the sign of peace before beginning the Agnus Dei. The latter is, of course, the accompaniment to the breaking of the bread for communion, something ritually distinct from the sign of peace.

Another issue, however, is mentioned in the historical section of the statement. It is the placement of the sign of peace within the whole Order of Mass. For historical, structural, and doctrinal reasons, liturgical purists often urge the relocation of the rite of peace—at the beginning of the liturgy of the Eucharist, for example, in order to relate it to the admonition in Matthew about reconciliation before bringing one's gift to the altar; or even at the very beginning of Mass as a sign of reconciliation in place of the penitential rite.

Of course, there are reasons on both sides of the argument, and the tradition of the Roman liturgy—the sign of peace and unity just before sharing in the sacrament of ecclesiastical unity—has been retained thus far. Curiously, many who are uncomfortable with the sign of peace before communion suggest by their reasoning that this location is indeed most desirable: It is quite wrongly urged that the sign of peace is a disturbing interruption of a period that should be devoted to interior recollection and personal, even private piety—the direct opposite of the meaning of the communal banquet, sharing at the table of the Lord in anticipation of the messianic banquet. Thus, though there are sound reasons for preferring another placement of the rite, its location, as the statement suggests, does maintain the profound meaning of communion with one another and with God in the sharing of the body and blood of Jesus.

This point can be made equally of all external signs of communal participation during the entire communion rite and especially of the communion song. It had been stated strongly in the Roman instruction on eucharistic worship, *Eucharisticum mysterium* (May 25, 1967: DOL 179):

Hence the Mass, the Lord's Supper, is at once and inseparably:
　　—the sacrifice in which the sacrifice of the cross is perpetuated;
　　—the memorial of the death and resurrection of the Lord who said: "Do this in memory of me" (Lk 22:19);
　　—the sacred banquet in which, through the communion of the body and blood of the Lord, the people of God share the benefits of the paschal sacrifice, renew the New Covenant with us made once and for all by God in Christ's blood, and in faith and hope foreshadow

and anticipate the eschatological banquet in the Father's kingdom as they proclaim the death of the Lord "until he comes."

This understanding of the Eucharist as holy meal of God's people has often been lost, either in the stress on the sacrificial and memorial dimensions or in the misconception of the Eucharist as a simple gift to the individual and isolated believer rather than the sacrament of the Church's unity. Thus, every sign and gesture, every word and song, that can better manifest the communal dimension of the eucharistic banquet is important liturgically and spiritually. In the Eucharist, we are the "table companions of God," his people who gather in anticipation of the banquet of the kingdom. This dimension of the Eucharist is supported by the sign of peace, as the statement of November 1976 demonstrates.

Introduction

The sharing of the peace of the kingdom was the risen Lord's first gift to the apostolic Church after his resurrection. His greeting "Peace be with you" extended the conviction of the risen life; it was a life made whole by the loving care of the Father.

When the early Church gathered for liturgy, a desire for peace marked its deepest longings. It was the peace of the risen Christ. The early community of believers saw the peace of Christ come to their lives for the building up of a new world. That world signed by peace was the will of the Father.

The peace of Christ must also be present in our lives today; it must be found at the very heart of our prayer. Indeed, there are many times in the liturgy when we express this conviction. The Word of God calls us to peace. The Lord's Prayer petitions the coming of the kingdom. The deepest human longing for peace and God's reign is expressed in the eucharistic prayer: "In the midst of conflict and division, we know it is you who turn our minds to thoughts of peace" (Eucharistic Prayer for Masses of Reconciliation II). When we eat and drink the body and blood of the Lord, we further extend the unity of the kingdom and its promise of peace. Whereas there are other similar expressions of this hope, the sign of peace in the communion rite stands out as a prime example.

The purpose of this statement is to look at the history of the sign of peace and the various expressions and meanings it has had. It is further the intention of the statement to present a rationale for a ritual gesture which, rooted both in the human longing for peace and in the conviction that true peace comes from the Lord Jesus, is now an important part of the revised eucharistic liturgy of the Church.

Early Tradition

The practice of extending a kiss of peace as a sign of respect or friendship is found in the Old Testament and firmly rooted in Jewish tradition. This practice is witnessed to in early Christian ritual, a borrowing from Jewish custom. For example, in the New Testament the kiss was a courteous preliminary to any ceremonial gathering, especially a meal. To omit it could cause remark or concern as when Christ said: "You gave me no kiss, but she has not ceased kissing my feet since I entered" (Lk 7:45). In the writings of St. Paul, the kiss is recognized as a token of Christian communion (Rom 16:16; 1 Cor 16:20; 2 Cor 13:12). In 1 Peter 5:14, there is mention of an embrace: "Greet one another with the embrace of true love."

The practice of the kiss of peace in the liturgy is first mentioned at Rome by Justin Martyr (c. A.D. 150) and is found in the Syrian Apostolic Constitutions (around the end of the fourth century). It was used in various prayer services and in the eucharistic celebration.

In the early Roman liturgical tradition, the sign of peace, or the kiss of peace as it was called, followed the celebration of the liturgy of the Word. When the liturgy of the Word became permanently joined to the liturgy of the Eucharist, the general tendency was to associate the kiss of peace with the presentation of gifts. The admonition in Matthew about reconciling oneself with one's brother before bringing a gift to the altar encouraged this positioning of the kiss of peace in the Mass. At a later stage, however, the kiss of peace was shifted to the conclusion of the eucharistic prayer, and finally, especially after St. Gregory the Great, it became an appropriate extension of the Lord's Prayer in preparation for communion. It was felt that since communion establishes and deepens the fellowship of Christ's Body, the Church, this gesture of peace and unity should be exchanged by all present before the actual participation in the body and blood of Christ. The revised Order of Mass retained this place for the sign of peace in the eucharistic liturgy of the Roman rite.

The Gesture as a Sign in the Entire Assembly

Early liturgical documents of the Church indicate significant variations in the particular manner of extending the sign of peace. In the earliest sources (Ordines Romani), it appears that the pax did not originate with the celebrant and then proceed in an orderly manner to the rest of the assembly. Rather, each member of the clergy exchanged a sign of peace with his neighbor while the faithful extended it among themselves. One source expressly states that as soon as the priest has said Pax Domini and all have responded with Et cum spiritu tuo, "the clerics and people offer the sign of peace among themselves where they are standing" (Capitulare ecclesiastici ordinis, Andrieu III, 124). Little need was felt to move around; each offered the sign of peace to the persons nearby.

Whereas the earliest guidelines regarding this rite stated that at the given signal those in the nave of the church greeted each other with the kiss, later formulations of the instructions introduced an inconspicuous but important change (Mabillon, PL 78, 945B, and later MSS). The kiss of peace was made to proceed from the altar and, like a message or gift, handed on from the celebrant "to the others and to the people." With this in view, it was only logical that the kiss of peace should come from the celebrant via the deacon as if from Christ himself. The celebrant was first to kiss the altar, or according to other sources, the missal, crucifix, chalice or the consecrated gifts, before extending the sign of peace to the others.

This amended procedure aptly agreed with the mentality of the middle ages and its tendency to clericalize everything in the liturgy. The assembly of the faithful, kept as a clearly distinct and separate body, was to be content with watching, assisting, and receiving. Accordingly, the sign of peace was to be received from a cleric and, even when communicated among the laity by means of the pax-board (a small tablet made of wood, ivory, or metal with the figure of Christ, a saint, or symbolic figures engraved or painted on it), it was understood as coming ultimately from the celebrating priest.

The present rite calls for a general greeting of peace proclaimed by the priest after the prayer for peace and unity within the Church. This prayer can be regarded as a communal seal and pledge of fellowship since it appeals to Christ for the peace and unity of his kingdom. When the celebrant or deacon says, "Let us offer each other the sign of peace," each person is invited to exchange the sign of peace with others nearby. The challenge is to make the sign of peace both genuine and reverent. It is not a mere greeting. It is a form of worship and of prayer—a personal and sincere pledge and sign of reconciliation, unity, and peace. It is a manifestation of faith in the presence of Christ in one's neighbor and a prayer that God may bless him or her. It is the opportunity to see one another afresh in God and to be reconciled in the way that only liturgy affords.

Pastoral Suggestions

The manner in which the sign of peace is exchanged is to follow the local custom. As a deeply significant part of the communion rite, this sign should not be used in a casual or introductory way, but should be maintained as a true gesture of the mutual peace that comes from one's union with Christ. The sign of peace may vary according to the type of celebration. In celebrations with large congregations, the handshake is the most common. Experience has shown that the use of both hands in extending the greeting creates an expression of greater warmth and distinguishes this rite from the ordinary handclasp associated with a social greeting. In celebrations with smaller groups, a handclasp is often used as well as the embrace. Some priests still employ the traditional *pax* of the Roman Rite. Often, words accompany the action, such as "Peace be with you" or some similar greeting.

It is also clear that the sign of peace is to be exchanged with persons who are rather close by (GIRM 112). Neither the people nor the ministers need to exhaust the sign by attempting to give the greeting personally to everyone in the congregation or even to a great number of those present. The sign remains just that—a sign of the peace that should exist among all those who celebrate the sacrament of unity.

The celebrant of the Eucharist may offer the sign of peace to the deacon or minister, that is, to those near the altar. In accordance with the intent of the ritual, the priest need not move from the altar to offer the sign of peace to other members of the assembly. The reason for this "limited sharing" is that the priest has already prayed for peace among all present and has addressed them with his all-inclusive greeting: "The peace of the Lord be with you always."

Unless the sign of peace is clearly tailored to a specific occasion, such as a marriage, ordination, or some small intimate group, the more elaborate and individual exchange of peace by the celebrant has a tendency to appear clumsy. It can also accentuate too much the role of the celebrant or ministers, which runs counter to a true understanding of the presence of Christ in the entire assembly.

Although the priest's greeting, "The peace of the Lord be with you always," is always included in the communion rite, the *General Instruction of the Roman Missal* (no. 112) indicates that the sign of peace need not be exchanged at every eucharistic celebration. However, its inclusion should become the norm.

Consideration for the overall ritual flow and rhythm should be an additional important factor in the use of the sign of peace. The time used to exchange the sign should be in proper proportion to the other ritual elements of the communion rite and should not create an imbalance because of length, style, musical accompaniment, or other elements that may give exaggerated importance to it. The celebrant, as the one who presides, must weigh such factors as local standards for propriety, size of the church, number of participants, character and intimacy of the assembly, lest the rite become a mere formality or deteriorate into a frivolous display.

Conclusion

All who gather to celebrate the Eucharist are called upon to form the worshiping community of faith and manifest by word and gesture to one another and the world that the Church is indeed a community of reconciliation, unity, and peace. The *General Instruction of The Roman Missal* (no. 566) therefore states that "before they share in the same bread, the people express their love for one another and beg for peace and unity in the Church and with all mankind."

26

A Call to Prayer: The Liturgy of the Hours

Statement, Bishops' Committee on the Liturgy
November 1977

The reform of the Roman liturgy of the hours has a longer history than most other elements of the liturgical renewal. The official introduction of an English version of the *Liturgia horarum* in the United States took place on November 27, 1977. Beginning with the *Constitution on the Liturgy* of 1963, this development took fourteen years—and breviary revision had been a major concern of the Commission on Liturgical Restoration created by Pope Pius XII in 1948. That commission had undertaken a consultation of the Catholic episcopate long before the Second Vatican Council and even prepared some modest simplifications of the divine office just before Vatican II began.

The *Constitution on the Liturgy* enunciates a strong and sound doctrine of ecclesial prayer as the worship of the entire community of the Church, but it also has a mindset that would complicate the actual reform of texts, the pattern of the canonical hours, and the very style of celebration of the Church's prayer. The problem, resolved neither in the actual revision nor in its application in church practice today, is a dichotomy between the prayer as ecclesial, public, and communal and the prayer as individual, personal, and ostensibly private—namely, a prayer that is largely the concern of the ordained ministers of the Church and of members of religious institutes.

This issue was evident in the conciliar debate on the text of the constitution's Chapter IV, "Divine Office." Some bishops were preoccupied with the office as the personal responsibility of ordained ministers and religious; laudably enough, they sought to increase its spiritual value to the individual, while maintaining it as a canonical discipline. With clearer ecclesial, historical, and liturgical insights, other bishops recognized that—however often the office was celebrated by a solitary individual—its communal elements and public character as ecclesial prayer have priority. They should be as rigorously maintained as in any other rites and services of Christian liturgy.

This is not the place to recite the complex details of the Roman revision. Again, a dichotomy was present: whether to develop or recover an office of prayer primarily suited for celebration in parochial and other communities of Christian people (perhaps in terms of what has been called a "cathedral office") or simply to introduce major simplifications and improvements. According to the latter course, which was indeed followed, the office would still follow the pattern of daily prayer in religious institutes (the so-called monastic office) but would be equally appropriate for the diocesan clergy—who do not regularly live in community and would celebrate communal prayer only by way of exception. It was to meet this situation, for example, that the hour of prime was suppressed, along with two of the other three lesser canonical hours (SC 89d and 89e) and the psalter spread over a four-week period instead of the monastic usage of one week (SC 91).

Despite such problems and with some compromises, the work of revising the old *Breviarium Romanum* of 1568 was accomplished. The result was a vastly improved quality of texts of prayers, songs, and readings for the daily prayer of the Church. The new liturgy of the hours was announced in a major apostolic constitution of Pope Paul VI, *Laudis canticum* (November 1, 1970: DOL 424). In his valuable discursive and descriptive treatment of the reformed office of prayer, the pope reaffirmed the canonical discipline but added a principle applicable to all ecclesiastical laws: Those mandated by the Church "should not only be moved to celebrate the hours through obedience to law but should also feel themselves drawn to them because of the intrinsic excellence of the hours and their pastoral and ascetical value."

In the first of the four volumes of the new divine office, the doctrine of the papal constitution was complemented by a lengthy document, the *General Instruction of the Liturgy of the Hours* (February 2, 1971: DOL 426), comparable in many ways to the *General Instruction of the Roman Missal*. The value of its doctrinal presentation of the ecclesial prayer of Christians can hardly be exaggerated, whether in the broad strokes of its chapters on the importance of the total office and the individual hours by which each day is sanctified or in the detailed treatment of the different elements and details of the celebration. From an advance text provided by the Holy See, a translation of this Roman document was distributed widely in the United States by the secretariat of the Bishops' Committee on the Liturgy in 1971, in the hope of moving forward general appreciation of the revised office ahead of its complete publication either in Latin or in the vernaculars.

The Latin *Liturgia horarum,* subtitled "The Divine Office according to the Roman Rite," was actually published in time for the liturgical year 1971–1972. The English version prepared by ICEL was completed in 1974 and then approved by the American conference of bishops, with Roman confirmation on December 6, 1974. With the actual publication of its four volumes, the official effective date was set for November 27, 1977.

In the long period from the conciliar decree of 1963 to 1977, during the working out of revisions and then translations, some limited steps had been taken, and these should be recorded as background to the statement of the Bishops' Committee on the Liturgy that is printed here.

First was the decision, in April 1964, to approve two existing English versions of the old breviary as official—so that, in turn, those obliged to the celebration of the office might use the vernacular with the requisite permission (SC 101). In practice, this permission was either granted or rather quickly taken for granted—not only in the case of individuals and of communities of women religious and lay men religious, as Vatican II had anticipated, but also in religious institutes of ordained men, the so-called clerical institutes.

If anything, this rather broad concession of the vernacular revealed the weaknesses and the complexities of the unrevised office of prayer, and the late 1960s saw an increasing number of those canonically obliged to the office finding the English version almost as much "a grave obstacle to their praying the office properly" (SC 101) as the Latin had been. A temporary expedient was found in various substitutions for the official liturgical prayer, often through formal commutations made by individual bishops. One example was a common concession that scriptural and other readings might be chosen at will to replace the daily office. Desirable enough as spiritual reading, this substitution hardly constituted a rite of prayer. The most satisfactory substitute was in the form of interim breviaries prepared under nonofficial auspices but in full conformity with the principles of liturgical reform.

Two of these interim breviaries were available in the United States, but it was the volume commissioned by the Federation of Diocesan Liturgical Commissions, *The Prayer of Christians* (New York, 1971), that enjoyed greatest favor. It was a single-volume edition, employing the *New American Bible* for the psalms and for a limited selection of readings. The other was British in origin: *The Prayer of the Church* (London, 1970), using the Grail Psalter and giving a list of biblical readings. Both volumes benefited from advance information provided by the Roman Consilium of implementation, so that they represented a kind of abbreviated form of the new Roman office not yet completed.

The Bishops' Committee on the Liturgy, in its *Newsletter* of April-May 1971, explained that no interim breviary was official or approved for the United States but such texts might be "approved by individual bishops for their dioceses, specifically as substitutes for the present divine office, under the usual conditions." This position, a combination of desire for maintaining the tradition of ecclesial prayer, especially by priests and religious, and recognition that the completed text of the *Liturgy of the Hours* would not be ready for several years, was further elaborated in a brief statement agreed upon in 1970 but only published in the *Newsletter* of April 1973:

In 1970, the members of the Bishops' Committee on the Liturgy addressed themselves to the question of the *Liturgy of the Hours* or breviary.

The interim breviary [*The Prayer of the Church*] was considered, namely, whether it should be officially adopted as an optional alternative to the Roman breviary. The bishops' committee decided not to recommend this course of action for several reasons: (a) The official adoption of a particular interim breviary would appear to give an unfair advantage to a single publisher. [*The Prayer of Christians* had not appeared in 1970.] (b) It does not seem desirable for the NCCB to give official approbation to a version with several limitations: the uncertain period of time (until the publication of the [revised] Roman breviary), the cost, style of translations, etc.

On the other hand, the bishops' committee agreed that there is an immediate need to satisfy the desires of very many priests and religious. These find the Roman office unsatisfactory and sincerely seek a better form of daily prayer. The experience of those who have tried the interim breviary, with its redistribution of psalms and new prayers of petition (*preces*), has been uniformly favorable when compared with the present Roman office.

Some bishops have already commuted the Divine Office in various ways, for example, commuting it to periods of scriptural reading. The Committee decided to give positive recommendation to the interim breviary as one form of commutation by the individual Ordinary (see SC 97).

Even in these significant efforts to provide interim liturgical opportunities for church prayer, the mindset mentioned above is still apparent. It takes the form of a preoccupation with the daily office as primarily the task of those with a mandate to pray or, better, a mandate to lead in prayer. The inevitable defect is that the actual prayer life of the church community as a whole becomes a secondary concern. And, the same problem arose with the publication of the official *Liturgy of the Hours*.

When finally it was possible to approve and have published a definitive English edition of the *Liturgy of the Hours,* the committee issued its own introductory statement in order to "provide a broad context for the responsibility of the entire Church to pray the Office." It is a straightforward statement, seeking at once to support an acceptance of the new office after a period of partial solutions and interim measures and to call for a return to ecclesial prayer by those with the Church's mandate to pray.

The statement is conscious of its own limitations. Because of the need that was felt to speak of the canonical obligation of prayer—expressed in the ameliorated terms of the *General Instruction of the Liturgy of the Hours*—it could do little more than give a broader setting for this role of the ordained and of religious and speak of the hoped for celebration of the prayer by the Church itself. Thus, the statement is realistic. It does not pretend that the daily prayer will easily become the authentic "prayer of the Church" simply because clergy and religious take up their burden of prayer more widely and more conscientiously. It tries to put prayer by clergy and religious in a broader context: the primary concern, which has hardly been accepted by the Church in the United States as yet, is that the community should join in communal prayer.

These comments would be incomplete without mentioning the continuing obstacles to any popular acceptance of morning and evening prayer, the principal hours, or of the office of readings, the other major and distinctive element of daily prayer. One, paradoxically, is the preference for the eucharistic celebration even in circumstances—such as evening meetings or on the occasion of large public gatherings of the Church—when the liturgy of the hours would be most appropriate.

Another obstacle is the form of the revised office, with all the progress

169

made in the revision. It is still, in the eyes of most, a highly stylized and rather rigid form of prayer, especially in its unadapted form. Its substance is far superior to the popular devotions of the preconciliar period, quite apart from its official and public character. Nevertheless, it is perceived as lacking the flexibility of certain sound but unofficial styles of communal prayer, and the Bishops' Committee on the Liturgy was correct in 1977 in its estimate of the likely future.

Introduction

The Lord Jesus, by word and example, taught his disciples that prayer is normative for the Christian believer. His life was spent in prayer: reflection alone in the desert, morning and evening prayer in the synagogue, praying with his disciples. Jesus was a "man of prayer" in every sense of the word, for communication with his heavenly Father was indicative of his whole life's work and mission. Even now, the risen Lord forever lives to make intercession for us (see Heb 7:25). He is the supreme and eternal Priest and our prayer is meant to be a participation in his heavenly liturgy. Prayer is the language of the city of God. Our motivation in prayer is to be joined to the Lord, to make his prayer ours, in the hope that ours will be his.

Christian prayer, like the prayer of Jesus, is living in the presence of God in an intimate communion of praise and thanksgiving, of reflection and supplication. The mighty works of God in the history of his people and in the personal history of the believer are the ground of all prayer. It is the creative and loving kindness of God in our individual lives and in the Christian communities that enables us to sing out his praises and makes us confident enough to place before him our most pressing needs, our most urgent desires, and our most anxious pleas.

Thus, whether it is the meditative prayer of the Christian alone in a room or the surging hymns and petitions of the liturgical assembly, Christian prayer finds its center in the person of Jesus Christ because it is in the name of the Lord Jesus that we pray, and in his name that our assemblies are formed.

The "necessity of praying always and never losing heart" (Lk 18:1) is the basis of the Christian's obligation to pray. From the earliest times, the Church has interpreted Christ's norm in two directions: personal prayer and liturgical prayer. The Lord's Prayer provided the model for personal Christian prayer. It is praise and petition, confidence and thanksgiving all in one movement offered to the Father.

Liturgical prayer, when the ecclesial assembly gathers together, also models itself on the life and example of Jesus. Jesus was ever attentive to the festivals of Israel. Attendance at Temple and synagogue expressed his own piety. His very act of redemption is given to us to celebrate in the context of the most basic of Jewish liturgical rites: the home seder. In the same way, the liturgy of the hours or Divine Office from the days of the early Church to own own, is modeled on the hinges of synagogue sabbath worship, morning and evening prayer. The Office is an expression of "the necessity of praying always," day after day, hour by hour.

The Second Vatican Council decreed a thorough reform of the liturgy of the hours so that it would truly express the sanctification of time and the consecration of the Christian's life in a rhythm not unlike that of the life of the Lord himself. By its nature, the Office is a priestly work of the whole Christian people and mirrors the eternal praise offered by the heavenly court. It is the rich source of personal prayer also. For, the liturgy of the hours familiarizes us with the psalms and Scriptures. It teaches us confidently to offer our petitions to the Lord day after day. In morning and evening we pray the Lord's Prayer and the gospel canticles proclaiming God's marvelous deeds. The Office nourishes us through song and prayer for the Sunday eucharistic assembly. Indeed, it is the prolongation of the central eucharistic theme of praise and thanksgiving. Ultimately, through the celebration of the hours, we are placed in more intimate contact with the mystery of Christ made present in the liturgical year.

In many ways, then, the liturgy of the hours is a school of prayer for all Christians. There we learn to pray. Through the Office, the community, that is the Church, is manifested. Thus, the obligation to pray the hours is serious for the whole Church, particularly those in orders who lead the assembly to celebrate this liturgy daily, and who have, in a special way, given themselves to public ministry within the Church.

The Liturgy Revised

The work of revising the traditional Roman Office took several years. The basic Latin text, prepared by the Apostolic See at the mandate of the Second Vatican Council, was published in 1971 and 1972 under the title *Liturgia Horarum*. In turn, this text was faithfully rendered into contemporary English by the International Commission on English in the Liturgy, sponsored by some eleven bishops' conferences and serving the Church in their countries and many other countries of the world. This translation, which was published in 1974 and 1975, is the only version approved by the National Conference of Catholic Bishops for the Church in the United States. It appears in editions issued by several publishers.

The new *Liturgy of the Hours,* whether in its complete form or in volumes of excerpts (*Christian Prayer*), has a number of distinctive features that show the goals sought by the Second Vatican Council: a simplified and somewhat abbreviated structure; a vastly enlarged range of biblical and nonbiblical readings, the latter not only from the Fathers and traditional writers but also from modern sources; psalm prayers to give a Christian reflection upon the Old Testament songs of praise; canticles from Scripture not used in the previous Office; new intercessory prayers in litany form; wide flexibility and adaptability in the use of texts. Even apart from the official approbation of Church authority, the Roman *Liturgy of the Hours* is a vastly improved collection of prayer services for the hours of each day of the Christian year.

The Liturgy of the Hours is preceded, as was the restored Order of Mass in 1969, by an important *General Instruction*. This lengthy document goes far beyond the introductory material of the old *Breviarium Romanum*. It gives not only necessary directions but also a careful description of all the elements that make up the liturgy of the hours and, still more important, the basic rationale for common services of prayer in the Christian community. The riches of the liturgical Office, the relation and flexibility of the parts, and the like are all explained in the *General Instruction*.

The Prayer of the Church

Perhaps the most difficult and challenging task is to make the liturgy of the hours in fact and practice, as well as in theory and doctrine, the prayer of the entire Church. It is several decades since the celebration of Sunday Prayer or Vespers practically disappeared from parishes in this country. The best efforts of the liturgical movement in the 1940s and 1950s to restore Sunday Vespers or Compline to parish use had only minimal success. The singing of Sunday Vespers was largely limited to seminaries; the singing of anything like the whole Office was largely limited to religious communities.

To introduce, in 1977, the common celebration of even some part of the Church's liturgical prayer in parishes and similar communities and gatherings will require extraordinary efforts, which are beyond the immediate purpose or scope of this statement to suggest. Such a development will be aided considerably, however, by the providential growth of groups, houses, and associations for prayer; by the practice among priests and others of voluntarily gathering to pray some part of the liturgy of the hours; by making it part of the prayer of meetings of priests' senates, diocesan and parish councils and of the prayer life of seminaries, rectories, and religious communities; and by greater familiarity with styles of common prayer similar to the official liturgy. Above all, it will be helpful if those accustomed to pray the Office alone, especially priests and deacons, gather others from their parishes to join with them in common prayer.

The Responsibility to Pray

As we look forward to the popular celebration of some hours of the liturgical Office, there remains the special question of the responsibility of the Church's ordained ministers to pray the liturgy of the hours. In the past, the canons of church law have indeed placed first stress upon the responsibility of common and choral celebration, but they have been likewise explicit about the individual responsibility of pastors, of professed religious, and of the clergy in major orders. If anything, the responsibility of the ordained ministers of the Church, the clergy, has been made more emphatic in recent years by asking that, upon admission to the order of deacons, each minister publicly commit himself to pray the liturgy of the hours. The clergy and religious must also bear in mind that the laity, with great confidence in the fruitfulness of prayers offered by their bishops, priests, deacons, and religious, often request these prayers. Furthermore, we cannot forget that the faithful, sometimes at great personal sacrifice, support their clergy and religious so that they may have ample time to fulfill their ministry of prayer for the entire Church.

As is well known, in the period immediately prior to the Second Vatican Council, the sense of obligation to pray the Office was somewhat eroded. This came about partly because some, perhaps very many, felt that the burden of the Latin Office was not commensurate with the prayerful purpose of the Church. Even after many bishops, in virtue of the Council's decision in 1963, had permitted the use of the approved English breviaries, other difficulties (such as the complexity, formality, and even archaic nature of the unrevised Office) were still felt—again by some and perhaps by very many—to be so great as to excuse from the obligation.

Many efforts were made to resolve these difficulties during the period between the enactment of the *Constitution on the Liturgy* and the appearance of the revised *Liturgy of the Hours*. In virtue of the conciliar decree, many bishops (and other Ordinaries) granted generous dispensations from the obligation of the daily Office, either in whole or in part. Such dispensations were most suitable when pastoral responsibilities, for example, occupied much of the morning hours when priests would have properly prayed Matins and Lauds. Even more frequently, and with great concern for the underlying need for prayer by the Church's ministers, many bishops permitted the commutation of the hours of the Office again in whole or in part, with other kinds of prayer and religious reading. The latter were intended to be suitable substitutes or commutations: purely reflective or meditative prayer, although of the greatest importance, is not the same as the psalter or the formal prayers of petition and intercession. Again, while spiritual reading, whether of the Scriptures or of religious writings, is of the greatest value, it has a different character when done in the setting of the liturgical hours of readings, with the traditional psalms of praise, responsive prayer, etc.

A very appropriate substitution during this period was the interim breviary of 1971. Patterned closely on the forthcoming revision, *The Prayer of Christians* provided perhaps the best provisional solutions to the various difficulties that had been experienced. The Federation of Diocesan Liturgical Commissions, which prepared this volume, deserves universal gratitude for its contribution to the Church's prayer life from all who have used *The Prayer of Christians* in common or individually.

Finally, many otherwise bound to the liturgical hours of the Office, felt that there were serious reasons that by themselves excused them from the daily Office on occasion or even regularly. There is, of course, a danger of self-deception in this kind of decision, but there are certainly reasons or causes that, considered objectively, do excuse from the Office as from other precepts of church law.

Such possibilities—dispensations, commutations, excusing causes—still remain now that the completely revised *Liturgy of the Hours* is available to the Church in this country. The difficulties and problems, however, that were associated with the form, text, style, and length of the Office no longer exist, and the interim breviaries themselves have been replaced. In other words, although dispensation, commutation or substitution, and excusing causes may well be appropriate in a reduced number of cases, difficulties intrinsic to the official prayer itself are few indeed.

The *General Instruction*, which introduces *The Liturgy of the Hours*, makes the point that the Lord's injunction to pray is not mere legalism; it should not be seen as a purely legal regulation. The same is true of the mandate to celebrate the liturgy of the hours, a mandate that is accepted by the ordained ministers of the Church and others. Communities and individuals should not pray the hours merely, exclusively, or even principally because they are so bound by custom or precept. On the contrary, the very goodness of praying in, with, and for the Church—which, as the redeemed people of God prays in union with the Lord Jesus himself and with his Holy Spirit—should be enough reason to celebrate the liturgical Office.

The canons that were replaced in 1971 by the *General Instruction of the Liturgy of the Hours*, defined the obligation for the clergy in very simple terms without qualification, namely, as "the obligation of reciting the canonical hours in their entirety each day according to one's proper and approved liturgical books." The *Constitution on the Liturgy* explicitly reaffirmed this precept, while lessening the quantity of the Office—by suppressing the hour of Prime and permitting the omission of two of the three other lesser hours.

The *General Instruction*, speaking of the mandate that ordained ministers freely accept on the occasion of their admission to the order of deacons, uses similar language of bishops, priests, and deacons who are to pray "the full sequence of hours each day" and to do this while respecting as far as possible the relation of the several hours of prayer to the appropriate times of day.

A special provision is then made for the responsibility of permanent deacons to pray the liturgy of the hours, which has been left to the conference of bishops to determine. In the United States, the Bishops' Committee on the Permanent Diaconate has simply encouraged the deacons to pray morning prayer and evening prayer "as expressing the praise of God from the entire church community." In view of the particular style of life and circumstances of most permanent deacons, it is appropriate that this be done with their families.

The Importance of the Various Hours

The *General Instruction*, however, deliberately departs from the canons by expanding the statement quoted above (to pray "the full sequence of hours each day") and by introducing distinctions. These distinctions suggest the varying weight of the different liturgical hours and the priorities among them, which are to be judged reasonably and certainly without scruples.

In harmony with the Council's decision and the intrinsic nature of the hours as revised, the *General Instruction* speaks first of the principal hours, morning prayer and evening prayer. Bishops, priests, and deacons should be careful not to omit these hours "except for serious reasons." This clearly means that such an omission by those who have the mandate to celebrate the Office should be exceptional. The *General Instruction*, however, is careful not to go further. It thus leaves to the ordained ministers the discretion to judge the seriousness of the cause that may allow the omission of one or both of the chief parts of the daily liturgy of the hours.

A secondary place is given to the still very important hour or office of readings, formerly called Matins and now to be observed at any convenient time of the day. With regard to it, the *General Instruction* says that bishops, priests, and deacons "faithfully" carry out this hour, the more so because, even when prayed by an individual, it is a liturgical celebration of God's Word. To receive that Word into our lives makes us "more perfect disciples of the Lord." Thus, without minimizing in any way this part of the liturgy of the hours, one may say that a lesser reason excuses from its observance than the serious reason mentioned in the case of the two chief hours, morning prayer and evening prayer.

Finally, the *General Instruction* speaks of the lesser hours for those who have accepted the Church's mandate to celebrate the liturgical prayer. These are the daytime hour (in effect, one of the three liturgical hours formerly called Terce, Sext, and None) and night prayer or Compline. Bishops, priests, and deacons "will have also at heart the recitation" of these two hours.

Conclusion

To speak at length on the specific details of the mandate to pray the hours, for those who have this responsibility within the community of the Church, may seem to contradict the more basic statement that it is the prayer itself rather than an ecclesiastical precept that should motivate the ordained ministers of the Church. It may seem to be a return to a legalism that the official texts avoid. Yet, the responsibility is a genuine one that we must not sidestep, and it reflects the Church's expectation that its ministers will be leaders of prayer and praise within the Christian assembly. It is with this understanding that, keeping in mind the proportion and relationship of the several hours of the daily Office, Pope Paul VI, in 1970, explained: "Those who have received from the Church a mandate to celebrate the liturgy of the hours are to complete its entire course dutifully each day, keeping as far as possible to the appropriate time of the day; first and foremost, they are to give due importance to Morning and Evening Prayer." And, he adds immediately that those in holy orders (and, similarly, religious) "should not only be moved to celebrate the hours through obedience to law, but should also feel themselves drawn to them because of their intrinsic excellence and their pastoral and ascetical values. . . . The public prayer of the Church should be offered by all from hearts renewed, in acknowledgement of the intimate relationship within the whole body of the Church, which, like its Head, cannot be described except in terms of a Church that prays."

All who lawfully dispense from the responsibility of the liturgy of the hours or permit some appropriate substitution for parts of it should be deeply aware of the intrinsic goodness of the liturgical Office when they weigh the reasons for exceptions to the ordinary expectation of the Church. All the more, this should be the concern of anyone who has accepted the mandate in making the judgment whether on occasion he or she is excused from this responsibility.

Contemporary circumstances may have eroded the sense of prayer and of liturgical prayer. Still more serious, the Church's prayer had come to be thought of as an individual and private task, often considered a burden undertaken purely because of the customary precept. Now, the interim period

175

of waiting for a refined and richer Office is over. In virtue of authority given it by the National Conference of Catholic Bishops, the Bishops' Committee on the Liturgy, with the concurrence of the conference's president, has set November 27, 1977, as the official effective date for the use of *The Liturgy of the Hours* in the dioceses of the United States. *The Liturgy of the Hours* is thus the single official version in English approved by the conference of bishops and confirmed by the Apostolic See for this country. After this date, only *The Liturgy of the Hours,* as it appears in several authorized editions, or the *Liturgia Horarum* in Latin may be used for the liturgical observance, whether in common or by individuals, of the Church's Office of prayer according to the Roman rite.

In the interim period, many communities and individuals in the Church have faithfully observed the daily liturgy of the hours, with the adaptations and substitutions permitted and with the help of such texts as the interim breviaries. The purpose of this statement is to introduce *The Liturgy of the Hours,* as explained so well in the *General Instruction,* into general and exclusive use as the public, common prayer of the Church. No one underestimates the pastoral challenge of celebrating even some small part of the liturgical prayer in communities such as parishes that are unfamiliar with it. It is both the responsibility and opportunity for priests, who are the leaders of the Christian community, to assemble the praying people of God and join with them in the Church's prayer. But, the first and necessary step is that the ordained ministers of the Church and others who have the Church's mandate to pray the Office, both in common and individually, should employ it to the full.

27

Christian Commitment

Statement, Bishops' Committee on the Liturgy
April 1978

(See also nos. 9, 28, 33, 34)

The frequency of formal statements issued by the committee declined as other means were found to engage in liturgical catechesis, such as the publication of the *Study Text* series. Another reason for fewer statements was the stricter norms adopted by the National Conference of Catholic Bishops for the issuance of statements; standing committees of the NCCB such as the Bishops' Committee on the Liturgy require authorization from the conference's Administrative Committee. These matters are now regulated according to norms revised in 1981, covering everything from joint pastorals to staff statements.

Although the number of statements became smaller, the breadth and often the quality increased. *Christian Commitment,* issued with the approval of the NCCB Administrative Committee, is a good example of this progress.

The term "commitment" has a stronger ring to it, in the development of religious language, than dedication or consecration. It was aptly chosen for this 1978 statement to pull together the liturgical elements, in various rites and celebrations, by which initial acceptance of the Lord Jesus by the church community and by each of its members is maintained, deepened, and enlarged. And, although the primary audience (pastors, catechists, and persons responsible for the Christian community's liturgical life, particularly the members of diocesan and parish liturgy committees) was a special one, the exposition is applicable to all the members of the Church. In a sense, it is a kind of seminal document, which needs frequent reiteration. Most of it speaks, and speaks eloquently, for itself.

The initial liturgical dimension of commitment is the sacramental sign of Christian initiation, including all the rites and services leading to and surrounding the initiatory sacraments. The interrelatedness of baptism, confirmation, and the Eucharist is a constant theme of liturgical scholars, sacramental theologians, and ecclesiologists. The reform of the rites of baptism and confirmation and of the catechumenate of Christian formation restored by the Second Vatican Council (SC 64) has an inescapable premise. This premise is the unity and sequence of the three sacraments. Even as a matter of church discipline, this is found in the new *Code of Canon Law:* canon 842 §2 speaks of the necessary coalescence of the three sacraments for the complete or total initiation by which the commitment of the Christian people to the Lord is first fully manifested.

In the background of the statement's exposition of commitment at initiation is the reform of the rites by the Apostolic See, in accord with the conciliar mandate. This was accomplished as an integral whole in the *Rite of Christian Initiation of Adults* (1972, with a provisional English version approved for the United States in 1974). It had been preceded by the preparation of parts of the full initiatory liturgy: the *Rite of Baptism for Children* in 1969, with a definitive English version published in the same year; the *Rite of Confirmation* in 1971, provisional English version in that year, definitive version in 1973. Underway also, and in its way as important as ritual revision, was the catechumenal program that has come to be identified with the ritual as RCIA (for the Rite of Christian Initiation of Adults).

The statement integrates the doctrine of Christian commitment with sacramental initiation. It does not move into an area of considerable tension among some pastoral and catechetical specialists, on the one hand, and some other specialists in the same fields, joined by the liturgical specialists and theologians mentioned above. The tension arises from either more or less attention being paid to the liturgical and specifically sacramental dimensions of initiation and from what is seen to be the peril of purely intellectual, psychological, and social formation—or even a religious and spiritual formation—without solid conviction about the centrality and priority of the liturgical celebrations of initiation into the community of faith.

Even more concrete, another underlying tension arises from the current sequence of the initiatory sacraments in common practice (baptism, Eucharist, confirmation—a sequence that becomes still more complex when penance is interposed between baptism and Eucharist). While the pastoral and disciplinary reasons for this modern sequence are well understood, it does upset the tradition of the Church and is difficult to reconcile with a Christian sacramental anthropology—much less with contemporary liturgical and canonical reform. In any event, the statement accepts the realities of church practice, while avoiding any compromise of principle.

A few years later, with the appearance of a definitive translation of the liturgical texts and rites for adult initiation (1986) and widespread growth of catechumenal programs, the Bishops' Committee on the Liturgy addressed such questions again, not in a statement, but in statutes or guidelines for the catechumenate, a number of liturgical adaptations, and a planned program to spread an appreciation of Christian initiation—all proposed by the committee and approved by the conference of bishops in November 1986.

In the 1978 statement, the committee was directly concerned with initiation in terms of commitment and especially the continuing commitment of the initiated Christian people, whether baptized in infancy or later. Here, the emphasis on the Eucharist in the text is to be understood in several ways.

First, the Eucharist is indeed a sacrament of initiation, in fact the culminating sacrament of initiation, as it is the summit of the liturgical manifestation of the Church's life. But, it differs from the other sacraments of initiation in that it is celebrated by the members of Christ again and again. It is the sacrament of the recurring event of conversion and com-

178

mitment. Thus, in terms of the statement's formal concern, Christian commitment, the Eucharist and especially the Sunday Eucharist is *the* moment of recommitment, rededication, and reconsecration to the Lord.

Here again, there is an underlying question that is carefully and correctly not challenged. It is the concept of a Christian commitment delayed or at least only inchoate until young adulthood, one rationale for the postponement of confirmation beyond the age of discretion, the age that has been the tradition and the norm in the Western Church. Instead of meeting this question head on, the statement wisely diffuses the issue by demonstrating that there are very many occasions and many signs in the liturgy for renewal and recommitment. In a way, this is the major achievement of the statement, to see in every liturgical celebration and especially in the Eucharist a renewal of baptismal commitment, while cautioning against diluting the force of the special and explicit annual renewal of "baptismal promises" at the Easter Vigil or on the day of Easter.

One sign of commitment, related to baptism by the liturgical text and the symbol of water, is not mentioned, although it is incorporated in the reform of the *Roman Missal* and stressed in the English versions of the Roman sacramentary. This is the sprinkling of blessed water on the assembly at the Sunday Eucharist as an alternative to the penitential rite. In the reform, this practice was extended as an option to all Sunday Masses—it had previously been restricted to the principal Mass—with two purposes in mind: First, it does concentrate attention on the Sunday Eucharist, as mandated by Vatican II, and this in a way to express continuity with Christian initiation by a simple style of renewal of baptism and baptismal commitment. Second, it was designed to relieve somewhat the burden of the introductory penitential rite, which is expressed only in words, by means of the liturgical sign of water, equally expressive of conversion or reconversion of life.

Finally, the statement's importance should be seen as intregrating so many liturgical elements and dimensions, services and observances. It does meet the challenge of a sometimes complex liturgy by relating the parts and the occasions one to the other in a whole, a whole in which Christian adherence to Christ by faith is affirmed again and again by his people, from initiation to eucharistic viaticum.

God's Call through History

For the Christian, the past is more than the prologue of the present. It is what makes us who we are today, both as individuals and as the community of God's people. Our history is the history of God working among us. More than a record of humanity's search for meaning or for the Ultimate, our history is the lived experience of God seeking out and summoning his people. The call of Abraham and the patriarchs, the call of Moses and the prophets, the call that Jesus of Nazareth received from his Father, the call of Christians of every age, all have one factor in common: the utterance of God's Word. "In the beginning was the Word; the Word was in God's presence, and the Word was God" (Jn 1:1). This is the Word that has given direction and purpose to the cosmos and to us who inhabit the earth. It is through the Word that God creates (Gn 1); through the Word he destroys and recreates (Gn 6:7; 8:15–17); through the Word that he forms history and gives it meaning. Christ Jesus is the fulfillment of that Word, the one who completes all that the Old Testament said the Word will do. He is the full self-revelation of the Father. As the Divine Word, he calls us to experience him (1 Jn 1:1–3) and so enter into union with him and through him, with his Father.

For both the community and the individual, the experience of the divine call is situated in history, conditioned and colored by specific cultures and circumstances. It is unique in each instance, both by virtue of those who are called, themselves unique, and by virtue of the One who calls, whose love is infinite and who loves each in an individual and special way.

The committed Christian attentively heeds God's call and is thereby able to respond through personal union with Jesus Christ, who is both the Word by which God calls and the individual's word of response. This personal union with Jesus has its sacramental beginning in Christian initiation.

Christian Initiation

The entry of the Christian into the mystery of Christ and his Church is achieved through participation in the paschal mystery of the risen Lord, who commanded his disciples: "Go, make disciples of all nations; baptize them in the name of the Father and of the Son and of the Holy Spirit" (Mt 28:19). This initiation of the Christian is a sharing in the event of the Lord's death and resurrection, which happened once and for all, yet constitutes an ongoing process for the Christian who seeks to observe all Christ's commands (Mt 28:20).

Christian initiation as a ritual event includes the sacraments of baptism, confirmation, and Eucharist (RCIA, nos. 2, 27–36). Through the celebration of these sacraments, the initiated ritually participate in the whole process of salvation history. New Christians join the pilgrimage of the entire people of God making their way through history to the fulfillment promised by the Lord Jesus when he returns. As individuals, the new Christians respond to the action of the Holy Spirit in their own lives, pursuing the unique call to follow in the footsteps of the Lord. The new *Rite of Christian Initiation of Adults* clearly sees the actual reception of sacraments of initiation in this context of a continuous, step-by-step movement along the "path of faith and conversion" (RCIA, no. 1).

The primary model for Christian initiation is the initiation of adults. Adults are capable of a mature response to the action of grace: "They hear the preaching of the mystery of Christ, the Holy Spirit opens their hearts, and they freely and knowingly seek the living God" (ibid.). This model of a mature adult seeking to enter the Christian life also includes the steps of preparation known as the catechumenate, a lengthy period of spiritual growth designed to assist the candidate experiencing conversion and making a commitment to the Gospel and to the community life of the Church. The point is this: The response of the individual to God's call is a dynamic, ongoing process, well symbolized by the image of a journey or pilgrimage. There can be no stopping or turning back. Each step, whether in the life of the sincere inquirer, the catechumen, the newly baptized, or the seasoned member of the Church, requires a continuing *metanoia* or conversion. Christian life must be a continuing response to the divine initiative by which God seeks to unite himself with a person created in his own image and in doing so to restore the divine image partially defaced and obscured by the human race through sin.

The current practice of the Church encourages the baptism of infants and postpones the reception of the other sacraments of initiation to a later time. This demands that a great deal of attention be given to the ways in which Christians are to renew and, one might say, even fully experience their initial sacramental meeting with the Lord. Therefore, it is essential to underscore those means available to help young Christians grow in awareness of their baptismal gift and of their need to accept and live it in a personal, committed way. Parents, family members, godparents, sponsors of confirmation, and, indeed, the whole local community are critically important in this regard. In different ways, they are responsible for providing the necessary Christian environment and the example of their own fervent Christian witness and their participation in the practical life of the Christian community. The seed of faith must be nurtured and lovingly cared for if it is to reach maturity. In fact, when there is no possibility that a child will enjoy a Christian environment and example, and no reasonable hope that the faith to be shared with a child will survive, baptism should be delayed until such time as reasonable hope does exist, except in danger of death.

Christians ought not to treat the faith life imparted in the sacramental event of initiation in the manner of the unenterprising servant who buried the talent his master left with him. Faith should live and grow. Its model is the mustard seed, the leaven in the dough, the fruit-bearing vine. For, either it continually grows and is shared or it suffers extinction. The faith life of the Christian must include a constant response to God's act of faith in the one he calls. Christian initiation, while happening once and for all through the initial participation in the paschal mystery of Jesus, must also be a moment-to-moment process of saying "yes" to the Lord at each step in life's pilgrimage.

Ways of Renewal

Eucharist

The paschal mystery is the foundation of the Christian life of faith. The Christian community most fully celebrates the paschal mystery in the Eucharist. By the Lord's command to make memory of him, the Eucharist captures all that he has given in faith to his people; for the Eucharist is ultimately the Lord Jesus himself, the whole Body of Christ, Head and members, offered to the Father. Thus, by its very nature each celebration of the Eucharist demands a total self-giving on the part of those who worship; Eucharist is not only the sacrifice of Christ, but, by that very reality, the sacrifice of the Church made one with the Lord.

The regular celebration of the Eucharist with the local church is the principal way in which the Christian consistently renews commitment to the dead and risen Lord. The theme of Christian commitment recurs throughout the Order of the Mass. The penitential rite, the silent and sung responses to the proclamation of the Word, the profession of faith, and, most important, the offering and reception of the body and blood of Christ, all express the Christian's renewal of baptismal faith at each Eucharist.

In a special way, the *Amen* proclaimed by the faithful at the end of the eucharistic prayer gives voice to a renewed acceptance of the new covenant and is a public profession of submission to its bond of love. Augustine poetically homilizes on this *Amen* in his sermon against the Pelagians: "My brethren, your *Amen* is your signature, it is your consent, it is your commitment" (Migne, PL 39:172). The same can be said of the *Amen* at the reception of communion. At each celebration of the Eucharist, the Christian is challenged to renew his commitment to the Gospel of Jesus Christ, to membership in his Body, the Church, and to the living of the covenanted relationship with the Lord manifested by a life of service to others. As such, the Eucharist is the repeatable sacrament of initiation.

Sunday

Eucharist is the primary liturgical event for the renewal of faith because it makes present and celebrates the paschal mystery. Similarly, the Lord's Day, Sunday, is the primary liturgical moment for the celebration of the Eucharist. The Church, in the *Constitution on the Liturgy* (no. 106), sees every Sunday as "the original feast day" and "the foundation and kernel of the whole liturgical year" when the faithful are to call "to mind the passion, resurrection, and glory of the Lord Jesus" and give thanks to God who "has begotten them again, unto a living hope" (1 Pt 1:3). Thus, the Sunday celebration takes a special place in any renewal of Christian faith, for it occasions a reliving of the paschal mystery.

Liturgical Year

The renewal of faith that Christians make each time they celebrate the Eucharist takes on a regular, rhythmed character through weekly association with the Lord's Day; and this is further heightened by the celebration of the seasons and feasts of the liturgical year.

Advent-Christmas is the time of anticipation and hunger for the presence of the Lord in our lives. The Christian is called to prepare not only for the feast of the birth of Christ but more especially for meeting the Lord in the many ways in which he comes: in Word, in sacrament, in people who are called to be temples of his presence, and in the situations that arise in the world. This preparation for the Lord's coming must focus particularly on the meeting with him, which occurs in the final human act of death. Then, sealing with a final "yes" the life he or she has lived, the Christian makes the commitment to the Lord an eternal one. Advent, then, is truly a season of commitment.

The forty days of Lent are the time *par excellence* for the Christian to renew commitment to the life of faith received in baptism. The rites of preparation for the sacraments of initiation are to be celebrated at the appropriate times throughout Lent. The Easter Vigil itself is the ordinary time for the actual reception of the sacraments of initiation and for the renewal of baptismal faith (RCIA, nos. 50–57). High points in the catechumen's journey into the Church are to be anchored in the renewal of baptismal faith made by the rest of the Christian community. The community, in turn, is challenged in its own faith renewal by the budding faith of the catechumen. "The initiation of catechumens takes place step-by-step in the midst of the community of the faithful. Together with the catechumens, the faithful reflect upon the value of the paschal mystery, renew their own conversion, and by their example lead the catechumens to obey the Holy Spirit more generously" (RCIA, no. 4; see no. 7f).

As the season of *metanoia* and Christian renewal, Lent is the time when every member of the Church is called upon to turn once again to the font of living water and drink deeply of the Spirit of the Lord. This process of renewal is most effectively accomplished when the faithful visibly express their sharing of faith with the newly baptized by participating both in the Easter Vigil and in the ceremonies throughout Lent, which lead up to it. So that all the faithful may share as fully as possible in this life-giving act, the Church insists that the whole community renews the vows of baptism during the Masses celebrated on Easter Sunday.

This is more than a pious practice. It is meant to be the climax of the whole Lenten season. The acts of prayer, mortification, and charity that have marked the previous forty days are now to bear fruit in a solemn, public reaffirmation of Christian faith. Each year, the Christian is called once again to solemnize and give expression to the choice of the Lord as center and master of his or her life and in so doing to reawaken an awareness of the divine presence and of his or her commitment to live as God wills. The community continues to celebrate this awareness and commitment in the fifty days of the Easter Feast crowned by Pentecost.

Sacrament of Penance

It addition to the Eucharist and the celebration of the liturgical seasons, the sacrament of penance is an obvious moment for the revitalization of baptismal faith. Each time the Christian turns to the Lord and the Church for this spiritual healing, the strength of the initial moment of grace is renewed and deepened. The rites of reconciliation involve more than the erasing of sin; key moments in the living out of the Christian covenant, they heighten in the penitent that awareness born of the Spirit—to see ourselves as God does.

Moments of Personal Decision

Coupled with and mirroring the various apostolates and works of charity performed by the whole community and by each individual Christian, the liturgical life of the Church forms the main path and substance of the Christian's life. This is especially emphasized by the fathers of the Second Vatican Council, who teach that the liturgy, although it "does not exhaust the entire activity of the Church," is nevertheless "the summit toward which the activity of the Church is directed; at the same time, it is the fountain from which all its power flows" (SC 9–10). This normal process in the Church's life is further augmented by key events in the lives of Christians. Such events can be liturgical or private.

Certain radical changes or new orientations in an individual's life naturally find expression in corresponding liturgical moments. This is the case, for example, with the sacraments of orders and marriage, religious profession or public commitment to any vow, and installation or recognition in liturgical or other public ministries of the Church, such as reader, acolyte, cantor, catechist. As special ways of living out the baptismal life of faith, these demand a renewal of faith in view of the new charge given by the community to the individual. These moments of personal dedication demand reflection, prayer, and discernment so that the decisions to be made may be truly responsive to God's call.

The nonliturgical events in the lives of individual Christians that call forth a renewal of baptismal faith are many and varied: graduation from school; the beginning of a new job; a retreat or participation in any one of many renewal experiences (e.g., Search for Christian Maturity, Marriage Encounter, Cursillo, entrance into a Charismatic community); serious illness; the death of a loved one, especially a spouse; and the making of any important decision, but especially the choice of vocation or career. All these special moments along the path of life demand decisions rooted in a Christian life of committed faith.

In preparation for and sometimes in conjunction with these liturgical events, it is very appropriate to renew formally the promises of baptism, those promises that accompanied our initiation into the mystery of Christ when we first said "yes" to his call. This can be done during the eucharistic liturgy as on Easter Sunday or in a specially prepared service of the Word. It is important that the significance of the renewal of the promises be explained and that the entire assembly be asked to pray for those renewing their baptismal commitment.

Several approved liturgical texts are available for use in the renewal of Christian commitment. Whereas the Nicene Creed, common to the Sunday eucharistic liturgy, is the most frequently used, the renewal of baptismal promises included in the Easter Vigil celebration and the Apostles' Creed may also be considered appropriate for use on a particular occasion.

It is important, however, that this ritual renewal of baptismal promises not happen so frequently as to become routine or detract from the primacy of the Easter renewal undertaken by the whole Church. Also, persons who are to make this public profession of their faith should always prepare seriously for doing so. Special times of retreat or recollection can encourage this necessary preparation and can even appropriately be the specific context for the liturgical renewal of baptismal promises.

The sacramental celebration of Christian initiation or of any liturgical renewal of that initiation must always be "worship in spirit and truth" (Jn 4:22–24). Arising from interior lives rooted in the Spirit, who binds us together in the Body of Christ, such worship must also be truthfully reflected in exterior lives of love and service. The liturgical renewal of Christian commitment must therefore be founded on that living faith, which manifests itself in good works. This is to say that worship must authentically mirror and support those acts of charity and mission that identify a Christian. Practical, consistent living-out of the Christian life is the ultimate proof of any liturgical renewal of Christian commitment, the test the Lord himself uses: "I tell you solemnly, insofar as you did this to one of the least of these brothers of mine, you did it to me" (Mt 25:40).

28

Fifteenth Anniversary of the
Constitution on the Liturgy
A Commemorative Statement

Statement, Bishops' Committee on the Liturgy
November 1978

(See also nos. 9, 27, 33, 34)

As its title indicates, this statement celebrates the fifteenth anniversary of the conciliar constitution promulgated on December 4, 1963. As its text indicates, it was also intended to commemorate the liturgical achievements of Pope Paul VI, who died August 6, 1978.

The statement requires little commentary in itself. The balance and the concern for the disaffected (and for those injured by recriminations against liturgical renewal) are apparent. Just as strong is the plea for liturgical catechesis and improved style of celebration.

The brief tribute to Pope Paul VI that is included has its own significance: first, for his own extraordinary fidelity to the Second Vatican Council in the difficult task of liturgical reform; second, as a response to (unmentioned) bitter critics of his decisions—although, more often than not, the critics did not blame him but rather attacked those who guided the Roman revisions. Particular objects of recrimination were Cardinal Giacomo Lercaro of Bologna, who headed the Consilium of Implementation from 1964 to 1968, and, above all, Archbishop Annibale Bugnini, who served as secretary of the Consilium from 1964 and later of the new Congregation for Divine Worship from 1969 until 1975.

It is impossible to assess the intangible effects of the reform of the Roman liturgy carried out by authority of Pope Paul VI, but there are measures of his impact in documents and books. One is the vast quantity of official constitutions and letters, addresses and homilies, along with the curial instructions and other material he reviewed personally and approved—all collected in *Documents on the Liturgy,* which is the source of English translations of Roman documents quoted in the present collection.

Another measure is to enumerate the official liturgical books of the Roman rite prepared by mandate of the council but under his direction, and, again, personally reviewed and approved by him. By the time of his death, the missal and breviary of the sixteenth century had been entirely revised and enlarged with a wealth of liturgical texts; all the major sections of the *Roman Pontifical* (1596) and *Roman Ritual* (1614) had also been revised, and all this had been done with a degree of pastoral and scholarly expertise that was not even remotely possible in the post-Tridentine reform.

The fullest account of the reform is given in a substantial, fully documented volume by Archbishop Bugnini himself, which constitutes a kind of tribute to Pope Paul VI's fidelity to the conciliar spirit and law. Published posthumously—Bugnini died in 1982 as apostolic pro-nuncio to Iran—the book begins with an account of the liturgical commission of Pope Pius XII but is mostly concerned with the postconciliar period. Entitled *La riforma liturgica (1948–1975)* (Rome, 1983), an English translation is being prepared for publication in the United States.

The commemorative statement of the American episcopal committee is, of course, principally a tribute to the Second Vatican Council, but it is very pragmatic in using the anniversary as an exhortation to healing for disaffected persons; appreciation for the sacred; preparation of liturgical ministers; catechesis; and respect for the arts. It is worth noting that two of the liturgical books are singled out for their "great promise for the revitalization of our communities, provided that proper catechesis is an integral part of their implementation." These are the liturgy of the hours and Christian initiation.

Of these two, the second has of course demonstrated much greater progress in the intervening years, as mentioned in the commentary on the statement, *Christian Commitment.* The restoration of a catechumenate of formation and probation for non-Christians who seek to move from initial faith to sacramental initiation has begun, as the statement forecast, to revitalize many parishes and even dioceses of the United States—as a program and process for catechumens, but especially as a providential means to involve the broad Catholic community, renewing itself as it welcomes and forms new members of Christ. It has also been the occasion of a parallel effort, properly but not always clearly enough distinct, to prepare baptized Christians from other churches and ecclesial communities for their welcome into the Catholic eucharistic community, as they enter the full communion of the Catholic Church.

In the case of the liturgy of the hours, the observations in the commentary on the statement *A Call to Prayer,* remain valid. At least in its appointed and official form, the new liturgy of the hours has not become the genuine prayer of the Church in many places or communities. On the one hand, there are positive signs of stronger Christocentric prayer with biblical and liturgical models and sources, in which the reform of the canonical hours of prayer—along with the "bible services" of the 1950s and 1960s and other celebrations of the Word of God—cannot be denied an impact. On the other hand, the expectation of popular celebration of morning or evening prayer in parishes has hardly begun to be fulfilled. And, perhaps more seriously, there has been little movement—despite the *Constitution on the Liturgy* and now canon 839 §2—in the needed reorientation of popular devotions of piety. The mind of the Second Vatican Council was clear on this matter:

Popular devotions of the Christian people [*pia populi christiani exercitia*] are to be highly endorsed, provided they accord with the laws and norms of the Church, above all when they are ordered by the Apostolic See.

Devotions proper to particular churches [*sacra Ecclesiarum particularium exercitia*] also have a special dignity if they are undertaken by mandate of the bishops, according to customs or books lawfully approved.

But these devotions should be so fashioned that they harmonize with the liturgical seasons, accord with the sacred liturgy, are in some way derived from it, and lead the people to it, since, in fact, the liturgy by its very nature far surpasses any of them (SC 13).

A final note is that the Bishops' Committee on the Liturgy, in a reflective style, touched the heart of many concerns in speaking of the Sunday Eucharist in the context of integrating the liturgy "with total ecclesial life and mission." The statement stands as one of many instances in which the teaching of the committee was sound and reasonable, even moving and eloquent, but the impact depends on the hearers and readers.

On December 4, the Church will celebrate the fifteenth anniversary of the promulgation of the *Constitution on the Liturgy*, the historic first document of Vatican Council II. As members of the Bishops' Committee on the Liturgy, we take this occasion to reflect upon these years of liturgical renewal within the household of God.

With gratitude, we look back; with honesty, we assess the present; with hope, we turn toward the future.

It is not difficult to believe that the Spirit providentially prepared the Church for that moment of liturgical renewal envisioned by Pope John. Popes, scholars and specialized centers had begun to study the liturgy in the light of new theological developments, especially in dogma, Scripture, and ecclesiology. Despite the leadership of Pius X and Pius XII, however, a comprehensive and universal liturgical renewal required the impetus of an ecumenical council, open to new developments and willing to plan carefully and to propose an agenda for renewing the liturgical life and practice of the universal Church.

We applaud the conciliar initiative for the reform we have witnessed, a reform seriously supported by the Fathers of Vatican II and directed by the labors of Pope Paul VI, the Consilium, and the Congregation for Divine Worship. The thrust of the constitution and its implementation has been authentically pastoral: the renewal of the prayer life of the Church. It is clear that the fundamental suppositions of the constitution were valid. That the liturgy is the action of the entire assembly of the faithful is basic; all liturgy is communal by nature. That "both texts and rites should be drawn up so as to express more clearly the holy things they signify" can hardly be disputed in light of our experience with communities that celebrate fully and actively.

We are indebted to the vision and agenda with which the Council and its decree have challenged the Church.

Few names stand out with more brilliance in the history of living worship and liturgical reform than that of Paul VI. While many individuals have contributed to the worship life of Christians throughout the centuries by their painstaking efforts in developing texts and ritual actions, handing them down from generation to generation, no one, not even the greatest reformers of the past, Gregory the Great and Pius V, have done more to enable Catholics to pray as a Church than Paul VI. Indeed, his accomplishments as a renewer of liturgical practice extend beyond the limits of our own Roman rite. The liturgical books, reformed during his papacy and actively promulgated by him, have influenced and initiated renewal in other Churches—those in union with Rome and those far from the liturgical tradition of the ancient Church.

It is not our intent to review all the major elements and achievements of the reform begun in 1963. We cannot but note, however, the rediscovery in the eucharistic celebration of a fuller ecclesial dimension, with a clarity, simplicity, and beauty of its own. The Church has already profited from a richer celebration of the liturgy of the Word, especially by the revision of the eucharistic lectionary in a three-year cycle that mirrors the themes and rhythms of the Christian year. The revised lectionary has been adopted and enthusiastically used by those Churches which for centuries shared with the Roman Church the one-year cycle; the excellence of its inherent rationale has also caused it to be widely used in other Churches, unaccustomed to a fixed lectionary. Thus, this lectionary, supported by the serious, positive criticism of biblical scholars has been of inestimable value in the promotion of Christian faith and witness. The other revised rites now in use throughout our country speak eloquently to people of faith. We have in mind not only the rites of initiation, but also of reconciliation and the pastoral care of the sick and dying.

As we look back, the achievements of these past fifteen years appear almost overwhelming. Nevertheless, the road of *aggiornamento* was not always easy or straight. We recall the hesitancy, the fears, yes, even the hurts of these years of change. But considerations such as these should not be allowed to overshadow the significant results of the years of toil by persons of good faith, openness, and generosity. The renewal has already begun to bear fruit abundantly.

It is a duty and a privilege for us to acknowledge the outstanding contributions of those who have worked closely with our own Committee on the Liturgy, as well as international and diocesan liturgical commissions, liturgical centers, associations, and publishers.

It is easier to recall the past than to evaluate objectively the present. Yet, we must attempt to determine where we stand, if we are to move with confidence into the future.

Sociological evidence assures us that the majority of the people, clergy and laity, have accepted the reform and renewal of the liturgy. This is to their credit; we thank them for their openness and willingness to accept change. There is overwhelming acceptance of the use of the revised liturgical books in the vernacular. The involvement of others in liturgical ministries is welcomed. New signs and symbols (e.g., the sign of peace, communion in the hand) are being employed with reverence and devotion.

Considering the brief period of time, the amount of change, and the quality

189

of present implementation, we can be proud of what has been accomplished. Our assessment of liturgical practice in our country is, for the most part, positive.

This essentially affirmative evaluation, however, does not blind us to the legitimate questions and problems of the disaffected. It does not mean there remains no work for the future. Nor does it imply that the reform has been completed.

The Church must always be concerned about its prayer life, the quality of every liturgical celebration. Therefore, there is an obligation to use every means possible to provide the opportunity to pray together in the manner that is best and most fruitful for the Church's growth in holiness and for the everlasting glory of the Father.

Looking to the future, we recognize areas of true concern and accept them as the new challenge. We cite but a few major changes.

Now is the time for healing. We realize that in the renewal process some— clergy and laity alike—have been hurt. There are those who were hurt simply by the phenomenon of change, the removal of the familiar and the uncertainty of the untried and untested. Still others were hurt by poor instruction, left ill-prepared for what was introduced, or misguided by the conduct of enthusiasts. Moreover, we cannot forget those who were hurt in the very process of implementing the reform—greeted with ridicule, hostility, at times refusal.

Confident of the soundness of the renewal, as designed by the providentially inspired guidance of the Church, we all must strive to overcome any divisiveness or rancor. Let time, humility, and love work in the hearts of all to heal the wounds so that we may remain united in belief and practice (see 1 Cor 1:11).

The sacred and the mystery must be safeguarded. The liturgy, as the action of the entire Church—head and members—is sacred. Its sacred character, an expression of the mysterious presence and self-manifestation of God in word and sacrament, must not be distorted or dismissed. The human or "horizontal" dimension, integral to liturgical prayer, must stand in awe at the presence of the divine, operative in the celebrating community of faith. With Christ, the one and eternal priest, all stand in reverence before the throne of the Father, offering the unceasing hymn of praise and thanksgiving. (see Heb 7:3).

The proper preparation of leaders of prayer must be assured. It is with great pastoral concern that we emphasize the need for the proper preparation of leaders of prayer. The liturgical preparation and formation of seminarians and deacons should be given that priority assigned to them by the *Commission on the Liturgy.* Lay ministers must be prepared to serve in a manner that befits the dignity of their task. Deacons and priests are encouraged to continue their study of the liturgy, both for their own growth and the spiritual benefit of those whom they serve. In this regard, liturgical preaching remains an area in need of particular attention, lest the proclamation of the Word be hindered by the failings of the homilist. Bishops, as "high priests of the flock," must see to it that the cathedral liturgy is always a model for the diocese and a source of edification for all.

Major catechetical efforts must be continued. All of the revised rites provide ample material for ongoing study and prayerful reflection. We have revised books, but we do not always witness a full understanding of their content. In a sense, the books must be "unpacked." More specifically, the Liturgy of the Hours and the Rite of Christian Initiation of Adults hold out great promise for the revitalization of our communities, provided that proper catechesis is an integral part of their implementation. These two revised rites of the universal Church offer considerable challenge for years to come.

The integrity of the Sunday celebration remains a major concern. In a sense, the Christian community gathered together on the Day of the Lord will always stand as a counter-culture sign. Yet, this is not to say that the liturgical life of the community can be bracketed out, consigned to a particular time or place. By its very nature, it seeks to give visible testimony to the relevance of Christ's saving power to all dimensions of life. We must, therefore, continue to integrate the liturgy with total ecclesial life and mission. Only when liturgical interiorization has occurred can the Church contribute significantly to the building up of the human community and the transformation of social structures.

The arts cannot be divorced from authentic liturgical action. The revised liturgical structures demand art forms proper to the culture and faith expression of our worshiping communities. The Church must continue to encourage the training of professional musicians and artists and support them in their pursuit of the beautiful in worship. In this regard, *Environment and Art in Catholic Worship* and *Music in Catholic Worship* remain guiding documents. It cannot be stressed enough that both sensitivity to the arts and willingness to budget resources to them are conditions of progress in the quality and appropriateness of liturgical prayer.

The challenge of the document *Sacrosanctum Concilium* will always remain clear: Make liturgy the true prayer of the entire Church. This task continues to engage all members of the Church; it is both a responsibility and a privilege. The aim of the Bishops' Committee on the Liturgy has been to assist in this undertaking; it remains the goal toward whose realization the committee will continue to contribute as best it can.

True, there are other matters that could have been raised in this commemorative statement to you, our brothers and sisters. We could, for example, have cited the pressing issue of ongoing liturgical evolution and adaptation; the responsibility to meet the needs of particular groups; the need to cooperate with other churches, etc.

As members of the Bishops' Committee on the Liturgy, we feel privileged to have served in this important area of the Church's life. We ask you, as we celebrate the anniversary of Vatican II's first document, to reaffirm your commitment to the renewal of the liturgy and to join us in a prayer of thanksgiving to God the source of all good.

191

29

Communion under Both Kinds

Proposal, Bishops' Committee on the Liturgy
November 1978

(See also nos. 8, 37)

There is no need to repeat the commentary on the 1966 statement under the same title, *Communion under Both Kinds*. In that commentary, the development of this liturgical reform was brought up to the present—and specifically up to 1984, when the Apostolic See confirmed the 1978 decree of the National Conference of Catholic Bishops on the subject. It was upon the confirmation of that American decision that the "norms and directives" in the publication *This Holy and Living Sacrifice: Directory for the Celebration and Reception of Communion under Both Kinds* (Washington D.C.: USCC Office of Publishing and Promotion Services, 1984) were issued by the Bishops' Committee on the Liturgy.

The text reprinted here is not in the form of a public statement. Rather, it is a proposal to the conference of bishops, with accompanying rationale. Although somewhat longer than most such texts, it is similar to the documentation that is regularly submitted to the NCCB by the episcopal committee with each proposal for action in liturgical matters. It has the special characteristic that it had to explain a second attempt by the committee—the first had been in 1970—to have communion under both kinds extended to any Sunday Eucharist and not merely to those Sunday celebrations that fell under one or other of the more specific concessions of the practice. This is the reason that the rationale includes both the doctrinal and liturgical exposition and also pastoral notes, the latter in the form of responses to difficulties.

There was a sharp contrast between the earlier decision (1970), extensive enough in itself, which was not challenged by the Roman Congregation for Divine Worship, and the 1978 NCCB decree enacted in the light of this proposal. Although the new decision was supported by some eight years of successful experience with communion under both kinds, the review by the Apostolic See, which was expected to be nominal, postponed the actual acceptance of the practice at Sunday Masses in many areas of the Church in the United States. In other dioceses, the 1978 decree was simply put into effect, with the expectation that it too would go unchallenged—and, indeed, that the formality of Roman review or confirmation would not be any obstacle.

The doubts and hesitations about communion under both kinds are hard to explain. It was understandable during the debate on the subject at Vatican II that there would be opposition arising from long memories of doctrinal errors and from fears of abuses in a practice that was then unknown in the Latin or Western Catholic Church. But the succeeding years rapidly overcame such hesitations, and the Apostolic See prompted the spread of this more authentic sign of eucharistic communion.

During this period, the anticipated abuses—of irreverence or worse—had not materialized. If they had occurred in some places, either they were undocumented or of such extraordinary rarity as not to justify limiting the Church in its liturgical life. As in other areas of church life and doctrine, however, extreme groups, often with substantial resources, have mounted campaigns out of disaffection with the letter and spirit of the conciliar *Constitution on the Liturgy* and the postconciliar liturgical discipline. That discipline developed under the guidance of Pope Paul VI and, for the national groupings of particular churches, by decision of the conferences of bishops as the council had desired (SC 22 §2).

The delay in reaching agreement with the Roman See over communion under both kinds on Sundays illustrates another change, having to do with the canonical status and operations of the conferences of bishops, with ramifications beyond liturgical norms and regulations. Most decisions of the conferences may be taken by simple majority vote—like the decrees of local or particular councils, the more formal and traditional style of such common episcopal action, which date back to the second century and long antedate the ecumenical councils of the Church. When Vatican II canonized the modern (nineteenth century) form of such common action, however, it placed some restrictions: decrees that would have the binding force of canon law were to require a two-thirds vote of all the members, were limited to specified areas of the conferences' competence, and required the review or confirmation of the Apostolic See. All this was determined in the decree on the pastoral office of bishops in the Church (known as *Christus Dominus*), no. 38; it was later repeated in the revised *Code of Canon Law*, c. 455.

From the close of the council, until his death in 1978, Pope Paul VI issued a long series of documents of implementation arising out of conciliar decrees. In most of these, he indicated, in full accord with the intent of the council, fresh areas of competence for the national and other conferences of bishops. These references to the conferences were very common in liturgical matters (especially in the introductions or *praenotanda* of the Latin liturgical books), but they covered all aspects of church discipline, from catechisms to distribution of clergy. In some instances, Pope Paul VI formally decided to forgo the right of Roman review, requiring only that the conferences of bishops send information about their decrees. Examples are particular legislation on penitential days and on the mitigated discipline affecting mixed marriages. In other cases, such as the minor liturgical adaptations permitted to conferences by the new *Roman Missal,* no formality of Roman review or confirmation was insisted upon beyond the routine transmittal of the minutes of the meetings of conferences or the general review and confirmation of the conference's approval of vernacular liturgical books.

When the proposal of communion under both kinds on Sundays, as described in the document reprinted here, was adopted by the American conference in November 1978—by 187 votes to 82—it was treated differently by the Apostolic See, which first insisted upon review and then was unwilling to confirm the decree until 1984. In a somewhat related matter, the question of communion in the hand, the conference of bishops had a much more satisfactory experience and indeed received ready Roman agreement with its decision.

The introduction of communion in the hand in 1977 was not the subject of a formal statement by the Bishops' Committee on the Liturgy, but it deserves recounting here because of its own importance and because it also illustrates a contrast with the later process initiated by the accompanying proposal on communion under both kinds.

The ancient and more traditional practice of communion in the hand had already been revived in many places when the Congregation for Divine Worship issued an instruction on the matter, *Memoriale Domini* (May 29, 1969: DOL 260), along with a form letter sent to conferences of bishops that sought an indult authorizing the official introduction of the practice (DOL 261). The instruction did not encourage the restoration. On the contrary, it recorded a consultation with the bishops of the Latin Church undertaken by Pope Paul VI; the response was negative from almost 60 percent of the bishops who responded. The papal decision was to retain the discipline of the past several centuries but, in view of the large minority of bishops open to the restoration, to leave the matter to decision by individual conferences, with the two-thirds majority required, as already described.

In view of pastoral practice—and, indeed, the positive reasons favoring communion in the hand—the Bishops' Committee on the Liturgy proposed the matter to the conference of bishops. After repeated failures to obtain the necessary two-thirds majority, the affirmative votes of the bishops present at the May 1977 meeting were supplemented by mail ballots submitted by the second week of June of that year. The Congregation for the Sacraments and Divine Worship (which had been established to succeed the two separate congregations in 1975) promptly sent the necessary confirmation, dated June 17. For its part, the committee initiated the necessary catechesis in time for a recommended effective date of November 20: a booklet, *The Body of Christ,* was published to assist priests, catechists, and teachers, together with an even more widely distributed leaflet of explanation.

In the August 1977 *Newsletter* of the committee, some practical considerations were offered. They are quoted to illustrate how, as with communion under both kinds in 1966 and 1970 and, finally, in 1984, every effort was made to precede such renewal with catechesis:

1. The decision to implement the optional practice of communion in the hand is left to the local Ordinary. Consultation with the diocesan liturgical commission and other informed representative diocesan bodies would be expected in the process.

2. Proper catechesis must be provided to assure the proper and reverent reception of communion without any suggestion of wavering on the part of the Church in its faith in the eucharistic presence.

3. The practice, once introduced, must remain the *option* of the

communicant. The priest or minister of communion does not make the decision as to the manner of reception of communion. It is the communicant's personal choice.

4. When communion is distributed under both kinds by intinction, the host is not placed in the hands of the communicant, nor may the communicant receive the host and then dip it into the chalice. Intinction should not be introduced as a means of circumventing the practice of communion in the hand.

5. Children have the option to receive communion in the hand or on the tongue. No limitations because of age have been established. As in the past, careful preparation for first communion will provide the necessary instruction.

Communion in the hand, besides being a more active, committed, and mature sign of sharing in the Lord's body, has proved to be a more reverent mode of communicating. In the event, the preservation of the freedom of the individual communicant and the ease of indicating one's preference to the minister overcame the hesitations that had been very strong. Together with the introduction of the response Amen made by each communicant (a practice decreed by Pope Paul VI, following the tradition of the Ambrosian rite) and the usual style of ritual procession to the minister of communion (rather than the minister moving along a line of kneeling communicants), it has improved the communion rite and largely eliminated the hurried routine of past practice.

All this suggests the contrast between the ease with which communion in the hand was introduced into church practice and the difficulties over the vastly more important practice of communion under both kinds in the Sunday eucharistic celebration. With regard to the latter, the allegations of abuses, real or potential, have proved false. Even in large congregations, careful preparation and the addition of enough eucharistic ministers have made communion under both kinds possible. Its spread remains dependent upon such efforts, but, just as with communion in the hand, the freedom of choice by individual communicants has removed any legitimate hesitations.

Introduction

In 1963, the Second Vatican Council restored the practice of Holy Communion under both kinds to the Roman liturgy. It left to the Apostolic See the determination of the instances or occasions for the practice; it left the actual introduction of the practice to the individual bishop (SC 55).

The development began with a listing of appropriate occasions for communion under both kinds (March 7, 1965), a listing that was gradually enlarged in 1967, 1969, and 1970. The present enumeration is that which appears in the *General Instruction of the Roman Missal* (no. 242). In addition, since it had become evident that the first stages of the restoration were successful, the Apostolic See left the determination of other cases or occasions to the conferences of bishops (June 29, 1970).

The National Conference of Catholic Bishops, which had earlier proposed that no restrictions of cases be placed upon the practice of communion under both kinds, took up the matter formally at its November 1970 meeting. It was agreed that, in view of the instruction issued that year by the Congregation for Divine Worship, further concessions would be made, always at the discretion of the Ordinary. These concessions, under four headings, are enumerated in the Appendix to the *General Instruction* in American editions of *The Sacramentary*, no. 240.

Communion under Both Kinds on Sundays

Holy Communion may be given under both kinds during Sunday Masses in any instance that falls within one of the categories already authorized. One of the concessions approved by the NCCB in 1970 was also stated very broadly to apply to "other members of the faithful present on the special occasions enumerated in no. 242 of the *General Instruction*."

Nevertheless, the NCCB voted in 1970 not to list the Sunday Mass as a reason *in itself* for the giving of communion under both kinds. At the time, it appeared that the large numbers of communicants at some Sunday Masses might create problems of order or be a source of inconvenience, a possibility to which the Roman instruction had averted. (In conceding communion under both kinds for Holy Thursday and the Easter Vigil, occasions when very large numbers might be present, the NCCB had insisted that the norms of the instruction concerning reverence and good order be observed.)

After the experience of more than eight years with the present enumeration of cases and the experience of more than fourteen years with the practice itself, it seems desirable to reappraise the question and remove even the appearance of a restriction upon communion under both kinds on Sundays.

Resolution and Explanation

On May 31, 1978, the Bishops' Committee on the Liturgy formally voted on introducing the practice of communion under both kinds on Sundays. The vote of both the advisors and the members was unanimously in favor of extending the practice as proposed. The proposed resolution read: "In addition to the instances already conceded by the Apostolic See and by the National Conference of Catholic Bishops, Holy Communion may be given under both kinds to the faithful at Masses on Sundays and holy days of obligation if, in the judgment of the Ordinary, communion may be given in an orderly and reverent manner (see instruction of the Congregation for Divine Worship, June 29, 1970)."

The effect of the above decision, which falls within the competence of the conference of bishops (in accord with the instruction cited), will be that the local Ordinary (or, for religious houses, the religious Ordinary) will be free to exercise the appropriate discretion in this matter for the future, not only for weekdays and special occasions, but also for Sundays.

1. The rationale for the conciliar decision to restore communion under both kinds is best expressed in the *General Instruction of the Roman Missal:* "The Sign of communion is more complete when given under both kinds, since in that form the sign of the eucharistic meal appears more clearly. The intention of Christ that the new and eternal covenant be ratified in his blood is better expressed, as is the relation of the eucharistic banquet to the heavenly banquet" (no. 240). (See Mt 26:27–29.)

2. Apart from the single problem of large numbers and possible inconvenience on that account, it should be at the eucharistic celebration on Sunday, the Day of the Lord, that the faithful should share most completely in the sacred banquet. The purpose of the Second Vatican Council in decreeing the reform of the Order of Mass was directed principally to the Eucharist on Sunday (SC 49), which it called the original or primordial feast day for the celebration of the paschal mystery (no. 106).

3. The possible inconvenience, because of the longer time needed for communion under both kinds, does not exist in smaller Sunday congregations. It can be avoided in moderately large or even quite large congregations if there are enough well prepared special ministers of the Eucharist. Any possibility of lack of order, which was the proper concern of the 1970 Roman instruction on the subject, can best be judged and then eliminated locally, under the immediate supervision of the bishop and his diocesan liturgical commission.

4. In many parishes and communities, communion under both kinds has become the usual practice on weekdays, and it may be said that the decision of the Council has been eminently successful. To avoid the anomaly of not encouraging communion under both kinds at the Church's principal eucharistic celebration each week, any apparent limitations should now be removed. Thus, more and more of the faithful, according to the judgment of bishops and pastors, will come to appreciate Holy Communion as the sacrificial banquet at which the Lord's gift of his body and blood is clearly signified.

5. It is impossible to measure the spiritual benefits of communion under both kinds, in devotion to the Eucharist, in devotion to the Precious Blood of Jesus, in the sense of the community gathered as "table companions of God." Nevertheless, the opportunity to increase these intangible results should be grasped.

Pastoral Notes

Why communion under both kinds? "The sign of communion is more complete when given under both kinds, since in that form the sign of the eucharistic meal appears more clearly. The intention of Christ that the new and eternal covenant be ratified in his blood is better expressed, as is the relation of the eucharistic banquet to the heavenly banquet." (GIRM 240).

How may communion under the form of wine be administered? The signs of sharing in the eucharistic sacrifice are those of the bread, broken and eaten, and the cup of wine from which we drink. Drinking from the cup is a clearer sign and response to Christ's words: "Take this, all of you, and drink from it." It is another means of fostering full and active participation of all present at Mass.

In addition to drinking directly from the cup, communion under both kinds may be given by intinction, from a tube or from a spoon (see GIRM 246–251). The last two options, however, have not been introduced in the dioceses of the United States.

Why extend this practice to Sundays now? Since 1970, when the NCCB extended the occasions when communion might be given under both kinds, the BCL has received requests that the practice be extended to include Sundays also. As the nature of Sunday as the principal celebration of the Resurrection of the Lord becomes more widely appreciated, the question is asked: Why not receive Holy Communion in the most complete manner?

Is the number of communicants too great on Sundays? Yes, in many places— especially the large urban/suburban communities—the number of communicants is significantly great. On the other hand, there are numerous parishes in the United States where the size of the community simply presents no problem for distributing communion under both kinds. Yet, unlike the situation in 1970, special ministers of communion may now be commissioned to assist the ordinary ministers when the number of communicants so requires.

Another change? Something else new? No, this is not really a change. At the present time, communion from the cup has become a widespread practice. Most Catholics are familiar with it and have experienced it either on weekdays or special Masses (e.g., weddings, funerals, etc.). Rather than a change in a practice, it is an extension of an already familiar practice, and a permission already granted for many occasions.

Is it new? No, even now communion may be distributed on Sundays under both kinds, as for example, when there is a baptism at the Mass, a concelebrated Mass, a retreat, conventual Mass of a religious community, etc. (see GIRM 240–42; American Appendix).

An option? Yes. First, the local bishop must decide whether the extended permission approved by the NCCB will be permitted in his diocese. Then, as at the present time, a pastoral judgment must be made by the celebrant as to the advisability of offering communion under both kinds. Finally, each communicant has the freedom either to receive from the cup or not when it is offered at Mass.

More catechesis? While all are concerned that the reception of communion be done with proper dignity, this will *not* be a time for extensive catechesis. Since many places have become familiar with receiving communion under both kinds, it is not totally new.

Is the practice hygienic? The American Medical Association, through its Department of Medicine and Religion has stated that: "It is the position of the AMA that, as far as we know, there have been no cases of transmission of germs to communicants using a common cup. The alcoholic content of the wine, plus the hygienic practice of wiping the cup and turning it to a new position for each communicant seems to remove any danger." It must always be remembered that the practice remains an option so that no one is under any obligation to receive from the cup.

What about intinction? Intinction is an approved form for receiving communion under both kinds. But, when it is used, it is not possible for the faithful to receive communion in the hand, nor is intinction as clear a sign of drinking as is the action of drinking itself. On some occasions, intinction may be preferred because of special circumstances, but on all other occasions, it would be preferable to receive from the cup.

30

General Intercessions

Statement, Bishops' Committee on the Liturgy
October 1979

(See also no. 20)

This 1979 statement is another instance of a more expansive treatment of an important liturgical element issued by the Bishops' Committee on the Liturgy after a period of years. There is no need to repeat the commentary on the guidelines on the general intercessions (1969), which are, as often as not, called the prayer of the faithful or, somewhat better, universal prayer. Only the first paragraphs of the earlier document are included in this collection—in favor of the later text reprinted here. Once again, in the background is the valuable booklet issued by the Roman Consilium of Implementation in 1965, *The Universal Prayer or Prayer of the Faithful* (DOL 239).

For the most part, the doctrinal and theoretical sections of the 1979 statement follow what has been said often about the intercessions or universal prayer. It is positive and encouraging, situating the rite as completing the liturgy of the Word, in accord with the revised Order of Mass, and insisting upon it as the petition of a priestly people, that is, the Church assembled for the Eucharist.

Some very positive elements are affirmed or reaffirmed, perhaps, above all, the importance of keeping the general intercessions a flexible element of the celebration. There is a clear concern for the sometimes stilted texts of intercessions given in books and leaflets—sometimes with an artificial or inappropriate response (such as "We thank you, Lord," or "Come, Holy Spirit"). Even in some of the cautionary notes of the statement, a positive recommendation is made, for example, the singing of the intentions or petitions by a cantor, or the possibility of spontaneous petitions in smaller communities—provided, it might be added, that these intercessions too are prepared in form, invite response, and can be heard by the entire assembly.

At the same time, it is evident that pastoral and liturgical practice needed—and still needs—some correction. The most important area is in the content of the petitions, especially that they should not be too particular to the neglect of the universal. Nor should they be didactic, partisan, or tendentious—all common enough weaknesses. The statement says firmly that the genre should always be respected: intercessions should not be composed "in a style that reflects other prayer forms, that is, prayers of thanksgiving, adoration, praise, or penitence."

Equally strong are some of the concerns for the structure of the intercessory prayer: the priest's introduction addressed to the gathered community and "never a prayer to God"; respect for the different roles (with preference for the deacon or cantor announcing the intercessions rather than one who has exercised the ministry of reading or the presiding celebrant himself); avoidance of wearying excess or disproportion in the number of petitions; style of intentions to invite a known response by the congregation (rather than an interruption to say, "please respond"); and, finally, the character of the concluding prayer of petition, in collect-style, by the presiding priest.

A further note can be added concerning the presidential prayer at the end of the intercessions. In the new Order of Mass, this prayer functions structurally to complete a major part of the rite, in this case, the petitions and the whole liturgy of the Word. Thus, it has a certain comparability to the opening prayer, which completes the introductory rite or rites; to the prayer over the gifts at the end of the preparatory part of the liturgy of the Eucharist; and to the prayer after communion, which concludes the communion rite. This structural function gives the prayer a weight and, perhaps, a solemnity that may seem at odds with its relative flexibility of composition: there is no strictly appointed text.

The consequence is that the presiding celebrant has to take great care that his prayer will be of sufficient breadth to encompass what has preceded, that it retains a petitionary character, that it truly sums up the general intercessions in some fashion. It may, of course, be topical, not unlike the opening prayer when it has reference to season or feast or even special ritual occasion such as a wedding or funeral; it may be desirable also that it echo some phrase or theme of the biblical readings. But, the concluding prayer should not be a mere repetition of the opening prayer, a point made in the statement. Above all, it should not be so particularized as to belie the name of the rite, "general intercessions," and its last words should naturally invite the Amen of the assembly in response and agreement. The general intercessions are the prayer of God's people, a people that shares in the priesthood of the Lord Jesus.

At every opportunity pray in the Spirit, using prayers and petitions of every sort. Pray constantly and attentively for all in the holy company.
Ephesians 6:18

The restoration of the general intercessions to the Roman liturgy of the Eucharist, to the liturgy of the hours, and to the other sacramental and liturgical rites was one of the principal elements of the liturgical reform of the Second Vatican Council (SC 53). God's priestly people gathered for praise and thanksgiving make intercession not only for the needs of the Church, but also for the world, for the oppressed, for peace, for the hungry, for justice, for the sick and the dying. The assembled community prays perseveringly, attentively, and "in a spirit of thanksgiving," (Col 4:2) ever obedient to the injunction of the Lord, who taught his disciples "the necessity of praying always and not losing heart" (Lk 18:1).

201

The purpose of this statement is to foster and encourage a proper and fuller use of the general intercessions as a prayer form in the celebration of the Eucharist and in other rites, and to suggest the meaning and significance of the general intercessions in all liturgical celebrations.

The needs for which we pray change rapidly. Even though the world moves so quickly and people's needs shift, the Church is convinced of the timeless value of intercessory prayer. In such a world, the Church seeks to be sensitive to the problems which individuals and communities face, bringing those concerns to the celebration of the paschal mystery.

In the Eucharist especially, we learn the meaning of Christian prayer, not only its depth and scope, but even how we must pray. The Spirit, in whose power we pray, "helps us in our weakness, for we do not know how to pray as we ought." And just as the Spirit makes intercession for us "with groanings that cannot be expressed in speech," so too the Spirit teaches us to intercede for the needs of all people when we gather to pray, and learn to pray, in the eucharistic liturgy (see Rom 8:26–27).

The recommendations in this statement about the general intercessions are not intended to introduce a static or rigid structure for this prayer form. A certain freedom, spontaneity, and flexibility are essential to the intercessions. At a time when creativity within prescribed norms is encouraged, the general intercessions should remain open and free, a legitimate expression of the desire to adapt the liturgical celebration to the local community. In many ways the intercessions form a profession of faithful dependence on God, a humble plea of each person in the assembled community of Christians.

The structure described in this statement reflects the norms of the *General Instruction of the Roman Missal* (nos. 45–47) and the best American usage. It should be recalled that the intercessions are an integral part of the eucharistic celebration and the final element in the service of the Word. Consistency with the whole celebration should be sought through the form, structure, length and style of the general intercessions, and their relationship with the service of the Eucharist which follows (SC 56).

It is not the purpose of these guidelines to recount the history of the general intercessions, nor to repeat all that has been said in the conciliar and postconciliar documents. The following statement from the *General Instruction of the Roman Missal* sums up much of what has been written in the documents of the liturgical reform:

In the general intercessions or prayer of the faithful, the people exercise their priestly function by interceding for all mankind. It is appropriate that this prayer be included in all Masses celebrated with a congregation, so that intercessions may be made for the Church, for civil authorities, for those oppressed by various needs, and for all mankind, and for the salvation of the world (no. 45; see also SC 53).

In fact, at this time, the practice of the Church has gone beyond the *General Instruction* that recommended the intercessions as "appropriate." The general intercessions have rightly become integral to the liturgy of the Word, even in weekday celebrations of the Eucharist.

Name

The restoration of the great intercessions to the Mass by the Second Vatican Council was not for historical or archaeological reasons. Rather, the prayer was reintroduced in the Roman liturgy for completely pastoral motives: to fill a genuine need and to correct an omission of long-standing.

Historically, the general intercessions have had many names. Although the phrase "prayer of the faithful" has become the common name for this intercessory prayer, its significance may more clearly be understood in the various other terms that have been used. In fact, the general intercessions are not *the* prayer of the faithful, in the sense of the principal prayer of petition made by the people. The Lord's Prayer is more accurately the "prayer of the faithful." Moreover, when catechumens are present, they are "dismissed in a friendly manner before the eucharistic celebration begins," that is, after the general intercessions (see RCIA, no. 19:3).

The general intercessions have sometimes been called the "common prayer" because, apart from the Lord's Prayer and the eucharistic prayer itself, they make explicit the common needs of God's people who are assembled for worship. However, tradition has reserved this title, "common prayer" (*oratio communis*) to the Lord's Prayer.

"Bidding prayers" is yet another name occasionally used to refer to the general intercessions. It is an expression that underscores the litanic form of the prayer, with the use of successive invitations, invocations, and petitions, a form that lends itself readily to congregational participation.

It seems more appropriate, however, to name this universal prayer the "general intercessions," to suggest that, however concrete and particular it may be, it always goes beyond the needs and concerns of the local assembly to the needs of the whole Church, of all the Churches, and indeed of the whole world.

The Nature of the Prayer

Some hesitation must be expressed about the recent development of this prayer in some places, and that is the problem of particularism. Important as it is for the local assembly to express the particular needs its members experience, the more crucial aspect is the universality and catholicity that finds expression in petitions for the whole of God's people. The Church is truly and fully present in each eucharistic community. Yet, the local Church must always relate its celebration of the Eucharist to the Great Church. The general intercessions are a sign of communion of the particular assembly with other assemblies and with the universal Church.

The Use of the General Intercessions

While the general intercessions must be included in all Sunday and holy day celebrations of the Eucharist (see SC 53), the importance of this intercessory and universal prayer indicates its incorporation in all celebrations of the Mass, even weekdays. The general intercessions are important also in celebrations of the sacraments and in other liturgical rites.

Provision is made in the Rite of Marriage for the general intercessions, when marriage is celebrated during Mass (no. 29) and outside Mass (nos. 49, 64). Intercessions are also a part of the celebration of the rites of Christian burial, the baptism of infants, confirmation, etc. In each instance, particular intercessions significant for the celebration are required. However, petitions of a more universal nature are to be included as well.

General intercessions joined to the Lord's Prayer are the fitting conclusion of services of the Word (see *Instruction* of the Congregation of Rites, September 26, 1964, no. 37), and may be a part of other services, whether these services take the form proper to the Mass, the liturgy of the hours, or to some other form.

Text of the Prayer

After several years of creative use, flexibility and spontaneity have been achieved by many parishes and communities that might not have otherwise been possible if fixed formulas had been imposed. Neither these guidelines nor the sources and texts that have already been published should be interpreted as restricting that freedom and diversity. The present intent is rather to review broad principles so that the general intercessions remain an effective element of the eucharistic liturgy and of other liturgical celebrations.

In the selection or composition of intentions, the *General Instruction of the Roman Missal* has made the following strong recommendations. At least one intention should fall into each of the categories of the general intercessions.

1. *The needs of the Church:* for example, petitions might be for the pope, the local bishop, all bishops and pastors of the Church, the Church's ministers, the missions, the unity of Christians, vocations to the priesthood and the religious life, etc.

2. *Public authorities and the salvation of the world:* for example, petitions might be composed for peace and justice, government officials, an end to war, good weather, a good and bountiful harvest, public elections, the solution of socioeconomic problems, etc.

3. *Those oppressed by any need:* for example, intercession might be made for those suffering religious or political persecution, for the unemployed, for the sick and infirm, for prisoners or exiles, for those suffering racial or other injustices, etc.

4. *The local community:* for example, intercessions might be composed for those absent from the community, for those who are to be baptized or confirmed, ordained or married, for the ministers of the local community, for first communicants, for a mission or week of renewal, etc.

In particular celebrations, such as baptism, confirmation, other rites of Christian initiation, marriage, Christian burial, the plan of intentions should be directed more closely to the individual occasion (see GIRM 46).

The reason for this pattern is clear. The Church is at once local and universal, and the balance between universality and particularity must be preserved. On occasion, the general intercessions may be most specific, for example an intention for the persons married at a nuptial liturgy. On all occasions, the intercessions should be open to local and particular needs, although the universal character of the prayer should never be neglected.

While it is not necessary to observe any single order in the arrangement of the intentions (either from general to particular or particular to general), the four categories already listed should be respected, and *at least one intention* be taken from each.

Because we do pray for universal as well as particular needs, the restoration of the general intercessions to the liturgy gives witness to the Church's concern for all people. *Gaudium et spes,* the *Pastoral Constitution on the Church in the Modern World,* summarizes the theology behind the general intercessions:

> The joys and the hopes, the griefs and the anxieties of [people] of this age, especially those who are poor or in any way afflicted, these too are the joys and hopes, the griefs and anxieties of the followers of Christ. Indeed, nothing genuinely human fails to raise an echo in their hearts. For theirs is a [human] community. United in Christ, they are led by the Holy Spirit in their journey to the kingdom of their Father and they have welcomed the news of salvation which is meant for [everyone]. That is why this community realizes that it is truly and intimately linked with [humanity] and its history. (GS 1)

The Church, present in each assembly gathered for worship, assumes its role as advocate of the human family.

Genuine necessities, real needs, should be the subject of the petitions for which the community prays. "Prepackaged" intercessions often fail to meet universal needs. Material prepared months in advance of the date of its use can hardly be expected to be current. Nor can the needs of the local community, which makes the prayer, ever be met by such material. A worshiping community must be sensitive to both the universal and the particular needs of the Church and the world. Current events should help shape the general intercessions for the community.

The Style of the Prayer

The style of the general intercessions is important for the impact that this form of liturgical prayer is to have in the assembly's worship. Intercessions are petitionary by nature and, as such, reflect the community that makes them. They are a people's prayer.

It may not be possible or even desirable in large liturgical assemblies, as it often is in smaller groups, to invite spontaneous and free presentation of petitions and intentions. However, ordinarily, some opportunity should be given to members of the community to submit intentions, which may then be formulated or summarized in preparation for worship.

Since the general intercessions are prayers of supplication and petition, it is not correct to compose them in a style that reflects other prayer forms, that is, prayers of thanksgiving, adoration, praise or penitence. Although these elements can never be excluded from any style or form of prayer, the clear and direct purpose of the general intercessions is petition to God, even though they are made "in a spirit of thanksgiving" (see Col 4:2). Therefore, declarations of praise and thanksgiving should not be included in the general intercessions. Praise and thanksgiving are the heart of the eucharistic prayer itself.

The general intercessions should never be didactic, as though they were announcements. Nor should the proposal of intentions ever become partisan or tendentious. The intercessions are not a substitute for the homily. While their style is not homiletic, they may reflect the Word of God in the proclamation of the readings and in the homily, but not as a summary of the homily. Petitions made "for a personal intention" can hardly elicit a good community response. If personal petitions cannot be adequately verbalized for whatever reason, they should be understood as being a part of a more global intention or a part of the collect prayer, which concludes the intercessions.

Imagery is important in all liturgical language, and biblical imagery is its most fundamental form in the liturgy. Therefore, images, metaphors, phrases, words, and other elements from the Scriptures should be taken into account in the composition of the intercessions. The imagery of the liturgical seasons or solemnity or feast being celebrated may also assist in the style of the intercessions. However, the intercessions are the community's petitions and should be neither abstruse nor unclear as to the purpose and intent of each of the petitions. The general intercessions must be concrete and to the point.

The Form and Structure of the Prayer

The form and structure of the general intercessions described here is the most common form as found in the *General Instruction*. It is not prescribed to the exclusion of other forms, especially at devotional services such as liturgies of the Word. For example, the most solemn form of the general intercessions, with lengthy invitations expressed by the president of the assembly, periods of silent prayer at the direction of the deacon, and collects, as used on Good Friday, should not be utilized in the ordinary circumstances of Sunday liturgy, but might be employed on occasion.

While examples of intercessions are offered in Appendix I of *The Sacramentary*, they were prepared to serve as models rather than as prescribed prayer texts.

Introduction

After the homily and/or the profession of faith, the president of the assembly (bishop or priest) should briefly introduce the intercessions in the form of an invitation to prayer.

This introduction is addressed to the gathered community; *it is never a prayer to God.* It may suitably give the broad purpose of the intercessions and serve to call forth the response of the assembly. It may or may not incorporate the simple invitation, "Let us pray."

The most important function of this preliminary invitation is to relate the general intercessions to the mystery being celebrated or to the feast or season of the day or to some particular aspect or theme of the Word of God proclaimed in the Scriptures. Thus, the introduction serves as a bridge between the proclamation of the Word of God and the response of the assembly in petition and intercession.

The introduction can also establish the particular and concrete application of the biblical message to the conditions of the assembly present for worship. It can express the link between the word as announced and preached and the rest of the eucharistic celebration.

If, however, this purpose is already achieved in the homily in some way, it is enough to use a general invitation to prayer such as, "Let us pray." This is especially true when the intercessions follow the homily immediately.

Intentions

After the presiding minister invites the assembly to pray, the intentions are announced by another minister, and the assembly responds to each petition. Ordinarily, the intentions are announced by the deacon, if one is present, or by another minister. It is not appropriate for the priest to make the intentions.

In the Roman rite prayer directed to God is made only by the one who presides at the Eucharist in the name of the people. Therefore, the deacon (or minister) does not address the intentions to God or Christ. In the general intercessions the prayer, directly addressed to God, is made by the priest or bishop in the concluding collect. The intentions then are formulated as *invitations* to the community to pray for a particular purpose, the phrase, "Let us pray," being understood.

Most simply, the intentions may be expressed as prayer "for" persons or some object, or more fully, with an indication of both the person(s) and the object, purpose or grace sought: "Let us pray for . . . that . . ." or just simply beginning, "For . . . that . . .," or even more simply, "That . . . " (see Appendix I of *The Sacramentary*).

It is very important that some clear and distinctive concluding formula be consistently added to each intention, especially if the intention is recited and not sung or chanted. This corresponds to the Latin *digneris* and invites the immediate response of the assembly. The most common way of ending each intention is with the expression, "Let us pray to the Lord," or "We pray to the Lord." Other formulas may, of course, be employed, provided they are consistently used and are known or become known to the community. The community should not have to guess at the response.

The length of the general intercessions is principally dependent upon the number of intentions. In ordinary circumstances, the intentions should be few, to retain the simplicity of the prayer, to avoid wearying the assembly, and to keep the prayer in proportion to the preceding elements of the liturgy of the Word. This should especially be borne in mind when the intercessions are to be sung.

Ordinarily, five or six intentions suffice; more rarely there might be seven or eight (see GIRM 46).

Response

In every case, the response to the intercessions must be made by all the members of the assembly, and not by a choir or other select group. Such was the intent of the conciliar restoration of the general intercessions, "in which the people are to take part" (SC 53).

Although there should be the greatest variety in the responses, normally only one is used on a given occasion. It is the task of the deacon or other minister to indicate any variation from the usual pattern before announcing the intentions. The announcement of a variation should not be done in such a way as to form an interruption between the presiding celebrant's introduction and the intentions which follow. Assemblies should be made aware of the possibility of variety in the response. The most commonly accepted responses in the United States are "Lord, hear our prayer"; "Hear us, O Lord"; "Lord, have mercy." When other responses are composed, the images of the day's readings might be reflected.

In multilingual celebrations, or when groups of various languages or rites join in the celebration, one recommended response is the venerable Greek expression, *"Kyrie eleison"* (Lord, have mercy). The assembly ought to be made aware of the importance of this response. It may even occasionally be used when the assembly is composed of one language group.

Silence

A brief period of silent prayer should be encouraged by the deacon or other minister at the end of the series of intentions, that is, before the concluding prayer. Such a period of silence provides the assembly the opportunity to reflect on the intercessions and to join any other intentions thus far unvoiced to the concluding prayer to come. The length of this period of silence should be indicated by the minister of the intentions and should be significant rather than a perfunctory gesture. The minister and the people may bow their heads as they pray in silence.

The *Constitution on the Liturgy* refers explicitly to the need for appointed times of silence in liturgical celebrations, when it speaks of the external expressions of active congregational participation: "And at the proper times all should observe a reverent silence" (no. 30). Just as silence should follow each of the readings, so too the whole assembly and its ministers should observe a silence at the end of the intentions.

Concluding Prayer

Following the intentions and responses, and after observing the period of silent prayer, the presiding priest or bishop sings or says the concluding prayer. He does not prefix this collect-style prayer with, "Let us pray," since he has already invited the community to pray in the introduction.

This prayer, like all the principal prayers of the Mass, is addressed to God the Father, and never to Christ, the Spirit, Mary, or the saints. It is composed and delivered in the style of a collect. However, it should not be a duplication of the Opening Prayer of the Mass, nor should it anticipate the Prayer over the Gifts.

The concluding prayer sums up and completes the general intercessions. Therefore, it is preferable that it not include new elements of petition not already mentioned in the introduction or in the intentions.

The concluding prayer should end simply in a brief formula such as "Through Christ our Lord" or "Grant this through Christ our Lord." The more lengthy, trinitarian formula is reserved usually to the Opening Prayer of the Mass.

Singing the General Intercessions

The Sacramentary as well as several hymnals and aids for congregational participation provide suitable tones for singing the general intercessions. A choir may accompany the assembly by singing a harmonization of the brief response. However, under no circumstances should the response be sung by a choir alone. As already mentioned, the whole assembly is to take part in this prayer.

The singing of the intercessions, as a musical element in the liturgy, should be done in balance and proportion with other musical elements in the service.

The Ministers of the Prayer

The several parts of the general intercessions are distributed as follows:

Priest (or Bishop)	Introduction
Deacon (or other Minister)	Intentions
Assembly	Responses
Priest (or Bishop)	Concluding Prayer
Assembly	Amen

The presiding minister (priest or bishop) introduces the general intercessions, as already mentioned, and sings or says the concluding prayer. It is not proper, except on Good Friday when the longer bidding prayer form is used, for the priest to announce the intentions, unless no other minister is available. The role of the priest is to preside over the people's prayer, and to pray in their name.

The proper minister to announce the intentions is the deacon. However, in the absence of the deacon another minister may be designated. Normally, the reader does not announce the intentions. When the intercessions are sung rather than recited, preference should be given to the cantor over another minister, even over the deacon, if he cannot sing or elicit a sung response from the assembly.

Position of the Ministers

The presiding priest or bishop directs the intercessions from the chair. There, he introduces the intercessions, makes the responses with the people, and sings or says the concluding prayer.

If this is not convenient because of the arrangement of the sanctuary area, the priest may direct the prayer from the ambo from which the readings were proclaimed and where the homily was given. For example, if there is no profession of faith, the priest may remain at the ambo after the homily and direct the intercessions. However, it is always preferable and more proper for him to preside over the assembly in this prayer from the presidential chair, from which he presides during the *entire* liturgy of the Word.

When the deacon announces the intentions, he may do so either from the ambo or from any other convenient place, for example, while standing at his usual place beside the priest, or from the edge of the sanctuary, nearer the people. Wherever he stands, care should always be taken that he be heard easily by all.

If another minister (cantor, leader of song, reader) announces the intentions, he or she ordinarily stands at a convenient place before the assembly where the minister may be seen and distinctly heard. Normally, the minister does not stand at the ambo from which the readings were proclaimed (see GIRM 272).

A Universal Prayer

Christians have, from the very earliest years of the Church's history, concerned themselves with prayer for the needs of the Church and for the needs of all humanity. The development of the general intercessions and their restoration to the Roman liturgy in our time testifies to the desire to incorporate universal prayer into the eucharistic liturgy, the heart of the Church's life. From the echoes of common prayer that we hear in the *Acts of the Apostles* (2:42) and in St. Justin's *First Apology* (65:1–3; 67:3–5) and in the epoch of Pope Gelasius I (492–496), when the general intercessions or universal prayer became a permanent part of the Roman liturgy of the Eucharist, this element of the Church's liturgy has been a principal means for the people to unite concrete, rapidly changing needs of Church and world to the timeless paschal mystery of Christ's death and resurrection.

Now restored to our worship, the general intercessions should be composed with care and earnestly prayed. For, the Church's power of prayer is great. The whole Church, the baptized praying with united voices and hearts, interceding for the needs, not only of its own, but especially for all humanity, is moving the world ever nearer to the kingdom of God's reign over the earth.

31

Composers of Liturgical Music

Letter, Bishops' Committee on the Liturgy
November 23, 1980

(See also nos. 4, 6, 10, 14, 15)

This statement was issued in the form of a letter addressed to composers of liturgical music in observance of the feast of Saint Cecilia. This accounts for its rather distinct celebratory and personal tone. It differs from most other documents in this collection in the directness and even warmth of its approach. It is consistent in speaking to the composers, consistent in praise of their contributions.

The starting point of the letter is in the *Constitution on the Liturgy* which, at the end of Chapter VI on music, spoke of the ecclesial role of composers:

Composers, filled with the Christian spirit, should feel that their vocation is to develop sacred music and to increase its store of treasures.

Let them produce compositions having the qualities proper to genuine sacred music, not confining themselves to works that can be sung only by large choirs, but providing also for the needs of small choirs and for the active participation of the entire assembly of the faithful.

The texts intended to be sung must always be consistent with Catholic teaching; indeed, they should be chiefly drawn from holy Scripture and from liturgical sources (SC 121).

In the intervening period, this particular exhortation of the council had not always been heard. It was designed as a balanced encouragement to great music for choral use, whether in large or small choirs, but never to the exclusion of music written for the whole assembly. The message had been heard best and clearest by composers who were writing music not only for congregations and cantors but also for choirs and congregations together, including more elaborate forms of music in which there would be a complementary but necessary part for the whole assembly.

It is more than evident that, like other and broader statements on music, this letter also reflected an actual situation: music continued to be composed and used that did not foster the active praying of the whole assembly, respect the liturgical genre of texts or even their language, or support adequately the revised liturgical rites.

In an effort to encourage composition of service music that was not being attempted by composers or commissioned by publishers—especially for the celebration of the sacraments other than the Eucharist and for the liturgy of the hours—the International Commission on English in the Liturgy had made a limited number of new compositions available as examples. The success of this effort was also limited, despite the quality of some of the compositions. The Bishops' Committee on the Liturgy was making, for the United States, a similar point, specifically mentioning the need for "acclamations in the *Rite of Christian Initiation of Adults,* the responsories in the *Liturgy of the Hours,* the antiphons in the *Dedication of a Church and an Altar.*"

One omission from the statement is the specific directive of the *Constitution on the Liturgy,* in the third paragraph of the text quoted above. This not only speaks of the doctrinal integrity of the texts to which music is set, but proposes biblical and liturgical sources of inspiration for new texts, such as hymns and responsorial music. Such a directive need not be a constraint upon composers. Already, some American composers have turned to New Testament texts for use in liturgical music, including texts that are themselves understood to have origins in early liturgical practice. And, so far as "liturgical sources" are concerned, the need for originality and creativity—while respecting the rites and the nature of Christian worship—has been forcibly recognized in comparison with translations from the Latin. Translations remain only a partial answer to the question of liturgical texts and, thus, to the musical settings for the singing of the Christian assembly. As far back as 1969, the Consilium of implementation made the point that may be quoted once again:

> Texts translated from another language [in the context, from Latin] are clearly not sufficient for the celebration of a fully renewed liturgy. The creation of new texts will be necessary. But the translation of texts transmitted through the tradition of the Church is the best school and discipline for the creation of new texts so "that any new forms adopted should in some way grow organically from forms already in existence" (instruction *Comme le prévoit,* no. 43: DOL 123).

What is said of verbal expression is as true of musical setting: respect for past traditions should be coupled with creative growth of new traditions.

Introduction

Through the efforts of numerous persons, the Church in the United States has experienced a healthy start in building a tradition of vernacular music for use in its worship. As composers, you have shown your sensitivity to the needs of the revised liturgy in the vernacular. Your creative efforts since the Second Vatican Council are to be truly commended. In so many cases, your compositions reflect an awareness of the culture in which people in this country worship. They also express your love for the liturgical prayer life of the

Church with its various forms. Furthermore, the results of your service to the community confirm, once again, both the genius of the Roman rite and the inspiration it can occasion, as witnessed through the centuries to the present day.

New Demands and Challenges

Liturgy, as ritual activity, employs language. In liturgical language, the good news of Jesus Christ is proclaimed, the paschal mystery celebrated, and the continual formation of the community of faith assisted. In recognition of this fact, convinced that language helps to bring about an intelligent and active participation in worship, during the Second Vatican Council, the Church approved the use of the vernacular in all liturgical celebrations of the Roman Catholic Church.[1] At the same time, it expressed concern for the proper translation of the texts of the revised liturgical rites and continues to protect their integrity, however they may be used, mindful of the ancient principle: *legem credendi lex statuat supplicandi* (the law of prayer establishes the law of belief).[2]

The introduction of English in the liturgy has placed new demands on the local Church. Translators have been directed to "be faithful to the art of communication,"[3] celebrants admonished to use only approved liturgical texts,[4] composers of liturgical music challenged to prepare settings that truly serve the Church at prayer according to the revised order.[5] These new demands have also presented new challenges, to be sure. Those who have responded with openness, generosity, and a willingness to meet the challenge of the day, must be commended. Yet, the challenge has not been exhausted; work remains to be done by all. Here, we consider briefly the challenge still before you as composers of liturgical music.

Music Is Integral to Worship

Whether in Latin or the vernacular, liturgical texts are integral to worship. Yet, they can become more noble and effective when set to appropriate music, as clearly affirmed by the declarations of the Second Vatican Council.[6] Musicians, singers, and instrumentalists are responsible for providing the direction and support by which the community can pray and sing well. For you, musicians who compose, the responsibility is equally clear: to be well-trained and sensitive to the liturgy, to provide musical settings for the approved

---

[1]Second Vatican Council. *Constitution on the Liturgy (Sacrosanctum Concilium*-SC), December 4, 1963, nos. 36 (3); 54.

[2]This axiom comes from the so-called *capitula Coelestini* which were annexed to a letter of Pope Celestine I (422–32), but probably are the work of Prosper of Aquitaine (c. 440).

[3]Consilium. *Instruction on Translation of Liturgical Texts,* January 25, 1969, no. 7.

[4]Congregation for the Sacraments and Divine Worship. *Inaestimabile Donum,* released May 23, 1980, no. 5.

[5]SC 121.

[6]SC 112, 113.

liturgical and scriptural texts, and to prepare music for hymn texts that enhance those moments of communal worship where they can be incorporated. In your work as liturgical composers, therefore, we recall two important working principles.

Compose to assist the assembly. According to the directives of the *Constitution on the Liturgy*,[7] music should assist the active participation of the faithful. The focus, therefore, in composing music is the entire assembly: the faithful with the ministers. Vocal groups and individuals, such as choirs and soloists, are a part of the assembly and the preparation of music for them must be treated accordingly. In the distribution of the architectural space, there is a real concern not to isolate the musicians from the community. Composers of music for choirs and soloists must also be conscious of the need to strengthen the unity of the community and the oneness of its worship. Therefore, as the primary role of all music ministry is to support the community in prayer, so the primary focus for composers of liturgical music is the entire assembly itself.

Respect the liturgical texts. The growing awareness on the part of composers of the inspiring treasures of Scripture is praiseworthy. Another source of inspiration is the corpus of approved liturgical texts of the revised rites. Here, however, a word of direction is in order. In writing music for specific liturgical texts, e.g., from the Scriptures, sacramentary, or rituals, the composer must respect the integrity of the approved text.[8] Admittedly, not all texts, as approved by the episcopal conference, easily lend themselves to musical composition because of their style, length, or translation. Nevertheless, composers may not alter the prescribed texts of the rites to accommodate them to musical settings. The Church is always concerned about the use of the approved liturgical texts be they written, spoken, proclaimed, or sung.[9] For texts not prescribed by the rites such as texts for songs, greater freedom is enjoyed by composers. Even here, however, composers need to select texts that truly express the faith of the Church, that are theologically accurate and liturgically correct. This area deserves widespread encouragement and support, as well as your creative efforts.

Needs of the Church

Liturgical action is always to be a harmonious whole. Music is no appendage, no decorative extra, or optional interlude. On the contrary, composers

---

[7]SC 121.

[8]Only one exception is provided, but it does not affect the preparation of new musical compositions. "In accord with no. 55 of the Instruction of the Congregation of Rites on music in the liturgy . . ., the Conference of Bishops has determined that vernacular texts set to music composed in earlier periods may be used in liturgical services even though they may not conform in all details with the legitimately approved versions of liturgical texts (November, 1967). This decision authorizes the use of choral and other music in English when the older text is not precisely the same as the official version" (*Appendix to the General Instruction of the Roman Missal*, no. 19).

[9]The basis for this concern is the Church's responsibility for safeguarding the doctrinal content of prayer texts. The *Constitution on the Liturgy*, no. 36 (4) states: "Translations from the Latin text into the mother tongue which are intended for use in the liturgy must be approved by the competent territorial ecclesiastical authority mentioned above" (i.e., episcopal conference, Holy See).

have come to recognize and respect the function of the several structural elements of the various rites and the role of liturgical texts which clothe the whole. Therefore, in the composition of music for particular texts, the musician needs to consider carefully the genre of the text (litany, acclamation, oration, etc.) and its purpose in the rite itself. Beyond the work you have already done in this area, we ask that you direct your attention and talents also to the needs of these diverse elements of service music found in all the revised liturgical rites. By way of example, one could cite the need for additional musical settings for the acclamations in the *Rite of Christian Initiation of Adults,* the responsories in the *Liturgy of the Hours,* the antiphons in the *Dedication of a Church and an Altar.* The amount of service music still required for the full experience of liturgical prayer in our country seems to have no limit.

We also encourage you to write new liturgical hymns to meet the demands of the new rites. Songs appropriate for use in the *Rite of Marriage, Pastoral Care of the Sick and Dying, Solemn Exposition of the Blessed Sacrament,* are but a few examples. We hope that you, as composers, will accept the challenge and address this need of the Church.

A final word needs to be directed to your publishers and to music publishers in general. We, as Church, owe them gratitude since over the past years they have made available, frequently at considerable financial risk, a wide variety of music for use in liturgical prayer. Their work, necessary for liturgical renewal in our country, gives them the responsibility to call forth from you, as composers, the best of your art in order to provide worshiping assemblies with quality music fitting for the great act of worship. Publishers need also to encourage new composers and be open to the publication of their work to provide an even greater richness of musical resources.

Finally, to all musicians, we offer words of gratitude and encouragement. Without your ministry, our liturgical prayer would be the poorer; with your service, our liturgical prayer becomes even more noble.

32

A Book of Prayers

Statement, Chairman of the Bishops' Committee
on the Liturgy
December 16, 1982

(See also nos. 2, 5, 13, 16, 35)

This statement explains very clearly the context: a collection of devotional prayers in English had received an absolute, but not a two-thirds majority, vote of approval from the National Conference of Catholic Bishops at its November 1982 plenary session. The statement was made on behalf of the Bishops' Committee on the Liturgy by Bishop John S. Cummins of Oakland, who chaired the committee from 1981 to 1984.

The origin and character of *A Book of Prayers* (Washington, D.C.: ICEL, 1982) should perhaps be described at a little greater length than in Bishop Cummins' statement. Generally, the textual program of ICEL has been confined to the translation of Latin liturgical texts and the composition of original texts for the liturgy itself. At the request of bishops from various countries—and at the direction of its own episcopal board—ICEL undertook this special project. Its purpose was to put into contemporary English some familiar and some not so familiar prayers of devotion. The hope was to encourage a renewed Catholic devotional life, personal and communal, in accord with the mandate of the *Constitution on the Liturgy*:

> But these devotions [the pious devotions of the Christian people and the sacred devotions of particular churches] should be so fashioned that they harmonize with the liturgical season, accord with the sacred liturgy, are in some way derived from it, and lead the people to it, since, in fact, the liturgy by its very nature far surpasses any of them (SC 13).

Many of the prayers in the collection had gone out of common use entirely or were available only in versions that were archaic and often incomprehensible. Other prayers, still fairly well known, existed in variant English forms—since the legitimacy of diverse private translations, included in private books of devotion with proper ecclesiastical permission, had never been questioned. The ICEL versions were fresh interpretations, made available to the conferences of bishops that constitute ICEL—although any diocesan bishop or local ordinary continues to have authority to permit publication of (nonliturgical) books and prayers of devotion and piety.

The collection has seven sections: "Mass and Holy Communion" (prayers before and after Mass); "Creeds and Canticles" (liturgical texts); "Consecrations and Litanies"; "Our Lady"; "Angels and Saints"; "Times and Occasions"; and "Invocations." Some examples of the work will help explain what was intended and accomplished.

Two lengthy modern prayers, "Act of Reparation to the Sacred Heart" and "Act of Consecration to Christ the King," had been intended for public as well as private use. For the first time, they were offered in simple, clear English and supplemented by acclamations to be used as a congregational refrain (respectively, "Praise to the Heart of Jesus, our Savior and our God" and "Praise to you, our Savior and our King"). Thus, in the best sense, they were made usable by the church community.

Among the fifty-three items in the collection, some ten are prayers to the Virgin Mary. In the Litany of Loreto, an effort was made to recover the strength of the invocations, for example: "Most honored of virgins (*Virgo virginum*); "Mother of chaste love" (*Mater castissima*); "Mother and virgin" (*Mater inviolata*); "Sinless Mother" (*Mater intemerata*); "Virgin most wise" (*Virgo prudentissima*); "Virgin rightly praised" (*Virgo veneranda*); "Virgin rightly renowned" (*Virgo praedicanda*); "Virgin gentle in mercy" (*Virgo clemens*).

One irony was that *A Book of Prayers* contains a fair number of official liturgical texts, such as opening prayers of the missal also used at the end of litanies, an act of contrition from the revised *Rite of Penance*, and creeds and canticles prepared by the International Consultation on Common Texts and adopted by ICEL. All of these had received canonical approbation from the NCCB and other conferences of bishops and had been confirmed by the Apostolic See. This fact did not deter the critics of the collection mentioned in the statement: They attacked both the translations, as inadequate and even heterodox, and also the notes on the liturgical texts in use for several years.

Another irony was that the texts, when presented to the NCCB in November 1982, already had received the approval of the eleven-member episcopal board of ICEL, which consists of bishops designated by the constituent conferences of bishops, and also of the American Bishops' Committee on the Liturgy. The collection had been incorporated in a publication authorized by the episcopal commission of Ireland and, in whole or part, by individual bishops. In fact, as mentioned above, even today the individual bishop is free to give the usual imprimatur to the devotional texts it includes; this is clearly within his authority in accord with canon 826 §3 of the 1983 *Code of Canon Law*.

ICEL had used as its guide in selecting texts a Roman collection, the *Enchiridion indulgentiarum*, issued by the Apostolic Penitentiary in 1968 (DOL 390). This, in turn, had been compiled in view of an apostolic constitution of Pope Paul VI, *Indulgentiarum doctrina* (January 1, 1967: DOL 386) on the doctrine and discipline of indulgences. ICEL, however, was not preparing its translations as a "collection of indulgenced prayers," and the indulgences were not listed. Instead, the book was offered only as a resource collection, primarily for the conferences of bishops but available for other purposes.

A Book of Prayers remains a valuable collection, with historical notes on some of the texts, Latin originals, and careful explanations of the more complex decisions on translation. It offers, moreover, a brief rationale for such a collection, of which the following may be quoted:

> A modified translation of these texts, with words and expressions congenial to our times, will encourage their use among new generations of Catholics. . . .
> Within the broad framework of Christian prayer, many forms have appealed at different times to people of various nations and cultures. This book contains some of these forms of prayer from the treasury of the Christian centuries. Believers living at the end of the twentieth century are invited to use those prayers, which help them join with Christ in praising the Father and in making intercession for the people of this world. In this way, we can continue working with the Lord Jesus to build up God's kingdom on earth (pp. vi–vii).

The introduction draws attention also to some guidelines for personal prayer—biblical, liturgical, ecumenical, and other criteria—that Pope Paul VI had proposed for Marian devotion; they are equally applicable to other devotional texts and practices. In harmony with part four of Chapter VIII of the *Constitution on the Church,* "Veneration of the Blessed Virgin in the Church" (*Lumen gentium* 66–67: DOL 4), Pope Paul VI had given these guidelines in an invaluable but neglected apostolic exhortation, *Marialis cultus* (February 2, 1974: DOL 467).

All in all, *A Book of Prayers* is a careful and conservative translation. As the statement suggests, it is unfortunate that improper criticism perhaps confused its initial reception, but need not stand in the way of future use.

In the commentary on the preceding document, *Communion under Both Kinds,* something of the complexity of procedures that attend decrees of the conference of bishops was recited. Ordinarily, English liturgical texts have been approved by the NCCB by overwhelming majorities of 80 percent and more. In this instance of a largely devotional "nonliturgical" collection, the fact that a simple majority of favorable votes was cast (125 to 115) was overlooked, and, unquestionably, a mistaken impression was created—as if the negative votes truly impugned the orthodoxy of the translations.

Whenever a vote is taken by secret ballot, it is difficult, if not impossible, to determine the motivating reasons for votes for and against. The statement carefully prescinds from judging the quality of the texts, which may indeed have resulted in some negative votes, in order to deal with an altogether unconscionable objection: that the texts were lacking in Catholic orthodoxy and, thus, that the translators were somehow unorthodox.

In a larger context, the statement is a rebuke to unconsidered criticism that may be unjust. Three years later, another chairman of the episcopal committee had to explain another misperceived vote of the American conference of bishops in the case of *The Revised Grail Psalter.*

At their general meeting last month, the U.S. bishops considered a proposal by their Liturgy Committee to approve a resource collection of devotional and liturgical prayers prepared by the International Commission on English in the Liturgy. A majority voted in favor of *A Book of Prayers*, but the volume did not receive the necessary two-thirds vote. There were 125 in favor and 115 opposed.

The book was offered by ICEL as a service to English-speaking episcopal conferences. The bishops had every right to make the decision they wished. The Liturgy Committee also has the right to reconsider the question and re-present *A Book of Prayers* to the bishops if later that seems timely and appropriate. The committee will be addressing that possibility in the months ahead.

In the meantime, however, I wish to take note of another matter pertaining to *A Book of Prayers*. Before the bishops' meeting, some groups conducted a campaign against the collection in which, implicitly or even explicitly, the orthodoxy of the translations—and therefore of the translators and those who approved the translations—was called into question. As a matter of correctness and also of justice, that cannot go unchallenged.

There is always room for honest disagreement about translations—their accuracy, their success in conveying the sense of the original in contemporary terms, their literary quality. But, something very different is at issue when the question of orthodoxy is raised. There are no grounds for impugning the orthodoxy of those responsible for preparing or proposing the translations in *A Book of Prayers*.

As noted, the collection was prepared by the International Commission on English in the Liturgy, a joint commission of English-speaking episcopal conferences around the world. This was done at the request and with the approval of ICEL's own episcopal board. Furthermore, a number of the translations are liturgical texts already approved by the U.S. bishops and confirmed by the Holy See.

Last May, *A Book of Prayers* was approved for use in the liturgy by the Irish Episcopal Commission on the Liturgy. As incorporated in a bilingual (English and Irish) publication of the Irish Institute of Pastoral Liturgy called *Exposition and Benediction of the Blessed Sacrament*, the translations are being used to help foster eucharistic devotion, especially contemporary revival of the traditional Forty Hours Devotion. The publication has met with much success in Ireland, as well as in England, Wales, and Scotland.

Moreover, *A Book of Prayers* was also carefully reviewed by the bishops who make up the NCCB Liturgy Committee before being offered to the U.S. bishops for their acceptance.

In short, these translations have been examined and approved by a large number of bishops from many English-speaking countries. It is significant that 125 U.S. bishops voted in favor of the collection last month. In view of all this, and leaving aside legitimate differences of opinion about the technical quality of the translations, it is hardly responsible to suggest that the orthodoxy of those involved in the preparation and approval of them is open to question.

219

33

The Church at Prayer: A Holy Temple of the Lord
A Pastoral Statement Commemorating the Twentieth Anniversary of the *Constitution on the Liturgy*

Joint Statement, National Conference of Catholic
Bishops (Prepared by the Bishops' Committee
on the Liturgy) ·
December 4, 1983

(See also nos. 9, 27, 28, 34)

The fifteenth anniversary of the *Constitution on the Liturgy* was observed by a substantial but not lengthy document from the Bishops' Committee on the Liturgy issued in November 1978. For the twentieth anniversary, the committee proposed and the National Conference of Catholic Bishops agreed to issue a joint statement emanating from the conference itself.

The text itself needs no comment. It is a profound treatment, following the chapters of the conciliar constitution but bringing matters liturgical into the present moment by doctrinal and pastoral reflections, embodying a deeper commitment of the bishops to liturgical renewal.

In some ways, this document might be compared with a much slighter effort on *Liturgical Renewal,* issued by the NCCB as a pastoral statement in April 1967. By the 1980s, however, a more elaborate procedure was in effect. According to the regulations of the conference, a document of this kind—whether called a joint pastoral or a formal statement—requires approval by a two-thirds majority of the members who have the right to vote, just as is required by the general church law in the case of decrees or laws enacted by the conference.

The commemorative statement was prepared under the guidance of a committee member, Archbishop Oscar H. Lipscomb of Mobile, and went through three drafts before presentation to the general meeting of the bishops. It was unanimously approved by the NCCB on November 17, 1983.

(The statement was also published in a Spanish version, *La Iglesia en Oración: Un Templo Santo del Señor.* In the English text, translations of excerpts from the *Constitution on the Liturgy* are taken from Austin Flannery, general editor, *Vatican Council II, The Conciliar and Post Conciliar Documents,* © 1975 by Costello Publishing Co., Inc. All rights reserved.

Introduction

1. Twenty years have passed since the Second Vatican Council solemnly promulgated the *Constitution on the Sacred Liturgy* (*Sacrosanctum Concilium*) on December 4, 1963. Responding to a deeply felt duty to provide for the renewal and fostering of the liturgy, the Council fathers issued this constitution as an altogether necessary step in its stated goal "to impart an ever increasing vigor to the Christian life of the faithful" (art. 1). The passage of a score of years now offers us an opportunity not only to commemorate so significant an event in the pilgrim life of our family of faith, but also to evaluate its effect, and to foster its continued importance for the future of the Church in the United States of America.

2. For us as bishops, no work can be more important. As the Council explained, "It is the liturgy through which, especially in the divine sacrifice of the Eucharist, 'the work of our redemption is accomplished' " (art. 2). In this *Year that is truly Holy,* this extraordinary Jubilee of the Redemption which coincides with the anniversary we celebrate, we are reminded by Pope John Paul II that the redemption is communicated

> through the proclamation of the Word of God and through the sacraments, in that divine economy whereby the Church is constituted as the Body of Christ, "as the universal sacrament of salvation" . . . (*Open the Doors to the Redeemer,* 3).

3. The generation after the Council is challenged anew to reaffirm God's close and intimate contact with each human life, to stress the importance of prayer, and especially liturgical prayer, as the principal means by which God interacts with his people, to recall the goals of the liturgical reforms mandated by the Council, to assess the strengths and the weaknesses inherent in the implementation of reform measures, to derive encouragement from liturgical achievements, and to specify the paths that lie before us in the vital work yet to be done in promoting the renewal of Catholic life and worship.

4. At the same time, we are mindful of liturgical abuses that have occurred, sometimes through unbridled zeal without theological formation, sometimes through personal whim or neglect. While lamenting these unhappy instances, we are hopeful that they will not prevent us from seeking with zeal and courage an authentic renewal of our liturgical life. What Pope Paul VI said in 1975 still applies today:

> In the course of our eagerness to rekindle the vitality and authenticity of religion in the life of individuals, but especially in the life of the people of God, we must revere and promote the liturgy in our times, in

ecclesial and collective life. . . . For us it suffices here to confirm the liturgical program that the Church has set before itself, to make stable and fruitful the idea and therefore the practice of liturgy. In that program lies the secret of a new vitality for the Church's tradition, the face of the Church's beauty, the expression of the Church's interior and universal unity . . . (Address to a General Audience, 6 August 1975).

This "liturgical program" continues to be our program for the Church in the United States of America, for its growth and vitality, for its participation in the great work of the redemption and reconciliation accomplished in Jesus Christ.

General Liturgical Principles

Christ is always present in his Church, especially in her liturgical celebrations (art. 7).

5. One of the primary concerns of the Second Vatican Council was to affirm the incarnational and the sacramental character of the Church. The Word of God who took flesh of the virgin of Nazareth continues to dwell in the world through the Church. Thus, what is central to the life and work of the Church is to build up that union with God made visible in Jesus Christ, a relationship made possible by his life, death, and resurrection. The paschal mystery is at the heart of the life of the Church. It is this mystery that the Church proclaims and shares with her members who are formed into the people of God through the outpouring of the Holy Spirit. The experience of this mystery is made possible through personal prayer but above all in and through the celebration of the liturgy.

6. The liturgy is a principal means by which God acts upon the Church to make it holy. That sanctification takes place through the presence of Christ in the power of the Holy Spirit, a presence manifested through the word of Sacred Scripture, through the community itself gathered in prayer and song, and above all through the sacraments, especially the Eucharist. The sanctification of the Church results in the creation of a community capable of continuing the saving work of Jesus Christ in the world.

7. The liturgy is the chief means by which the Church, through Jesus Christ and in the unity of the Holy Spirit, responds to God's saving presence in thanksgiving, praise, petition, and longing. In the liturgy, the members of the worshiping community are united both inwardly and outwardly with Christ: inwardly by being conformed to Christ in his disposition of humble, self-giving service of the Father and his people; outwardly by expressing both in word and action that interior conformity with the attitude of Christ. In responding to God's gift of his life offered in Christ, the Church recognizes the mystery of the Father's love entrusted to "vessels of clay." It is our challenge in faith to live the paradox of this human element which leaves the People of God in this world always an imperfect community, always inad-

equate in its acceptance of God's love, thus always in need of reform and renewal. In this sense, the Church is always a community of penitents.

8. The primary purpose of the liturgical reforms in which we have been engaged in a special way for the past twenty years has not been simply a change in sacramental rites. Rather, the reform of the rites has been distinguished by a noble simplicity which both protects and proclaims the core of our Christian tradition so that authentic tradition might grow in the lives of present-day Catholics and bear fruit in the future. The goal is above all to enrich the Church's life of prayer and worship so that those who believe in Christ and are members of his Church might be empowered and motivated to proclaim the good news that God has offered salvation to all in his Son Jesus Christ.

9. The worship that is given to God does not consist simply in the externals of liturgical rites but rather includes the very lives of those who celebrate the liturgy—lives which should manifest what the liturgy expresses, which reveal the life and love of Christ to others, and which call them to share in the Spirit of God and in the work of building up God's Kingdom on earth. For as we noted in our reflections commemorating the fifteenth anniversary of the *Decree on the Apostolate of the Laity* in 1980,

> The quality of worship depends in great measure on the spiritual life of all present. As lay women and men cultivate their own proper response to God's call to holiness, this should come to expression in the communal worship of the Church (*Called and Gifted: The American Catholic Laity*, p. 3).

10. Liturgical renewal, then, implies an ever deeper involvement of the whole Christian community in the paschal mystery of Jesus Christ. The primary means to achieve renewal is that liturgical formation which enables all those who take part in the liturgy to become more and more imbued with its spirit and power. Liturgical formation is as necessary for the laity as it is for the clergy. For

> as lay persons assume their roles in liturgical celebration according to the gifts of the Spirit bestowed on them for that purpose, the ordained celebrant will be more clearly seen as the one who presides over the community, bringing together the diverse talents of the community as gift to the Father (*Called and Gifted: The American Catholic Laity*, p. 4).

The secondary means is an ongoing reform of the liturgical rites themselves to ensure that the words and actions of the liturgy express more and more adequately the holy realities which these words and actions signify. Liturgical formation and the continued reform of the rites therefore bring about that complete, active, and conscious participation in the liturgy required of the assembly and its ministers.

11. Properly trained ministers and programs for such training must be available for liturgical formation. To provide for the future, seminarians and those beginning their lives as religious must be properly formed both aca-

223

demically and spiritually in the spirit of the liturgy. In this regard, we direct the attention of those responsible to the norms and guidelines set forth in the Instruction on Liturgical Formation in Seminaries issued by the Sacred Congregation for Catholic Education in 1979. Bishops, priests, and deacons must be helped also to understand better what they are doing when they celebrate the liturgy, to live the liturgical life more profoundly, and to share it effectively with others. They have a special responsibility to be formed in the spirit of the liturgy. As leaders in the Christian community and in the liturgical assemblies, bishops and priests have as one of their principal tasks to preside at worship in such a manner that the other members of the assembly are led to pray. In a sense, they should be transparent images of what it means for a Christian to die and rise with Jesus.

12. Deacons and other liturgical ministers likewise require a formation that is at once personally profound and directed toward their service within the assembly. The laity must not only be helped to participate fully both internally and externally in the liturgy, but they must also be encouraged to use and develop their various ministerial gifts in the liturgical celebration.

13. In recent years, we have seen a renewed interest in traditional and newer forms of prayer, but special effort must be made to assure that the spirituality of individual Catholics is both Christian and liturgical. The way the Church prays and worships should be the way individual Christians pray and worship. In that sense, the liturgy is normative for Christian spirituality. The personal prayer of individual Christians is important because it ensures that they will come to the liturgy with the proper dispositions. In liturgical celebrations, their minds and hearts will be in tune with what they say and do. Personal prayer, however, does not displace the liturgy nor is it a substitute for it; rather, it should lead Christians to the celebration of the paschal mystery and, in turn, be nourished by that mystery.

14. We do not worship God primarily to become better people; the very nature and excellence of God demand worship. But when we worship, by the grace of the redemption, we can be transformed into better people. And so the worship of the Church is a moment in which Christians are formed as moral persons. The liturgy helps to form Christian character, and, as a result, those who celebrate the liturgy are empowered to relate to one another in justice and peace and to involve themselves in the establishment of God's kingdom on earth.

15. The Eucharist especially teaches us the meaning of God's peace and justice. For as we have said in another pastoral letter, the Mass is

> a unique means of seeking God's help to create the conditions essential for true peace in ourselves and in the world. In the Eucharist we encounter the risen Lord, who gave us His peace. He shares with us the grace of the redemption, which helps us to preserve and nourish this precious gift (*The Challenge of Peace: God's Promise and Our Response,* 295).

God's gifts of justice and peace, indeed all those gifts which strengthen our moral life, are summed up in the liturgy, especially in the Eucharist as a sacrament of reconciliation. As God loves us and shares this new life with us, so we are enabled to love and serve one another. In the liturgy, the divine story of creation and redemption is told and retold; that revelation is reinforced by ritual patterns which communicate Christian meaning and values in verbal and nonverbal ways. As a result, a Christian vision of life is shared. It is a vision framed and permeated by faith. In celebrating the liturgy, Christians do not leave their everyday world and responsibilities behind; rather, they enter into God's real world and see it as it actually is in Jesus—a place where God's providence and love are indeed at work.

16. In order that the Christian vision may be available to all members of the Church, efforts have been made in the past twenty years to adapt the liturgical rites and symbols to the diverse cultures of the world. If the Church is to become incarnate in every culture, the liturgy must express the paschal mystery, which lies at the heart of the Church, in some symbols derived from these diverse cultures. In our own country, special care must be taken to adapt the liturgy so that it is perceived as inclusive of women and responsive to the needs of persons of diverse ages, races, and ethnic groups. Liturgical adaptation is not simply a concession granted by the *Constitution on the Sacred Liturgy*; it is rather a theological imperative of liturgical renewal that the paschal mystery may be celebrated for all people and that all may be able to bring their talents to the service of the liturgy.

17. A renewed appreciation of the centrality of worship in the life of the Church with its emphasis on God's initiative in offering unity and peace to his people through his Son has increased our sensitivity to the need for greater ecumenical activity among all Christians. While working to overcome doctrinal and structural differences, Christians have been encouraged to pray together and to celebrate those rites which have been authorized for common celebration, especially celebrations of the Word of God, so that Christian unity might be more readily and effectively achieved.

18. In our own country, the rediscovery by other churches and ecclesial communities of liturgical sources and traditions common to our Christian heritage encourages all Christians. Recent liturgical reforms in many churches of North America, especially in the rites of the Eucharist, already point to a convergence and unity of liturgical prayer that gives hope for eventual doctrinal agreement. That many churches now use a similar three-year cycle of Scripture readings for the Eucharist based on *The Roman Lectionary* means that the majority of American Christians hear the same Word proclaimed each Sunday. The liturgy has already become a source of unity and a sign of hope for even greater unity.

The Eucharistic Mystery

At the Last Supper, on the night he was betrayed, our Savior instituted the eucharistic sacrifice of his Body and Blood. This he did in order to perpetuate the sacrifice of the Cross throughout the ages until he should come again, and so to entrust to his beloved Spouse, the Church, a memorial of his death and resurrection: a sacrament of love, a sign of unity, a bond of charity, a paschal banquet in which Christ is consumed, the mind is filled with grace, and a pledge of future glory is given to us (art. 47).

19. It is by means of the liturgy that the Church touches its members at the principal moments in their lives. Baptism and confirmation, penance and anointing, orders and marriage each reveal and reflect for Catholic Christians a particular facet of the paschal mystery of Christ and make possible a vital transforming relationship with Christ in his Church. However, it is the Eucharist which is the preeminent celebration of the paschal mystery. In the Eucharist, the victory of Christ over death is made manifest, enabling the community to be one with Christ and to give to the Father, in the unity of the Holy Spirit, all honor and glory.

20. The revised liturgical books, along with numerous decrees relating to the Eucharist have been issued in the past twenty years. These documents have resulted in a renewed appreciation of all aspects of eucharistic theology and spirituality: the celebration of the sacrifice of the Mass, the reception of Holy Communion, and the reservation of the Blessed Sacrament whether for the communion of the sick and dying or for devotion on the part of the faithful. Just as there has been a renewed appreciation of the Eucharist as both sacrifice and meal, so too the Eucharist is the "school of active love for neighbor," as Pope John Paul II stated in his letter *On the Mystery and Worship of the Eucharist:* "The Eucharist educates us to this love in a deeper way; it shows us, in fact, what value each person, our brother or sister, has in God's eyes, if Christ offers himself equally to each one, under the species of bread and wine" (no. 6). The Eucharist is therefore the bond of charity and unity which unites Christians in God's love.

21. The revised Order of Mass sets out a rite that is simple and uncluttered, a rite which underscores the unity and bond of the assembly. This enables the symbols to speak with clarity but also necessitates great care on the part of the ministers so that the celebrating community will be drawn to a reverent experience of the mysterious presence of Christ in word and sacrament. A recent evaluation project, centered on the structural elements of the Order of Mass, was sponsored by our Committee on the Liturgy and the Federation of Diocesan Liturgical Commissions. It provided an excellent opportunity both for liturgical formation concerning the Eucharist and for suggesting ways to improve the celebration.

22. Certainly, for Roman Catholics, one of the most significant achievements of the contemporary liturgical reform has been a retrieval of the riches of Sacred Scripture and the breadth of exposure to the Word of God set out in the new lectionary. The importance of the homily as an effective way of relating that Word to the contemporary lives of the community has been stressed by our Committee on Priestly Life and Ministry in its document *Fulfilled in Your Hearing: The Homily in the Sunday Assembly.* We urge those charged with the ministry of preaching the homily to study that document carefully and to make even greater efforts to preach a well-prepared homily at both Sunday and daily celebrations. Likewise, the restoration of the general

intercessions has offered an opportunity to relate the Eucharist to the universal Church and the world.

23. The introduction of vernacular languages into the liturgy has enabled the faithful to make the liturgy truly their own through greater understanding of the rites. We must also continue our efforts to preserve the treasures of our liturgical patrimony in Latin. Regular reception of Holy Communion as an integral part of the eucharistic celebration, a more frequent availability of communion under both kinds, and the extension of the practice of concelebration have also contributed to the desired effect of greater participation in the eucharistic liturgy. Nevertheless, as bishops charged with the promotion and custody of the liturgy, we urge priests, deacons and lay people to give more of their energy to an even greater and more profound participation in the Church's eucharistic mystery.

The Sacraments and Sacramentals

For well-disposed members of the faithful the liturgy of the sacraments and sacramentals sanctifies almost every event of their lives with the divine grace which flows from the paschal mystery of the passion, death, and resurrection of Christ. From this source all sacraments and sacramentals draw their power. There is scarcely any proper use of material things which cannot thus be directed toward the sanctification of men and the praise of God (art. 61).

24. In revising other aspects of the liturgy, efforts have been made to help the faithful develop an integral view of the sacraments and sacramentals as related components of Christian liturgy and as manifestations of the Church which is itself a sacramental community. The rites have been carefully related to the paschal mystery of Christ, to the Eucharist as the principal celebration of that mystery, and to the critical experiences of individual Christians and communities. The Liturgy of the Word has been restored as an integral component in all sacramental celebrations and other liturgical rites.

25. The *Rite of Christian Initiation of Adults* is only gradually being implemented and appreciated in our country, but already many parishes have discovered the benefits that are available not only to the newly initiated members of the Church but also to the parish community as a whole. Above all, the rites of initiation have affirmed the importance of a vital ecclesial community in the life of Christians and have shown the essential relationship among the doctrines Christians believe, the worship they carry out, and the responsible moral lives they live. The *Rite of Baptism for Children* also has stressed the importance of the faith community as the essential environment in which the infant grows toward a personal faith commitment as well as the primary responsibility of both parents and godparents for nurturing that faith in the life of the child.

26. Although pastoral, liturgical, and theological questions continue to be raised about the sacrament of confirmation, the introduction of a new rite for this sacrament of initiation has contributed to a renewed appreciation of the

role of the Holy Spirit in Christian life. As pastors and theologians continue to study the sacrament, it should be stressed that although the sacrament of confirmation may be an occasion for giving testimony to a religious commitment, it is above all the outpouring of the Holy Spirit, "the seal of the gift of the Holy Spirit," who operates in a powerful transforming way in the life of the baptized Christian.

27. Although intensive study and discussion preceded formulation of the revised *Rite of Penance,* pastoral problems continue to surround the sacrament. The new rites of reconciliation emphasize the reality of both personal and social sin in the Christian community and affirm that Christians are reconciled with God through the ministry of the Church. The fact is, however, that the importance of this sacrament has declined in the lives of many Christians, who are not likely to recover appreciation for it unless they are once again convinced of its role in their lives. In spite of the evil so obviously rampant in our world, a genuine sense of sin in our lives is often absent. Greater pastoral efforts must be directed toward a recovery of that sense of sin joined to a more profound understanding of the merciful forgiveness and reconciliation offered to us in Christ Jesus.

28. We urge our priests and those who have charge of catechesis to greater efforts in leading all of us toward a deeper faith in the healing power of God who, in his Son Jesus Christ, has reconciled us. That faith can only be deepened if we understand the existence of sin in our lives, "for the members of the Church . . . are exposed to temptation and often fall into the wretchedness of sin" (*Rite of Penance,* 3). As individuals and as a people, we must come before God seeking pardon and reconciliation. As individuals, we need to experience healing, reconciliation, and forgiveness, an experience that comes preeminently through the ministry of the Church. And as a people we must experience this same forgiveness:

> In fact, people frequently join together to commit injustice. But it is also true that they help each other in doing penance; freed from sin by the grace of Christ, they become, with all persons of good will, agents of justice and peace in the world (*Rite of Penance,* 5).

Therefore, not only should great attention be given to celebrations of the sacrament with individuals, but pastors should also assure communal celebrations of penance, especially in Advent and Lent, according to the norms of the rite, remembering that inner conversion embraces sorrow for sin and the intent to lead a new life.

29. The revised rites for the sick and the dying, known as *Pastoral Care of the Sick: Rites of Anointing and Viaticum,* convey with sensitivity and power the Lord's healing love. These rites have been deeply appreciated because of their pastoral sensitivity and the consolation and strength they have brought not only to the sick and dying but also to their families and friends in time of crisis. In keeping with the revised ritual, priests, deacons, other ministers, and those engaged in any ministry to the sick in homes, hospitals, and hospices should avail themselves of the riches and variety of these liturgical texts and rites, never contenting themselves with brief or "emergency" forms

228

unless absolutely necessary. The sick and the dying are members of the Body of Christ, greatly in need of the Church's pastoral care.

30. That same consolation has been experienced through the revised *Rite of Funerals* which carefully relates the death of Christians to the death and resurrection of Christ. Although the funeral rites honestly acknowledge the dread of death as a result of sin and evil in the world, above all they stress the right of Christians to hope for triumph over death because of Christ's resurrection. In that trust, we wish to make clear our responsibility to pray for the deceased so that freed fully from their sins they may experience the joy of God's light and love. At the same time, we urge continued effort by pastors, deacons, musicians, and other ministers toward better celebrations of the funeral rites so that these will console the living and demonstrate the community's faith in the saving death and resurrection of Christ.

31. In the revised rites of ordination, emphasis has been clearly placed on the candidate's responsibility for proclaiming the Word of God, presiding over the liturgy, and ministering the sacraments. An unclouded understanding of these basic ministries sets a firm foundation for other pastoral and liturgical services, fosters commitment on the part of the laity, and cultivates the development of Christian community. Of special significance has been the restoration of the permanent diaconate and the emergence of lay involvement in a number of ministries which were until recently performed only by the ordained clergy. Continuing education and formation in the liturgy is therefore all the more important for priests, deacons, and lay ministers. Liturgical renewal and spiritual growth need "mystagogues," men and women themselves well-versed in the ways of the Lord, to lead others to drink more deeply from the refreshing waters of divine life, always eager to live the Christian life as though newly baptized.

32. The revised rites for the sacrament of marriage acknowledge human friendship as one of the most basic symbols of God's loving presence to human life. In marriage, Christian men and women sacramentalize the covenant relationship of commitment between Christ and his Church, between God and humankind. Their love is expressed in their self-gift to each other, in children who manifest the creative nature of love, and in their witness of fidelity in a world where lifetime commitments are increasingly rare. The revised rites and liturgical texts for Christian marriage underscore the totality of the mutual gift involved in this sacrament which St. Paul calls a "great mystery" and Pope John Paul II recently called a "memorial," for marriage calls to mind the great works of God in creation. Likewise, marriage is a communion which specifically represents Christ's incarnation and the mystery of the covenant. For all that is human in marital love signifies the intimacy of our relationship with God (*Address to a General Audience,* 3 November 1979). When couples are preparing for marriage, their attention should be directed toward the proper choice of liturgical texts, music, and rites. They should also be shown how the *Rite of Marriage* itself expresses the bond and covenant into which they are about to enter.

33. In the Church, the vocation to Christian marriage is complemented and strengthened by the vocation to celibacy ratified in the revised *Rites of Religious Profession* and the *Rites of Consecration to a Life of Virginity.* These rites, so little known to most Catholics, reflect the positive value of celibate love.

Liturgical Prayer

The Church, by celebrating the Eucharist and by other means, especially the celebration of the divine office, is ceaselessly engaged in praising the Lord and interceding for the salvation of the entire world (art. 83).

34. By both word and example, the Lord Jesus taught his disciples that prayer is necessary for Christian believers. Like the prayer of Jesus himself, it should flow from the experience of living intimately in the presence of God. Such a communion is one in which we, as God's people, share in the divine life and love and, in turn, respond to these gifts with praise and thanksgiving, petition and longing. To foster that spirit of prayer the Liturgy of the Hours or Divine Office has been reformed. Although a special mandate has been given to bishops, priests, and deacons to celebrate the Liturgy of the Hours, it is also clearly desired that all the faithful take part in this liturgical prayer of the Church, especially Morning and Evening Prayer. The theological and liturgical thrust of the Liturgy of the Hours should be a model and an ideal for the way in which all Catholic Christians pray.

35. This communal experience of liturgical prayer will be new for many; its effectiveness will depend to a great extent on liturgical formation and the experience of well-structured and prayerfully executed celebrations. Unfortunately it must be acknowledged that the revised Liturgy of the Hours, which has been designed especially for communal celebration, has not yet become a vital prayer form for many priests and religious who do not reside in liturgically structured communities. In order that extended psalmody and patristic readings be experienced as inspiring sources of strength for ministry, it is necessary to provide adequate scriptural, theological, and liturgical background. Similarly, more realistic efforts must be made to adapt the Liturgy of the Hours to the actual situations which prevail in parishes. Where the responsibility to pray in the spirit of the Church has been taken seriously and time and effort have been put into the preparation and celebration of the Liturgy of the Hours, the experience has been very rewarding. This is an area which calls for much more attention on the part of pastors and prayer leaders in our Catholic communities.

Liturgical Time

Once each week, on the day which she has called the Lord's Day, Holy Mother Church keeps the memory of the Lord's resurrection. She also celebrates it once every year, together with his blessed passion, at Easter, that most solemn of all feasts.

In the course of the year, moreover, she unfolds the whole mystery of Christ from the incarnation and nativity to the ascension, to Pentecost and the expectation of the blessed hope of the coming of the Lord. Thus recalling the mysteries of the redemption, she opens up to the faithful the riches of her Lord's powers and merits (art. 102).

36. The life of the Church is sanctified not only by the Liturgy of the Hours but also by the celebration of the liturgical year. In revising the liturgical calendar, each liturgical season is focused on the paschal mystery of Christ as the center of all liturgical worship. Hence, the feasts of the Lord, especially the celebration of his death and resurrection, have been given preference. These mysteries are celebrated in a special way during the Paschal Triduum but also on Sunday which, since early centuries, has been observed as the "Lord's Day."

37. Lent has been restored to its proper observance as a preparation for the celebration of the paschal mystery. The primary features of this season are the purification and enlightenment of catechumens and works of prayer, alms-giving or service to others, and penance, especially fasting and abstinence. Through the celebration of the forty days of Lent and the fifty days of Easter, the main lines of the Church's Year of the Lord are clearly established; it is essentially a celebration of the saving work of Christ.

38. Throughout the rest of the year, the various aspects of that saving mystery unfold. Of special importance is the celebration of Christmas. During the Christmas season, the mysteries highlighted in the gospel infancy narratives are celebrated. The solemnity of the Epiphany of the Lord reveals the universal saving mission of Christ the Messiah. The feast of the Baptism of the Lord, which marks the beginning of Christ's public ministry, brings the Christmas season to an end. The season of Advent is celebrated with joyful expectancy as a reminder of God's fidelity and care culminating in the first coming of Christ, and as preparation for his second coming at the end of time.

39. The Sundays of the Year ("Ordinary Time") and the feasts and sol-emnities of the Lord are always celebrations of the same paschal mystery commemorated in the "great seasons." Yet, all too often little attention is given to these "ordinary times." In view of the increasing secularization of the Lord's Day, we suggest that full celebration of the Sundays of the Year be promoted, since they are essential and crucial to the development and deepening of the Christian life. In addition, we urge our people and pastors to make greater efforts in planning the whole liturgical year in such a way that each season, memorial, feast, and solemnity is given its proper significance and importance. Furthermore, we must all be reminded of the close link between liturgy and devotion, liturgy and popular piety. The devotion which surrounds the solemnity of Corpus Christi, for example, is a model of the proper relationship between liturgy and popular piety in the liturgical year. True and authentic piety can only help us to be more devoted to the liturgy.

40. Special care has been taken to stress the role of Mary, the Mother of God, in the life of the Church, as we have stated many times, especially in our pastoral letter on the Blessed Virgin Mary (*Behold Your Mother: Woman of Faith*, 21 November 1973). The great Marian feasts and solemnities of the revised calendar relate the life of Mary to the mystery of her Son; in this way, she is honored both as the Mother of the Church and as a model for Christian discipleship.

41. The new calendar significantly reduces the number of saints' days so that the mystery of Christ may not be overshadowed. The *Constitution on the Sacred Liturgy* prescribed that only saints of universal importance should be proposed to the whole Church for obligatory commemoration. Every nation,

indeed every diocese, has its own particular and proper calendar celebrating certain mysteries, saints, and days of prayer.

42. In the United States, for example, the Church honors Mary in a special way under the title of the Immaculate Conception as patroness of the United States and under the title of Our Lady of Guadalupe as patroness of the Americas. American holy men and women such as Isaac Jogues and companions, Kateri Tekakwitha, Elizabeth Ann Seton, John Neumann, Frances Cabrini and others testify to holiness in America. Thanksgiving Day, while not a liturgical feast, nevertheless is celebrated liturgically by American Catholics as a day of prayer and thanksgiving for the gifts God has bestowed upon us.

43. Efforts must also be made to relate the liturgical year to the secular calendar so that the ordinary lives of Christians may be sanctified. Ecumenical discussions have raised a number of important questions concerning the possibility of a fixed date for Easter and a common calendar shared by various churches and ecclesial communities; these are questions that require and deserve further study by the whole Church.

Liturgical Music, Art, and Architecture

Holy Mother Church has always been the patron of the fine arts and has never sought their noble ministry, to the end especially that all things set apart for use in divine worship should be worthy, becoming, and beautiful, signs and symbols of things supernatural (art. 122).

44. In matters of liturgical music, art, and architecture, only directives of a very general nature have been issued in the past twenty years; and rightly so, for the creation of art is something that can be neither clearly defined nor readily mandated. In this regard, our Committee on the Liturgy has issued statements which have been well received and proven very useful, especially *Music in Catholic Worship; Liturgical Music Today;* and *Environment and Art in Catholic Worship*. The norms and guidelines of these documents should be followed by pastors and all those engaged in the liturgical arts. Our churches must be homes for the arts and houses pleasing to the Lord.

45. Artists, architects, artisans, and musicians who work for the Church should be competent in their own right and should have a clear understanding of the theology of the liturgy and the role of their proper arts in liturgical celebrations. We must continue to search for appropriate ways to enrich our liturgies both by retrieving our artistic tradition and using it appropriately, being open to new forms of the artistic imagination, and by utilizing the cultural heritage of the diverse ethnic and racial groups of the Church in America. While we continue to make efforts to alleviate world poverty, it is important that some of the Church's material resources, even in the case of financially impoverished communities, be allocated to the development of the liturgical arts because they nourish the human spirit and bear witness to the preeminence of the sacred in human life. They enable Christians to grow more

and more into that holy temple wherein God can dwell and empower people to transform the world in his name.

Conclusions

> Mother Church earnestly desires that all the faithful should be led to that full, conscious, and active participation in liturgical celebrations which is demanded by the very nature of the liturgy, and to which the Christian people, "a chosen race, a royal priesthood, a holy nation, a redeemed people" (1 Pt 2:9, 4–5) have a right and obligation by reason of their baptism (art. 14).

46. There have been many significant liturgical gains in the past twenty years, but there remain many areas of unfinished liturgical business. Liturgical reform must move more and more toward genuine Christian renewal. That means above all that we must continue to make efforts to appreciate and open our hearts to the spiritual and prayerful dimensions of the liturgy.

47. Much progress has been made over the past generation through great personal and pastoral effort to help people develop a sense of communal prayer. Yet, in many cases, piety continues to be individualistic and untouched by the richness and treasures of the liturgy. Even specialized programs in spiritual renewal are at times only minimally related to experience of Christian worship and sacraments.

48. The liturgy should be the primary school for Christian prayer and spirituality, enabling Christians to live justly, peacefully, and charitably in the world. Often, we fail to understand that the celebration of the liturgy is the Church's ministry of worship and prayer, calling people to conversion and contemplation, inviting them into communion with God and with each other. And the more professional we become in the area of liturgy, the more we may be tempted to become preoccupied with external forms and aesthetic experiences. The end result may simply be a new form of ritualism.

49. Liturgical ministers themselves must be people of prayer. If sometimes there is a gap between liturgical ministers and the larger Christian community, it may be because the ministers may not appear to be praying people. Liturgical ministers must be spiritually and personally involved in the mystery of Christ, and they must show outwardly this involvement if they are to lead people into that same experience.

50. If, in the last analysis, a great part of the responsibility for liturgical formation and renewal falls on the individual Christian, there is nevertheless a need for help from others in this regard. Parish liturgy committees, diocesan liturgical commissions, and offices of worship also have a great task before them to continue the work begun twenty years ago when the *Constitution on the Sacred Liturgy* was first promulgated. Parish liturgy committees should assist priests, deacons, and other liturgical ministers such as readers and ministers of communion in fulfilling their roles. At the same time, through planning and careful attention to the norms of each of the rites, they will help

lead the assembly toward a more profound worship of God and communion with Christ and one another.

51. The diocesan liturgical commission or office of worship must assist the bishop in carrying out his functions as promoter and guardian of the liturgical life of the diocese. First convened by our Committee on the Liturgy in 1968, the Federation of Diocesan Liturgical Commissions, especially through the annual national meeting of liturgical commissions and worship office personnel, should continue to assist us on a national level. In this way, all those engaged in the great work of liturgical renewal will ensure not only the continuation of "that full, conscious, and active participation in liturgical celebrations," but also help the Church always to be a Church of pilgrims, ever renewed and ever being renewed in its life and worship.

52. We must continue to struggle to overcome our selfishness, our closed-mindedness, our indifference, our timidity, and our lack of trust in God and one another. Both Christian life and worship presuppose community—a willingness to learn from others and to be open to others in generosity and love. Only on such a base can liturgy really be said to affect and deepen the sense of community. In its language, symbol, style, and spirit, today's liturgy is a growing sign and instrument of community, people at one with each other and with God.

53. This score of years has witnessed the most sweeping changes in liturgical life that the Catholic Church has known in centuries. When we observe similar shifts in culture, values, and attitudes elsewhere throughout the world, we can have no doubt that the Council acted under the guidance of the Holy Spirit. Liturgical flexibility and adaptation have made it possible for the Church's proclamation of the Good News to challenge our times with a realistic chance for a hearing and an impact. Above all, the liturgical reform has helped the Church to come into the presence of the all-holy God in languages, signs, and gestures spoken and made by contemporary Catholics without loss of its tradition—truly a gift of the Holy Spirit.

54. For older generations, acceptance of liturgical changes has been a true venture in faith; it is a sign of the Church's vitality that the vast majority has endorsed and taken to heart the reforms initiated by the Council. For a newer generation, the provisions of the *Constitution on the Sacred Liturgy* have offered hope that worship and world, liturgy and life, can be harmonized and truly become the gift of the Father who has loved us through the Son and empowers us to return that love in the Spirit.

55. Mindful of our own responsibilities as bishops to carry out the office of sanctification in the Church, we pledge renewed efforts to continue the great work of the Council in liturgical renewal and in the renewal of prayer, penance, and worship in the life of the Church. This anniversary and this holy year of the redemption must lead us all to a "renewed and deepened *Spirit of Advent*," a prayerful spirit of expectation, as our Holy Father John Paul II reminds us (*Open the Doors to the Redeemer,* 9). We urge, therefore, our helpers in the ministry, priests and deacons, our lay ministers in the liturgy, our liturgists, but above all our liturgical assemblies to engage themselves continually with faith and trust in that holy work which is the liturgy, and always to remember these words of the *Constitution on the Sacred Liturgy* as we await the coming of the Lord:

In the earthly liturgy we take part in a foretaste of that heavenly liturgy which is celebrated in the holy city of Jerusalem toward which we journey as pilgrims, where Christ is sitting at the right hand of God, minister of the holies and of the true tabernacle. With all the warriors of the heavenly army we sing a hymn of glory to the Lord; venerating the memory of the saints, we hope for some part and fellowship with them; we eagerly await the Savior, our Lord Jesus Christ, until he our life shall appear and we too will appear with him in glory (art. 8).

34

Twenty Years of Liturgical Renewal in the United States of America: Assessments and Prospects

Report, Chairman of the Bishops' Committee on the Liturgy
Rome, September 30, 1984

(See also nos. 9, 27, 28, 33)

This statement, in the form of a report, is a second response of the Bishops' Committee on the Liturgy to the 1983 anniversary of the *Constitution on the Liturgy*. The first response was the 1983 pastoral statement prepared for the NCCB, *The Church at Prayer: A Holy Temple of the Lord*. The occasion for the report was a congress held a year later in Rome (October 23–28, 1984), to which the Congregation for Divine Worship had invited the presidents and secretaries of national liturgical commissions throughout the world.

For this congress, the American episcopal committee submitted two reports under the title given above. The first and lengthier report, not reprinted here, described the current activities and personnel of the committee and responded at length to a series of questions posed to all the national commissions by the Roman congregation. The questions were listed under several headings: languages and liturgical books; adaptation of the liturgy to local cultures and traditions; pastoral liturgy; other problems; and expectations of the Congregation for Divine Worship by the national commissions.

In addition, a synthesis was prepared on behalf of the committee and presented both in writing and orally by the chairman, Bishop John S. Cummins of Oakland, who participated in the congress together with the executive director of the committee's secretariat, the Reverend John A. Gurrieri.

Both reports are appended to the collected volume of the committee's *Newsletter* for the years 1981–1985 (Washington, D.C.: USCC Office of Publishing and Promotion Services, 1987); they also appear in the proceedings of the congress issued by the Congregation for Divine Worship, *Atti del Convegno dei Presidenti e Segretari delle Commissioni Nazionali di Liturgia* (Padua, 1986; pp. 315–340 and 340–348, respectively). The same volume of proceedings includes a report from the International Commission on English in the Liturgy (pp. 881–893), since ICEL, like the other international or "mixed" commissions, was also invited to be represented at the congress. Only the second report from the Bishops' Committee on the Liturgy is reprinted here.

The special value of this statement is its clear and realistic, even pragmatic, presentation of liturgical renewal and progress in the United States twenty years after the great beginnings in the conciliar constitution. It was an opportunity to draw back a little and to describe the realities in the Church of the United States in terms that could be appreciated universally. Equally, it was an opportunity to speak explicitly about the needs of the future (in the section, "Specific Pastoral Questions")—both those matters that the committee can influence and others in which the Congregation for Divine Worship was asked to move forward.

The congress itself provided an occasion for formal addresses and communications, as well as for the participants from the principal language groups to meet separately and offer their respective contributions in the form of recommendations. In previous years, the International Commission on English in the Liturgy had sponsored three meetings of the secretaries and other staff executives of national liturgical commissions from countries where English is spoken. In Rome, in 1984, this meeting of the English-language group was a different kind of opportunity, under the auspices of the Roman congregation, for both presidents and secretaries of the English-language countries to come together. From this group, a brief statement was formulated that is worth quoting, as the common submission of representatives from countries where English is spoken; it too appears in the proceedings or *Atti* of the congress (pp. 947–948):

The group [of presidents and secretaries from English-language countries] was composed of representatives of 32 conferences of bishops; 27 bishops, 29 secretaries. After discussion, the following resolutions were proposed and adopted:

1. It was unanimously resolved that the Congregation for Divine Worship be respectfully requested to convoke a plenarium of its members, in keeping with the norms of *Regimini Ecclesiae,* and that the *Consulta* be called together beforehand to prepare for such a meeting. And further, again in keeping with those same norms, a plenarium be called every year.

2. It was resolved that the Congregation for Divine Worship be informed of the grave concern, regret, and dismay with which news of the letter of 3 October 1984 of the Congregation concerning the concession of the Missal of 1962 ("Tridentine Mass") was received. Among the particular concerns voiced by the English-speaking group were the following:

—The concession appears to be a movement away from the ecclesiology of the Second Vatican Council with its insistence on the involvement of the whole People of God (according to their different functions and ministries) in the Eucharist.

—The indult seems to give support to those who have resisted the liturgical renewal and seems to demonstrate a lack of consideration for all those who, at great personal cost and with great difficulty, did in fact accept the liturgical reform and who, in time, whole-heartedly embraced the desires of the Council.

—The concession seems to violate the collegial sense of the world-wide episcopate, 98 percent of whom, when asked their opinion by the Congregation on this question, responded that this was not a problem in the Church but rather only the concern of a tiny minority who have contrived to create the impression that it is a much greater issue than in fact it is.

—While the Apostolic See by law is required to confirm the decisions of episcopal conferences in liturgical matters, this concession appears to be a subversion of that principle in that the responsibility of both the Apostolic See and an episcopal conference is removed, and the authority over so important a liturgical question is left to the local bishop; in this case neither the *approbatio* of an episcopal conference nor the *confirmatio* of the Apostolic See is required.

3. It was unanimously resolved that a strong statement reaffirming the work of all those engaged in liturgical renewal according to the principles of Vatican II is respectfully requested of His Holiness Pope John Paul II. We ask that the rights and competence of the local Church to take initiatives in matters of divine worship be clearly endorsed. Local bishops, conferences of bishops, liturgical commissions, and all others engaged in the work of liturgical renewal need the support and encouragement of the Holy Father and of a strong, efficient, and well-staffed Congregation for Divine Worship.

4. It was resolved that the recent division of the Congregation for the Sacraments and Divine Worship posed a potential threat to the ongoing work of liturgical renewal because of a seeming return to a preconciliar understanding of the sacraments. As the work of Christ in his Church, as the "summit and source of the Church's activity" the liturgy must not be relegated to pure concerns of ritual and rubrics. Recent experience with letters concerning general absolution and reconciliation rooms confirms these misgivings, since the interpretation on these questions came from Congregation for the Sacraments rather than the Congregation for Divine Worship. On the local level, these matters are handled by the national liturgical commissions and diocesan liturgical commissions.

5. It was unanimously resolved that the Congregation for Divine Worship should address the question of cultural adaptation in the immediate future by:

—reaffirming the "Magna Charta" of liturgical adaptation, *Sacrosanctum Concilium,* nos 37–40;

—responding to the past legitimate proposals and requests for liturgical adaptation submitted by various episcopal conferences;

—encouraging the reestablishment of centers of liturgical experimentation and adaptation on the level of the local Church.

6. It was unanimously resolved that the Congregation be requested to choose its consultors from around the world, assuring the nomination not only of Europeans and North Americans, but also experts from Asia, Africa, Oceania, and Latin America.

7. It was resolved by a majority of those present, six members

being in opposition, that the intervention of Bishop John S. Cummins (USA) concerning *Ministeria quaedam* be acted upon by the Congregation, viz., that since the ministries envisaged in that document are specifically defined as lay ministries, they should be open to all lay persons, men and women.

These resolutions have a distinctive character. As is evident, they are expressed more strongly than would be likely if they came from a single conference of bishops or from a single national liturgical commission. They reveal some of the tensions existing in the relationships of ecclesiastical authorities in matters liturgical. Although not emanating from the American committee, the resolutions reflect some of the committee's concerns—and also the influence of the American participants in the 1984 Roman congress (specifically in no. 6 of the resolutions).

Resolution no. 2 is the longest and the most fully argued. It expresses an American concern and one equally felt in other countries where English is a liturgical language, although the issue of the so-called Tridentine Mass is not a language question. Perhaps, the contrast between the (limited) concession of the preconciliar rite of Mass in 1984 and the much earlier concession of communion in the hand needs to be spelled out.

The revival of a venerable ritual practice, receiving the holy Eucharist in the hand, could hardly be challenged on the basis of incongruity with the liturgical renewal. As noted in commentary on the 1978 proposal, "Communion under Both Kinds," the Apostolic See had canvassed the opinion of the Catholic episcopate on that subject, only to find that there was substantial division among the bishops, about 60 percent generally opposed, 40 percent generally favorable. The Roman instruction in that case took a middle course, maintaining the existing discipline but respecting the large minority and leaving the decision to the conferences of bishops (*Memoriale Domini,* May 29, 1969: DOL 260).

The decision concerning the return to the preconciliar rite of Mass in certain well-circumscribed cases was announced just before the 1984 congress, as resolution no. 2 notes. It was in sharp contrast to the 1969 decision on communion in the hand: difficult indeed to reconcile with the letter or spirit of the *Constitution on the Liturgy,* contrary to the judgment of some 98 percent of the episcopate.

This, together with other issues, rather obviously colored the character of a congress that was highly positive in its purpose and basic orientation. The report, given in writing and orally by the chairman of the Bishops' Committee on the Liturgy, stands also as a positive contribution to the dialogue of the particular churches and the Apostolic See—and sums up the situation of the liturgical renewal in the United States two decades after the *Constitution on the Liturgy.*

Introduction

The twenty years that have passed since *Sacrosanctum Concilium* was solemnly promulgated on December 4, 1963, at the Second Vatican Council

239

have made prophetic for the Church in the United States the words spoken by Pope Paul VI on that occasion: "The first achievement of the Council must be treasured as something that will quicken and put its imprint on the life of the Church. The Church is above all a worshiping society, a praying community."[1]

Catholics in the United States of America responded enthusiastically to the promulgation of the *Constitution on the Sacred Liturgy*. They embraced the postconciliar reforms that renewed the use of Scripture in prayer, introduced the vernacular, called for vocal and interior participation, and initiated the development of ministries. Pastors supported by bishops, liturgical committees, and resources embarked on the new adventure. In 1963, the ground was already fertile for reform since many American Catholics were involved in the liturgical movement or were affected by its goals and hopes. The "spiritual treasury" uncovered by the postconciliar reforms as a result of the implementation of the decrees of the Council changed the life of the Church in this country. Though hard for some, met with hesitancy by others, and controverted at times, worship once again became the center of Christian faith and practice.

Our report shows only as a partial reflection of the vitality that is characterized, and continues to characterize, the implementation of the Church's liturgical program wherein lies "the secret of a new vitality for the Church's tradition, the face of the Church's beauty, the expression of the Church's interior and universal unity."[2] The report can only allude to the countless initiatives and achievements of local churches, clergy, diocesan liturgical commissions, the various centers of pastoral liturgy, and the many other societies, organizations, institutes, and schools that have contributed so greatly to the renewal of the Church's liturgy and the many contributions of thousands of individual Catholics who work untiringly and with great love for the liturgy.

The Importance of Sunday Worship and Active Participation

Historically, the greatest liturgical concern of the Church in the United States has been to create the most favorable conditions possible for the dignified and devout celebration of the Sunday Eucharist in a society that was for many years inimical to the Roman Catholic Church. Such was the case only a few years after the founding of the Republic, when John Carroll, the first bishop of Baltimore, in his pastoral letter of 1792 urged clergy and laity to greater efforts for a more "dignified" Sunday worship celebrated with "all reverence and becoming respect," in which nothing "used for the Holy Sacrifice would be of the meanest materials."[3]

Sunday worship and the celebration of the feasts and solemnities of the

---

[1] Pope Paul VI, *Address to the Fathers at the End of the Second Period of Vatican Council II*, 4 December 1963: AAS 56 (1964) 31–40. English translation from *Documents on the Liturgy, 1963-1979: Conciliar, Papal, and Curial Texts* (=DOL) (Collegeville, Minn., 1982), 134.

[2] Pope Paul VI, *Address at a General Audience*, 6 August 1975 (DOL 550).

[3] Pastoral Letter of the Right Reverend John Carroll, Bishop of Baltimore, 28 May 1792, Statute V in *Pastoral Letters of the United States Catholic Bishops* (Volumes I-IV), Volume I: 1792–1940 (Washington D.C.: USCC Office of Publishing and Promotion Services, 1984), p. 23.

year formed the basis and nourished the spirituality of American Catholic life in early colonial times and in the first fifty years of American independence. A spirituality based in the liturgy was the legacy of our English Catholic origins. Because of that heritage, the fullest and most active kind of participation in the liturgy, according to the norms of the day, was always encouraged and supported by the bishops as the keystone for other dimensions of Catholic life.[4] In many respects, this central role of Sunday in the life of American Roman Catholics was reinforced by a similar concern for the Lord's day within American Protestantism. The tradition, therefore, of committed Sunday observance among American Catholics is rooted in the heritage of the colonizers and also in the pluralism of American society. Such commitment to the Lord's day was a factor enabling Catholicism to grow steadily in the more than two hundred years of American history. Pope John Paul II recently, in an address to a group of American bishops, paid tribute to the faith of American Catholics when he stated: "Throughout the United States there has been a superb history of eucharistic participation by the people, and for this we must all thank God."[5]

Because of this strong historical tradition of Sunday observance, the liturgical reforms of *Sacrosanctum Concilium* found a sure and certain footing in our country. Active participation in the liturgy very quickly became widespread since the liturgical movement had already influenced the Church on a grass-roots level in the parishes in preconciliar days through the "dialogue Mass," the use of vernacular hymns, Latin participation through the use of "hand missals," and many other factors.

Such participation affected all other dimensions of Christian existence. Worshipers discovered that the liturgy is the model for participation in the life and ministry of the Church on every level of its existence. Sunday worship, therefore, had a particular importance and enveloped not only singing and making the acclamations in the liturgy but assisting in the preparation of Sunday worship through parish liturgy planning teams and groups. Participation, from the very beginning of the reforms, also meant that lay persons would fulfill those ministries open to them, such as reader, minister of communion, cantor, psalmist, musician, and other responsibilities. Lay liturgical ministries, therefore, quickly became rooted in the Church in the United States and continued to grow and have an effect on all levels of Catholic life. Ministers developed an excitement and appreciation for worship. They have grown in understanding their tasks as they grow in a new level of shared faith because of such large numbers involved. The effect has been felt in the parishes.

Additionally, liturgy intertwines with programs of spiritual renewal at the parish and diocesan levels. Some of these are worldwide such as the Cursillo, Marriage Encounter, and the Charismatic movement. Some are more dis-

---

[4]The decrees of various councils testify to such an outlook. See *Concilia Provincilia Baltimori habita in anno 1829 usque ad annum 1849, Editio altera* (Baltimore, 1851); *Concilii Plenarii Baltimorensis II. In Ecclesia Metropolitana Baltimorensis a die VII. ad diem XXI. Octobris A.D. MDCCCLXVI, habiti et a Sede Apostolica recogniti, Acta et Decreta Concilii Baltimorensis Tertii, A.D. MDCCCLXXXIV* (Baltimore, 1886).

[5]Pope John Paul II, *Address to the Bishops of the United States of America during an Ad Limina Visit, 9 July 1983* in *Ad Limina Addresses*, April 15–December 3, 1983 (Washington, D.C.: USCC Office of Publishing and Promotion Services, 1984).

tinctively American such as RENEW and Genesis II. Others are very local, particularly the growing and intense interest in the Scriptures. Some of these are aimed particularly at young people and have been richly productive. Special mention should be given to the Rite of Christian Initiation of Adults that adds to the Church through its neophytes and candidates for full admission but renews the parish through the ministry of sponsors and catechumenal teams.

Active participation in the liturgy is also greatly fostered by the Federation of Diocesan Liturgical Commissions, established by our conference seventeen years ago. Through the resources of the national federation, each diocesan liturgical commission is able to share its experience and efforts with others. Under the leadership of the federation and our committee, the commissions meet annually to consider a special theme and offer suggestions to the conference for its actions. Such participation in the work of our committee by the diocesan commissions greatly facilitates a national effort for liturgical renewal.

Liturgy and Language

The introduction of the vernacular has served us well toward conscious participation in the liturgy, especially for devout participation in the worship of God. Its introduction, perhaps, forced us to make too rapid a change, leading to a neglect of Latin hymns and overshadowing, as well as leaving aside, many of our popular devotions. That temporary eclipse is moving back into view now. What has been of great benefit is a vernacular not just in Sunday liturgy but in the Liturgy of the Hours, deeply appreciated by our religious communities and becoming a frequent occurrence in parishes and other institutions.

Our conference is grateful to the International Commission on English in the Liturgy, the joint commission of Catholic bishops' conferences. Nearly all the liturgical books issued by the Apostolic See have been translated by ICEL, approved by our conference, and received the confirmation of the Apostolic See. Prior to canonical approbation, the translations undergo a thoroughly careful and widespread consultation. With few exceptions, the translations have been praised for their quality and high standards, an important fact when one considers that ICEL is charged with the task of producing translations for countries with literary traditions that vary from nation to nation. This task points to a subject that is very important to our committee: the development of liturgical language.

The production of vernacular translations over the past twenty years has demonstrated that the development of a contemporary "liturgical English" is an arduous task, subject to development and evolution. Other Christian churches in the English-speaking world engaged in revising their liturgical books are also aware of this fact. Their rich experience can be of great assistance to our own Church as it prepares new texts in a liturgical English that is simultaneously contemporary and reverent, accessible to all and able to be sung or spoken by the ministers and the assembly.

One should also add the following point with regard to liturgical language. As an international language of business, diplomacy, and the arts, English, perhaps more than any other European language, is subject to a rapid evolution expressed in new styles, phrases, words, and sensitivities. Among these are problems that relate to gender, race, and ethnicity. Liturgical translations must be sensitive to these questions, which have their roots in cultural history rather than in language or theology per se. For nearly a decade, our conference has been concerned about this pastoral problem. Initiatives have been taken to avoid even the appearance of offensive or insensitive language that may be construed as racist, anti-Semitic, or sexist.

From colonial times, the United States has been a nation of many peoples. The liturgy is celebrated in countless languages Sunday after Sunday. Since 1964, with the approval of the Apostolic See, local ordinaries have been able to permit non-English vernaculars that were approved by a competent ecclesiastical authority of that language. Our conference, too, has faced the situation of the languages of native Americans. Two native languages, Navajo and Choctaw, have been approved of by the bishops and the Apostolic See. Action is presently being considered with regard to other indigenous languages, and greater pastoral efforts are being made to relate language and cultural adaptation.

In the case of the use of Spanish in the liturgy, several versions of other episcopal conferences are available to us. However, a substantially uniform version has been deemed pastorally desirable by our conference for a variety of reasons, not the least of which are the continuing migration of peoples from Central and South America and the development and the need to unify, liturgically, Catholics of Hispanic descent.

Cultural Adaptation of the Liturgy

The fathers of the Council made very wise provision for the adaptation of the liturgy to the culture and genius of peoples. By its nature, liturgy in the vernacular demands adaptation and inculturation. Liturgical adaptation to the general culture of the United States over the last two decades has been limited primarily to those liturgical texts, ritual elements, and rubrical directives that the liturgical books themselves permit. Adaptation of the liturgy in our country has not gone as far as what was envisioned or proposed in *Sacrosanctum Concilium*. The need to inculturate the liturgy in the United States is now more evident after twenty years of experience.

While our conference has made minor adaptations in the Mass, the Rite of Funerals, the Rite of Marriage, the Rite of Baptism for Children, the Rite of Penance, Pastoral Care of the Sick, the Rite of Confirmation, and the Liturgy of the Hours, we must give attention over the next several years to an examination of these and other rites in terms of greater pastoral application and future adaptation according to the norms of *Sacrosanctum Concilium,* nos. 37–40.

One final point worthy of consideration in this regard is the influence of other Christian churches and ecclesial communities. Ecumenism has given rise to new and unforeseen questions. The Roman liturgical reform has influenced nearly every major church or ecclesial community in this country. Most churches use an adapted form of the *Roman Lectionary* in their eucharistic rites or are contemplating its use. The Roman eucharistic prayers, collects, and other liturgical texts and rites have deeply influenced the liturgical reform of these churches. Through dialogue, research, ecumenical-liturgical societies, joint projects such as the proposed *Order of Readings* of the North American Consultation on Common Texts, a healthy cross-fertilization of ideas and principles takes place among the churches of the United States of America. The unexpected progress of this facet of liturgical development is a cause for great rejoicing and one of the unexpected fruits of the conciliar reforms.

May we suggest that a process of regulated experimentation be considered. There seems to be value in trying out adaptations in genuine liturgical settings. Such a process should lead to very authentic developments.

Specific Pastoral Questions

From the point of view of our committee in the United States, we suggest the following areas for consideration:

1. *Liturgical formation of ministers.* While commendations are in order for many seminaries, lay ministry programs, and parish developments, this area still needs a great deal of attention. The focus obviously must be on the continuing education of priests and deacons, especially in leadership style. Lay people are making significant progress in their understanding of roles and the competence with which they serve. There is room here for greater development.

2. *The importance of the homily.* While the history of the Church in the United States indicates strong episcopal leadership in urging improved quality of preaching, the performance has evidenced often enough a mediocre practice. The understanding is growing of the integral place that preaching has in the liturgy. Much attention has been brought to this question. The Bishops' Committee on Priestly Life and Ministry has developed a document on preaching. There are workshops throughout the country on this matter. There remains, too, despite the clear statement from *Inaestimabile Donum,* occasional inquiry on the part of many religious and some laity for nonordained preachers.

3. *The importance of the assembly.* Though conscious, full, and active participation is a highly regarded value and in many places an achieved goal, there still remains much experience of the passive congregation and the attitude on the part of some liturgical planners that leaves the assembly largely in the position of spectators.

4. *Authentic liturgical signs and symbols.* Liturgical reform and renewal require more authentic signs and symbols in our worship, as noted especially in the *General Instruction of the Roman Missal* and in the *praenotanda* of other ritual books. There is a growing desire in our country that the signs, symbols, gestures, and other elements be more genuine so that their very authenticity may lead worshipers to a truer understanding and faith in what they are doing in liturgy. (The controversy over "eucharistic bread" in our country was symptomatic of that yearning for authenticity.) Signs and symbols as well as liturgical text bear the Church's tradition, therefore, "renewal requires the opening up of our symbols, especially the fundamental ones of

244

bread and wine, water, oil, the laying on of hands until we can experience all of them as authentic and appreciate their symbolic use."[6]

We are also cognizant that the ministers of worship must be formed and educated to a greater sensitivity to artistic expression as well as to symbols, gestures, and signs. Our committee has produced guidelines in its books, *Music in Catholic Worship, Liturgical Music Today,* and *Environment and Art in Catholic Worship,* in order to give greater encouragement to artists and the place of art in liturgy.

5. *The role of the laity in liturgy.* Lay men and women in the United States, as already noted, participated well in the liturgy and many thousands are involved in the several liturgical ministries open to them. The shortage of priests in seminaries of the country has made the need for lay persons to assume leadership in liturgical ministry an issue, and one that may become more pressing as the years go by. While vocations to priesthood remain the fundamental issue in this regard, it may become necessary to address the liturgical dimensions of this question more directly through clear guidelines on how a conference of bishops may deal with the matter on the level of the local church.

6. *Extraordinary ministers of the Eucharist.* Thousands of lay persons have been trained for this ministry. They assist at the Sunday Eucharist and, more importantly, they bring communion to the sick and the homebound on a weekly and, often enough, on a daily basis in collaboration with the priests and deacons. However, apart from these incidences and the context of our experience, it is felt that consideration should be given to the use of special ministers of the Eucharist in certain circumstances when there are enough priests and deacons present as a sign of the Church's diversity of ministries and gifts among the baptized, both men and women.

7. *The place of women in liturgy.* American women are active in every level of society, whether in business, the arts, politics, or other areas of life. Women have played significant roles in the life of other Christian churches and movements in the United States since the seventeenth century. Catholic women especially have influenced the life of the Church in the United States in the establishment of the Catholic school system and the Catholic hospital system. The contribution of women religious has been immeasurable. It is within this context that the role of women in the liturgy in the United States must be understood.

With few exceptions, women have equal access to all liturgical ministries open to lay persons, apart from the instituted ministries of acolyte and lector. Women have an active role in the liturgy in the dioceses of the United States as readers, extraordinary ministers of the Eucharist, cantors, musicians, diocesan directors of liturgical commissions, directors of liturgy planning teams, as well as national roles in organizations concerned with liturgical renewal. For this reason, most American Catholics, women and men alike, find it difficult to understand, appreciate, or accept the prohibition repeated in *Inaestimabile Donum* concerning the service of women or girls at the altar. Many American Catholics perceive the prohibition symbolically exhibits a

---

[6]Bishops' Committee on the Liturgy, *Environment and Art in Catholic Worship* (Washington, D.C.: USCC Office of Publishing and Promotion Services, 1978), no. 15.

245

discriminatory dichotomy between lay men and lay women, rather than a theologically based discipline.

Attention might well be given also to the institution of women into the ministries of acolyte and reader.

8. *Rite of penance.* In the estimate of most people, participation in the sacrament of reconciliation has declined in the past several years. Interest remains high, however, in penitential practice, both from the active observance of Lent and the interest on the part of many in the Synod of Bishops on the subject of penance and reconciliation last October. We are aware of some of the questions raised at that synod, such as the extent and use of the third form of the sacrament with general confession of sins and general absolution; whether there should be a simpler form of absolution for the celebrations of the Rite of Penance with children; and the sequence of first confession and first communion, still a matter of concern for pastors and catechists. Our committee recognizes that these are all pastorally and theologically sensitive issues. We are most interested in seeing the Rite of Penance serve the more frequent use of the sacrament by our people, but particularly to restore the authentic significance and tradition of the sacrament of reconciliation in the life of the Church.

9. *Second editions of ritual books.* Some of the liturgical books promulgated in the early years of the liturgical reform deserve further consideration. Some attention can probably be given to those rites such as marriage and the baptism of children, which lack the fuller and richer pastoral and theological *praenotanda* present in later liturgical books. Greater attention may be given to delineating more clearly the role of the conference of bishops in the regulation and adaptation of the rites in these second editions of the liturgical books, especially with regard to the provision of original vernacular texts and other ritual elements drawn from the cultural experience of the particular churches.

Conclusion

We present this report filled with experience of a quality of worship over these past years that has been perceptibly nourishing of faith. We note and we commend the energy that parishes and dioceses are exerting with consistency and conviction in this work of central importance in the life of the Church. We believe that worship has moved us to a new depth of prayer that is rich and vibrant.

Our committee is grateful for the opportunity to participate in this congress, to give an oral report, and to share our concerns. We are sure that we can enlarge one another's opportunities toward greater efforts to continue the great work begun in *Sacrosanctum Concilium* more than twenty years ago. To that end, I can, on behalf of the bishops of the United States, pledge our best efforts.

35

The Revised Grail Psalter

Statement, Chairman of the Bishops' Committee
on the Liturgy
March 1, 1985

(See also nos. 2, 5, 13, 15, 21, 32)

Like the 1982 statement made by his predecessor on *A Book of Prayers,*
the accompanying statement of Archbishop Daniel E. Pilarczyk of Cincinnati arose because of a misinterpretation of a decision by the National
Conference of Catholic Bishops. At the general meeting of the NCCB in
November 1984, the Bishops' Committee on the Liturgy proposed that a
revised version of the Grail Psalter be approved for liturgical use. The
revision, done by the original translating body, had as its distinctive feature
the elimination of consciously exclusive language, that is, language dis-
criminating on the basis of gender where this was not required by the
text in the original language.

The Grail translation of the psalms, in its unrevised form, was and is
one of four English psalters approved for official liturgical use in the United
States—the others are the psalters of the *New American Bible,* the *Jerusalem Bible,* and the *Revised Standard Version, Catholic Edition.* It is
the only psalter approved for the liturgy of the hours in English.

When the committee's recommendation failed to receive the requisite
two-thirds majority of affirmative votes, the decision was wrongly taken
to mean either a repudiation of the revised translation as a whole or,
equally problematical, a repudiation of the principles of revision. As in
other instances, it was difficult to tell what motivates negative (or affirmative) votes in a secret ballot; the statement tries to sum up the discussion
at the NCCB plenary session: "The principal reason put forward by those
who opposed authorization of the revised psalter was the lack of clarity
concerning which psalms were messianic in character, either in themselves or in the exegesis given such psalms in traditional liturgical usage,
and whether such psalms should or could be revised for inclusive language."

In some instances, there have been slight revisions of biblical translations that are made from one printing to another or from edition to
edition. These are ordinarily understood to be covered adequately by the
general approbation given to the original edition. Such, for example, has
been the case with the *New American Bible,* the translation of which is
one of those approved for use in the readings at the Eucharist and other
rites. From time to time, minor adjustments and corrections have been

made by editors and proprietors of the texts, and these need hardly be the subject of entirely new decisions by the NCCB.

In the case of this psalter, prepared and later revised by the Ladies of the Grail (England), it was thought that the character of the revisions was such that they should be brought to the attention of the conference of bishops as a whole. After careful study, the Bishops' Committee on the Liturgy made its positive recommendation, but this was not accepted. The official position, explained in the statement, was that after further study the matter might be taken up again and resubmitted.

Fortunately for those desirous of using the revised version of the Grail Psalter, it may be used in nonliturgical services like other "unofficial" texts, which as devotional texts ordinarily have only local ecclesiastical approval. Indeed, it may be used in those parts of the liturgy for which prescribed or appointed official texts may be replaced almost at will, for example, by hymns or other songs with appropriate texts.

Thus, the revised version of the Grail Psalter is excluded from the psalmody of the liturgy of the hours, for which the unrevised Grail Psalter alone is prescribed. It is likewise excluded from the lectionary, from which the responsorial psalm is read or recited.

On the other hand, the new version may well be used at the eucharistic celebration as a substitute for the appointed texts of the entrance and communion processions—along with hymns and various responsorial songs, which are rather freely chosen. This choice was allowed by the NCCB as far back as November 1968: So far as "other collections of psalms and antiphons in English" are concerned, it is permissible to include "psalms arranged in responsorial form, metrical and similar versions of psalms, provided they are . . . selected in harmony with the liturgical season, feast, or occasion." Then in November 1969, the NCCB made a further concession to allow, in accordance with specific criteria of choice, "other sacred songs not from the psalter."

Only the first of these concessions is applicable to the responsorial psalm after the first reading, which is to be a psalm or psalm-based—a qualification clearly satisfied by the Grail Psalter in revised as well as unrevised versions. But, it does extend the potential use of the Grail Psalter while the questions of its liturgical use are resolved.

To return to the formal statement from the committee's chairman, the chief concern was to correct the misunderstandings along two lines: first, that the failure to adopt the revised psalter was a general rejection or repudiation; second, to praise the revision of the Grail Psalter and, perhaps above all, the principle of inclusive liturgical language.

Even though the question was narrowed down to the instances of messianic language in the psalter, whether in the original text or in traditional use, the broader issue at stake is that of inclusive language in general. There has been a gradual realization, coincidental with the liturgical renewal of the past thirty years, that changes in the meanings of words in the English language, as well as the perception of those meanings, have to be taken seriously. The notion of exclusive language, whether it works to the exclusion of women or is a discriminatory allusion to some group or race or people, has to be attended to. Any generic references must now be carefully scrutinized, even though they may well be un-intentionally exclusive or may have been appropriately understood as generic a generation ago.

The liturgical texts in English produced by ICEL in the years prior to the mid-1970s illustrate this clearly. In some texts from that period, there is an evident effort to embrace the total community of the Church or of humankind (for example, the use of "brothers and sisters" as an alternative to "brethren"). In other texts, the much more common use of "man" or "men" and the masculine pronouns to refer to both women and men survived and now grates on the ear. This is true not only in North America, as is sometimes wrongly alleged, but increasingly throughout the English-speaking world.

The problem is apparent—and the good intentions are also apparent—in some prayers from the earlier ICEL corpus in which one line is carefully written to speak of "men and women" or "brothers and sisters" and, two or three lines later, an expression such as "family of man" is unconsciously used. The most celebrated example is the use of the phrase, "for all men," in the eucharistic prayers: intended as a reference to all of humankind, to all women and all men, it soon became almost obsolete in that sense and had to be changed to "for all" by ICEL and then by the NCCB and other conferences of bishops, with the agreement of the Apostolic See.

Beginning in the early 1970s, with a greatly raised consciousness con-cerning the question, the ICEL texts—and thus the texts approved by the American conference of bishops at the recommendation of its episcopal committee—were translated or composed with a careful avoidance of exclusive language. Often, this fact is not even noticed, but it becomes an issue when an existing English text is revised to expunge exclusive or sexist language.

The first formal recognition of the problem by the International Com-mission on English in the Liturgy is worth noting; it dates from August 1975: "The Advisory Committee recognizes the necessity in all future translations and revisions to avoid words that ignore the place of women in the Christian community altogether or that seem to relegate women to a secondary role." Since enlarged and refined, the principle has been applied to new translations and revisions and to original liturgical texts submitted by ICEL to the conferences of bishops in the English-speaking world. In the case of the eucharistic prayers, slightly revised in 1980 to reflect this concern, the American conference of bishops quickly approved the revision, but their decision and those of a number of other conferences have not yet been confirmed.

The case of the Grail Psalter is somewhat parallel, although emanating from a source different from ICEL. While the revision was not accepted, it gave the Bishops' Committee on the Liturgy the chance to affirm strongly, through its chairman, support for the principle of inclusive language, especially in the concluding paragraph of the statement reprinted here.

At its last plenary meeting in November 1984, the National Conference of

Catholic Bishops considered a proposal of the Bishops' Committee on the Liturgy that an inclusive language version of the psalter prepared by the Ladies of the Grail (England) be approved for liturgical use in the dioceses of the United States of America, namely, in the *Liturgy of the Hours,* in *The Lectionary for Mass,* and in other ritual books in which the psalms are used. This proposal did not receive the required two-thirds vote necessary for canonical approval by the conference of bishops. The principal reason put forward by those who opposed authorization of the revised psalter was the lack of clarity concerning which psalms were messianic in character, either in themselves or in the exegesis given such psalms in traditional liturgical usage, and whether such psalms should or could be revised for inclusive language.

On March 1, 1985, meeting in Chicago, the Bishops' Committee on the Liturgy reconsidered the matter at the request of GIA Publications of Chicago, American agent for the Grail Psalter. (GIA is preparing a new edition of *Worship,* a service book and hymnal.) While the Bishops' Committee on the Liturgy looks favorably upon the revised version of the psalter, the following points were made concerning its approval and use in the liturgy in the near future:

1. It had been judged in 1984 that the revised psalter requires canonical approval by the entire National Conference of Catholic Bishops. Such action cannot take place until the November 1985 plenary assembly of the bishops, too late for the requirements of GIA's new edition of *Worship.*

2. The National Conference of Catholic Bishops has favored the use of inclusive language in liturgical texts and has approved such language since 1978. Consequently, nonauthorization of the revised Grail Psalter at this time should not be construed as insensitivity to the question. Rather, the Bishops' Committee on the Liturgy wishes the matter of inclusive language in biblical texts, when such texts refer to the liturgical assembly ("horizontal language"), to be the object of further study before presenting any revisions to the National Conference of Catholic Bishops for its consideration.

3. The Bishops' Committee on the Liturgy maintains its commitment to those plans and projects of the International Commission on English in the Liturgy in which liturgical texts are revised or translated with inclusive language in mind.

4. The Bishops' Committee on the Liturgy applauds and commends the work of The Grail in this first attempt to prepare a carefully revised inclusive-language version of the psalter. The Committee likewise commends the efforts of GIA Publications of Chicago for its efforts to seek authorization and approval of the revised psalter. Although the psalter was not authorized for liturgical use, the Bishops' Committee on the Liturgy looks forward to the publication of the revised psalter as a volume apart from any liturgical book or participation aid so that this version of the psalter may be tested and reviewed by biblical, liturgical, and musical experts.

5. Finally, the Bishops' Committee on the Liturgy wishes to make it known that the question of inclusive language is a matter that deserves attention in the Church because of the cultural development of the English language in the United States and in other English-speaking countries. The Bishops' Committee on the Liturgy applauds the recent initiative taken by the Congregation for Divine Worship, namely, the establishment of a special international

commission that will study this question. As its own contribution to this effort, the Bishops' Committee on the Liturgy intends to commission a scholarly review of the elements inherent in the inclusive language issue. The Bishops' Committee does not understand the matter of inclusive language as a "women's issue" only, as is thought by some. Rather, the Bishops' Committee on the Liturgy understands inclusive language to be a question of the cultural development of the English language and therefore important to all worshiping members of the Church. It is the hope of the Bishops' Committee on the Liturgy, therefore, that an inclusive language version of the psalter be authorized for liturgical use in the dioceses of the United States after further study of the questions raised in November 1984 and since by bishops, biblical scholars, and liturgists.

36

"Clown Ministry" and the Liturgy

Statement, Bishops' Committee on the Liturgy
November 10, 1985

(See also nos. 9, 11)

In the brief note that introduced this statement in the November 1985 issue of the committee's *Newsletter,* the background is explained. After discussing the "growing phenomenon of 'clown ministry' and its use in liturgical celebrations," the committee wished "to make known that the ministry of clowns is not appropriate to liturgical worship. . . . It should be noted that the Congregation for Divine Worship has also expressed its concern in this matter."

The measured and careful statement, prepared by the Secretariat of the Bishops' Committee on the Liturgy and approved by the members, avoids the outright condemnations that characterize the other extreme in dealing with liturgical developments. It includes a positive affirmation of the evident sincerity and good will of those who have introduced the presence of clowns into liturgical rites and who have employed, perhaps loosely, the term "ministry" to characterize such participation.

Certainly, ministry has its own diverse meanings, from the total activity of the total people of God to the highly specialized activity of those who are ordained to ministry or instituted in official ministry. In the case of the style and action of clowns, the term might well be broadly applicable—and certainly outside the public liturgy this kind of ministry may easily have its own recognition and even official encouragement. The real problem arises with elements and associations of the actions of clowns in our society that seem inextricable from entertainment, circuses and other theatrical occasions, televised shows, and the like.

No one should read this statement to suggest that the episcopal committee was unaware—as some of the extreme critics of clown ministry doubtless are unaware—that mime is a serious art form or that the figure of a clown may have the most profound human and religious meaning. It is simply that the ordinary and common acceptance of clowns cannot normally be separated from the world of entertainment and the comic, often farcical.

This is the reason for the committee's precise conclusion: "While special pastoral reasons may sometimes suggest the use of clowns or mimes in certain celebrations for small children, it is not normally appropriate for clowns to function in any way in celebrations of the Mass or in other liturgical rites." This is the central sentence in the statement, and it should be read very carefully—so that the door is not closed absolutely to legitimate creativity or to future development.

The reference to the concern of the Congregation for Divine Worship suggests a parallel case, which was not made the subject of any formal statement. Another concern of the Roman congregation was handled in a different and perhaps less satisfactory way. The April/May 1982 issue of the committee's *Newsletter* reprinted a brief essay on "Dance in the Liturgy." This document, translated from the Roman congregation's journal, *Notitiae* (11 [1975]: 202–205), was printed to respond to queries and criticisms not unlike those concerning the so-called clown ministry. Of course, it is never too clear how widespread such phenomena are—either clowns or dancers as participants in the liturgy—nor whether they constitute real aberrations or abuses in a concrete liturgical situation.

Even more than in the case of the performance of clowns, the role of dancers and dancing in the liturgy has to be evaluated in terms of what is a genuine art form, often with the most profound human and religious significance. It may be folk dancing, individual interpretative dancing, or ballet itself, but no one questions the legitimacy of dance, and no one should question the legitimacy of religious dance. Its regular admission into the public and official liturgy may be another question.

Again, there are serious reasons for concern and hesitation, particularly because of the associations that some kinds of dance have. The addition of dance to the liturgy may seem bizarre to many communities and congregations. No doubt, some attempts at liturgical dance have been poorly conceived and more poorly executed. An equal possibility is that liturgical dance will be only a show witnessed by a liturgical assembly.

Nevertheless, the essay from *Notitiae* concerning dance was seriously weakened by an arbitrary and unhistorical dismissal of liturgical dance as if unprecedented in Western Christian liturgy and as if totally uncongenial to Western religious culture. Even in citing the precedents from Scripture and from non-Western cultures, including Christian rites of the East, even in interpreting favorable indications from conciliar documents, the essay appeared to be arbitrary in rejecting liturgical dance utterly—and even appeared to be patronizing to other Christian cultures.

A more sympathetic and sound treatment would have recognized, first, the relationship of dance to other forms of bodily movement, posture, and gesture that do have a place in Western liturgy; second, the presence of processions and, indeed, dances in the Western liturgical tradition; and third, the sound intentions and sometimes great talent of those who have tried to introduce some form of dance into the liturgy.

All this is by way of saying that the statement on clown ministry issued by the episcopal committee in 1985 is a far better way of dealing with a problematical phenomenon in the liturgy. It recognizes objectively the potential and good purpose but points out the problems that, at least normally or ordinarily, rule out a liturgical ministry of this kind.

Since the inception of the liturgical reform over twenty years ago, the Church has welcomed and given renewed attention to a variety of art forms and styles not previously associated with worship. The statement of the Bishops' Committee on the Liturgy, *Environment and Art in Catholic Worship* (1978), gave positive and strong encouragement to the service of the arts in worship in keeping with the Church's traditional support of the arts: "Christians have not hesitated to use every human art in their celebration of the saving work of God in Jesus Christ, although in every historical period they have been influenced, at times inhibited, by cultural circumstances" (no. 4). Yet, art in the service of worship must also respect the nature of liturgy: "If an art form is used in liturgy it must aid and serve the action of liturgy since liturgy has its own structure, rhythm, and pace" (no. 25).

In recent years, new and old art forms have come into the service of worship in the Church in the United States. Among these has been what has come to be known as "clown ministry." The sincerity of those involved in "clown ministry" is not to be questioned, but it must be made clear that they have no liturgical function. While the clown has a place in the world of entertainment, or may be involved in works of charity such as visiting the sick in hospitals or those confined to nursing homes or homes for the elderly, or as a pedagogic aid in schools or in the religious education of children, or even in certain traditions of Christological reflection, the clown as such is not to be understood as a liturgical minister. While special pastoral reasons may sometimes suggest the use of clowns or mimes in certain celebrations for small children, it is not normally appropriate for clowns to function in any way in celebrations of the Mass or in other liturgical rites.

In making this statement, the Secretariat of the Bishops' Committee on the Liturgy does not intend to impugn the good intentions or motives of those involved in "clown ministry." Nor does the Secretariat wish to stifle genuine adaptation and authentic creativity where permitted by liturgical norms. Nevertheless, certain approaches which derogate from the nature of liturgy must be avoided: "for example, a too-personalized style, illicit omissions or additions, rites invented outside the established norms, and attitudes unfavorable to a sense of the sacred, of beauty, and of recollection" (Pope John Paul II to the members of the Congregation for Divine Worship, October 17, 1985).

While "the liturgy of the Church is rich in a tradition of ritual movement and gestures," it should be recalled that "these actions, subtly, yet really, contribute to an environment which can foster prayer or which can distract from prayer" (EACW, no. 56). The use of clowns during the liturgy personalizes the liturgy too much and detracts from that prayerful atmosphere necessary for the good order of a community's sense of the transcendent in worship." *Appropriateness* is another demand that liturgy rightfully makes upon any art that would serve its action. The work of art must be appropriate in two ways: (1) it must be capable of bearing the weight of mystery, awe, reverence, and wonder which the liturgical action expresses; (2) it must clearly *serve* (and not interrupt) ritual action which has its own structure, rhythm, and movement" (EACW, no. 21).

The Secretariat of the Bishops' Committee on the Liturgy, therefore, calls upon diocesan liturgical commissions and offices of worship and all responsible for liturgical celebrations to recall these principles of *Environment and Art in Catholic Worship* with respect to the phenomenon of "clown ministry."

37

Communion under Both Kinds and Certain Health Concerns

Statement, Bishops' Committee on the Liturgy
November 10, 1985

(See also nos. 8, 29)

This statement was published in 1985 with the approval of the Executive Committee of the bishops' conference. It may seem like an anticlimax to profound questions of liturgical celebration taken up in other statements. Nevertheless, the issue is itself extremely grave, related as it is to the transmission of communicable diseases, potentially one of epidemic proportions.

In accord with the statement, it has to be said at once that the issue of contagion because of communion from the cup has been raised repeatedly in the past and as often dispelled. Both in the United States and elsewhere, studies have shown that the danger of serious infection does not exist if the minister is careful to wipe the cup after each communicant and follows the practice of rotating the cup a quarter turn or a third turn after each communicant. Even subsequent to the statement, the same position has been stated explicitly by health authorities in relation to the transmission of Acquired Immunodeficiency Syndrome (AIDS).

The questions arising from AIDS, which continues and may be expected to continue for many years, understandably lead to concern. Church authorities properly take the same position as health authorities, combining caution with every effort to avoid excessive reactions. The tone of the statement is both pastoral and reassuring; fortunately, it is able to place the new threat of AIDS in the context of the precautions described in the 1984 norms, which were given in *This Holy and Living Sacrifice: Directory for the Celebration and Reception of Communion under Both Kinds.*

The simplest response is to remind persons hesitant about receiving communion from the cup that, in every case, this is a free choice of the individual communicant. One fearful of contagion (of any kind) may choose to receive under the form of bread alone; one who is especially susceptible to infection, including those with Acquired Immunodeficiency Syndrome, are equally free to refrain from communion from the cup.

Another possibility is mentioned in the statement: that of communion by intinction. This mode of communicating has obvious limitations in expressing authentically the full eucharistic sign of drinking as well as eating. These limitations have led liturgical and pastoral specialists almost unanimously to deprecate intinction. (The kind of intinction recently introduced into the Roman liturgy cannot properly be compared with the practice of intinction in the Eastern Churches: In the Byzantine liturgy, for example, the minister communicates the individual by using a spoon with which he takes the eucharistic bread—leavened, of course—from the cup containing the consecrated wine and places it in the communicant's mouth.) It also limits the freedom of individuals who choose to communicate under one kind only if communion is given exclusively by intinction.

The liturgical concern remains to encourage the fullest expression of the religious meal, the form in which the eucharistic sacrifice was instituted by the Lord and so to encourage communion under both kinds—if possible, from the cup. Providentially, the Second Vatican Council restored this usage to the Church, a usage that had not been lost by the other Christian Churches and ecclesial communities.

At first, in particular cases, examples of which were given in the *Constitution on the Liturgy* (SC 55), and then gradually more and more widely, communion under both kinds has become appreciated and accepted in the Catholic community. It is far, far from universal in ordinary parochial use, but it may now be said to be generally appreciated and accepted. The principal change is that communion under both kinds, with a preference always for the use of the shared cup that signifies the unity of the Christian people, is the basic exemplar rather than the rare privilege or exception. While respecting the freedom of each communicant and supporting every proper precaution, the statement continues to seek the goal of the eucharistic renewal.

"The Eucharist has always been a source of Christian love and the center of ecclesial life, daily building up the life of all Christians."[1] Because the Eucharist is so important in the life of Christians, "the Church is concerned with all aspects of the eucharistic celebration, particularly the rite of Holy Communion."[2] In Holy Communion, the faithful are joined to Christ and to one another through the reception of the Body and Blood of the Lord. The Eucharist is therefore the "sacrament of love, a sign of unity, a bond of charity, a paschal banquet in which Christ is consumed, the mind is filled with grace, and a pledge of future glory is given to us in the memorial of Christ's death and resurrection."[3] Under no circumstances, therefore, should the Eucharist ever become a source of anxiety or contention or controversy.

In the Church's long history, however, there have been times when anxiety and worry and even fear have attended upon the reception of the Lord's eucharistic Body and Blood. There are times when sickness prevented a

---

[1] *This Holy and Living Sacrifice: Directory for the Celebration and Reception of Communion under Both Kinds (= Directory)*, (Washington, D.C.: USCC Office of Publishing and Promotion Services, 1984).

[2] Ibid., no. 4.

[3] Second Vatican Council, *Constitution on the Sacred Liturgy (Sacrosanctum Concilium)*, December 4, 1963, art. 47.

communicant from receiving one or both species. There have been times when epidemics have prevented large numbers of Christians from approaching the Lord's table for fear of becoming infected with disease. In the last several months, a similar concern has come into being among some Catholics with regard to the transmission of Acquired Immunodeficiency Syndrome (AIDS) and other communicable diseases when receiving the sacred Blood of Christ from a common chalice.

As a liturgical practice, communion under both kinds was recently restored among Roman Catholics in the United States. It has been and continues to be a gift of great spiritual benefit. When first implemented according to the norms of *This Holy and Living Sacrifice: Directory for the Celebration and Reception of Communion under Both Kinds,* the bishops of the United States affirmed the Church's traditional preference for reception of the Blood of Christ directly from a chalice: "Because of its ancient sign value *ex institutione Christi,* Communion from the cup or chalice is always to be preferred to any other form of ministering the precious blood."[4]

At the same time, however, the *Directory* also cautioned ministers of the chalice to take ordinary precautions for hygiene: "After each communicant has received the Blood of Christ, the minister shall carefully wipe both sides of the rim of the cup with a purificator. This action is both a matter of courtesy and hygiene. It is also customary for the minister to move the chalice a quarter turn after each communicant for the same reasons."[5]

The usual requisites for hygiene and cleanliness are always to be observed when ministering the chalice to several communicants. The *Directory* also repeats the general legislation of the Church with regard to other forms of receiving the Blood of Christ, most notably the method of intinction."[6]

The genuine concerns about communicable diseases, along with the increased, and often misleading, publicity given to them require further pastoral response from the Church. The Bishops' Committee on the Liturgy therefore encourages diocesan liturgical commissions and offices of worship to recall the norms of the *Directory* and, at the same time, to take note of the following information concerning the transmission of communicable diseases as stated by the Centers for Disease Control of the U.S. Department of Health and Human Services:

Since laboratory studies have shown that bacteria and viruses can contaminate a silver chalice and survive despite the alcohol content of the wine and wiping or rotating the cup, the potential exists for an ill parishioner or asymptomatic carrier to expose other members of the congregation by contaminating a common cup. If any diseases are transmitted by this practice, they most likely would be common viral illnesses such as the common cold, but transmission of other illnesses cannot be entirely excluded. During the past four years since AIDS has been studied, there has been no suggestion of transmission of the virus that causes AIDS by

---

[4]*Directory*, no. 44.
[5]Ibid., no. 47.
[6]Ibid., nos. 50–52.

257

sharing utensils, including the common communion cup, or through any other means involving saliva.

We are not aware of any specific episodes or outbreaks of any illness that have been associated with use of a common communion cup. However, it is important to understand that health officials would only become aware of a health risk from such a practice if it resulted in the transmission of unusual diseases or large clusters of common illnesses and subsequent investigations were successful in determining the vehicle of transmission. Viral respiratory disease might be transmitted frequently by a common cup, but the association may not be recognized or the disease may be attributed to respiratory or other forms of person-to-person contact. We are not aware of any epidemiological studies that have attempted to study the importance of a common communion cup in disease transmission. The lack of documented occurrence of disease is reassuring that the practice is not gravely hazardous, but it should not imply that there are no risks.

In summary, we cannot quantitate a risk for disease transmission by use of a common communion cup nor can we provide an absolute endorsement that the practice is safe.[7]

In view of this statement, the Bishops' Committee on the Liturgy does not believe that parishes need to suspend communion under both kinds. The committee, however, encourages those who may feel compelled to change their practice in this regard to minister the Blood of the Lord by the method of intinction, until further medical evidence warrants a return to their former practice. At the same time, pastors should advise those who are fearful that they have the option of receiving Christ under the species of bread alone. "For Christ, whole and entire, exists under the species of bread and under any part of that species, and similarly the whole Christ exists under the species of wine and under its parts."[8]

Pastors should exhibit common sense and pastoral solicitude both for the concerns of their people and for the liturgical practice which enables the faithful to experience the fullness of the Lord's presence in both the signs of bread and wine. Pastors should also advise communicants who have communicable illnesses to refrain from drinking from the chalice and to receive by intinction or receive the consecrated bread only.[9]

It should also be noted that persons with AIDS are more at risk from

---

[7]Letter from Donald R. Hopkins, M.D., Assistant Surgeon General and Acting Director of the Centers for Disease Control (Atlanta) to Rev. John A. Gurrieri, Executive Director, Bishops' Committee on the Liturgy, September 4, 1985.

[8]Council of Trent, *Decree on the Most Holy Eucharist*, C. IV: *Transubstantiation* (DS 1640).

[9]The methods of administering communion under both kinds by the use of a common cup and by intinction are set forth in the *Directory*, nos. 44–52. If communion under both kinds by intinction is to be offered to the communicants, then no. 52 of the *Directory* must be followed: "If communion is given by intinction the communicant may never dip the eucharistic bread into the chalice."

opportunistic infections than those who do not suffer from suppression of the immune system. The Church must demonstrate great pastoral care and solicitude for those who suffer from this affliction, through prayer and works of charity.

As the "sacrament of love" and the "bond of charity" the Eucharist must always be the source of our unity in the saving death and resurrection of the Lord Jesus, who cared for the sick and afflicted. It is all too easy in our concern for our own well-being to forget or ignore the needs of those in our midst who suffer from illness or even to attempt to exclude the sick from our midst out of fear. But, the love of God and the eucharistic food of heaven, Christ's Body and Blood, compel us to ever greater acts of love for our fellow human beings.

Looking Forward

It is thirty years since the Bishops' Committee on the Liturgy was established, about a quarter of a century since its first formal statement on liturgical renewal. The diverse documents in this collection chronicle the period in a way different from the committee's monthly *Newsletter,* now reprinted in three volumes, two of which (Volume II [1976–1980] and Volume III [1981–1985]) are still available from USCC Office of Publishing and Promotion Services. Some undertakings of the committee have not formed part of this record, including some that are very important indeed, such as efforts to support Hispanic and black liturgies. The same is true of its collaborative work with other bodies, official or not, and in its routine but significant day-to-day activities through its secretariat. By and large, however, the breadth of the committee's work shines through its statements, some slight, some substantial.

We are too close to the events of the day to say whether the end of three decades is a turning point, but the matter of liturgical renewal is a continuing process in the life of the Christian community—and a good many of the concerns of 1957, above all, liturgical catechesis in all its forms, remain constant.

What is new and for the future is not only consolidation of liturgical progress but fresh progress. Certainly, a first phase of postconciliar reform has been completed: the thoroughgoing revision of the Roman liturgy and its first and basic translation into contemporary language, accompanied by minimal cultural diversification and massive efforts at broader and deeper participation by the whole people of God.

Just as certainly, this is only a beginning. And, the desirable consolidation of what has been achieved can hardly be permitted to freeze the liturgy at a given moment of postconciliar achievement, as tragically happened during the four centuries after the Council of Trent. Today, there are many new and better names, theories, and potential applications of what the *Constitution on the Liturgy* called liturgical adaptation, but the liturgical renewal cannot become static or closed.

In the years recorded by the collection of its statements, the Bishops' Committee on the Liturgy, like Christian worship itself, has had its own remarkable progress. This has been both in its bishop-members and in its staff, both in its breadth of understanding and in its varied activities. Properly, this is only a beginning, as the Second Vatican Council was only a beginning.

About the Editor

REV. MSGR. FREDERICK R. McMANUS, a priest of the Archdiocese of Boston, is presently ordinary professor of Canon Law at The Catholic University of America (Washington, D.C.), a position he has held intermittently since 1958. Ordained in 1947, he holds a B.A. from St. John's Seminary (Brighton, Massachusetts) and a J.C.D. from The Catholic University of America. In his career at CUA, Msgr. McManus served as dean of the School of Canon Law (1967–1973) and as vice provost and dean of Graduate Studies (1974–1983).

Msgr. McManus is currently the editor of *The Jurist,* the magazine of the Canon Law Society of America, a position he has held since 1959. He served as director of the Secretariat of the Bishops' Committee on the Liturgy, National Conference of Catholic Bishops, from 1965 until 1975, at which time he was appointed "permanent" staff consultant to the Secretariat. From 1960 to 1962, Msgr. McManus served as consultant to the Pontifical Preparatory Commission on the Sacred Liturgy for the Second Vatican Council and then as peritus to the Council from 1962 to 1965. In addition, he has been a consultant to the Consilium for the Implementation of the Constitution on the Liturgy (1964–1970); consultant to the Pontifical Commission for the Revision of the Code of Canon Law (1967–1983); treasurer and member of the Advisory Committee of the International Commission on English in the Liturgy (1964–   ); consultant to the Secretariat for Promoting Christian Unity (1979–   ); president of the Societas Liturgica (1979–1981); and member of the Board of Directors of the Association of Catholic Colleges and Universities (1979–1980), chairman of the Association (1980–1982), and immediate past chair of the Association (1983–1984).

Msgr. McManus has authored numerous books, most recently *The Rite of Penance* (with Ralph Kiefer), and is a frequent contributor to a variety of periodicals and collected works. He is a member of several canonical, theological, and scholarly organizations and serves on the Board of Directors of the Institute of Medieval Canon Law (Berkeley, California), as well as on the Board of the American Council on Education. Msgr. McManus has been awarded numerous honorary degrees from colleges and universities. In addition, he has been the recipient of many scholarly prizes including the Role of Law Award (1973); the Gerald Ellard Award (1976); the Michael Mathis Award (1978); the Berakah Award (1979); the Prelate of Honor of Pope John Paul II (1980); and the Presidential Award of the National Catholic Educational Association (1983).

Index

Acclamations
    in *A Book of Prayers* 217
    before the gospel 37
    in the liturgy of the Eucharist 103
    as part of texts 100
    in the rite of Christian initiation of adults 212, 215
    in the rites of ordination 117
Acolyte 121-27, 134, 155, 184
Acquired Immunodeficiency Syndrome (AIDS) 255, 257-58
Acta Apostolicae Sedis 8
Actio pastoralis 67
Ad pascendum 121-24
Advent 141, 182, 228, 231, 234
Allocation of roles (in the liturgy) 37-38, 40, 41
Ambo 32, 137, 210
Amen
    in eucharistic prayer 182
    the great 103, 182
    as response 195
American Guild of Organists (examination program) 45
American Medical Association 198-99
Anaphora, eucharistic 47, 82
Antiphons 153-54, 212, 215
Apostles' Creed 184
Apostolate (liturgical) 3, 5-7
Architecture 94, 232
Arts, The 34, 43, 94, 191, 232, 253
"Authentic celebration" 26, 93, 96, 112, 139, 244

Baptism 8, 177-78, 180-81, 204, 227, 243, 246
    Sunday renewal of 143, 147, 179, 182
Benedictine Liturgical Conference 4
Bernardin, Joseph L., Archbishop 158-59
Bible services 27, 74
Bidding prayers 133, 203. *See also* General intercessions;
    Prayer (prayer of the faithful)
Bilingual rituals 5, 82
Bishops
    conferences, history of 3-5
    councils 3, 4
    as leaders 224
    named in eucharastic prayer 154
    ordination of 113-16
Bishops' Committee on Ecumenical and Interreligious Affairs 13
Bishops' Commission (Committee) on the Liturgical Apostolate.
  See also Bishops' Committee on the Liturgy
    composition of 12
    formation of (1958) 1, 3
    implementation of *Constitution* 10-11

263

Distribution. *See* Allocation of roles (in the liturgy)
Divisive movements 66, 76
Documents on the Liturgy 1963-1979: Conciliar, Papal, and Curial Texts 16, 37, 46, 67, 85, 93-94, 121, 130-31, 135, 143, 161, 186, 194, 200, 212, 218, 239
Doxology 38-39, 78, 86-87
Dworshak, Leo, Bishop 21

Easter 230-32
Easter Vigil 5-6, 55, 179, 183-84, 196
Eastern Church
    communion by intinction in 256
    communion under both kinds 56
    concelebration in 48
    faithfulness to gospel tradition 58
    minor orders, tradition in 122, 126-27
    role of dance in liturgy of 253
Ecumenism 243-44
Enchiridion indulgentiarum 217
English (language)
    manner of speaking properly 29
    use in liturgy 23, 108, 213, 242
    use in the *Sacramentary* 138
    words in music 34
Entrance rite (Mass) 38, 101-2
Environment and Art in Catholic Worship 15, 94, 191, 232, 245, 254
Environment for Worship: A Reader, The 95
Eucharist. *See also* Communion; Concelebration; Mass; Music
    for adults 67
    application of the principles of celebration 101-4
    celebration of, in family home 67
    for children 67, 146, 195
    clericalization of 47-48
    disciplinary and doctoral instruction 53, 56
    instruction on 78
    modes of receipt 54
    mystery of 56, 225-27
    as sacrament of initiation 178-80
    as sacrament of reconciliation 58, 224
    as sacrificial banquet 56-59, 61
    as source of Church's strength 58
Eucharistic banquet 53, 56, 58-59, 69, 86, 162, 197
Eucharistic fast 155-56
Eucharistic mystery 225-27
Eucharistic prayer (canon) 25, 32, 73, 100, 103
    definition of 85-86, 102-3
    the great Amen 103, 182
    introduction in English 80, 84, 88
    manner of proclaiming 82, 85, 87-88, 103
    prefaces 33, 140
    relation to Lord's Prayer 85
    unity of 39
    use of English in 111, 138

267

use of Latin in 26, 111
weaknesses of 86
Eucharisticum mysterium 53-54, 78, 161-62
Euchological texts 82-83, 107, 139
Evangelization 100
Evening prayer 174-75, 230
Exclusive language 136-37, 243, 247-51
Exorcists 121, 125

Federation of Diocesan Liturgical Commissions (FDLC) 14, 92, 94, 173, 234, 242
Funeral Masses 9, 55, 134, 144, 229, 243

Gallagher, Joseph, Monsignor 84
Gaudium et spes 136-37, 205
Gelasius I, Pope 210
General intercessions 129-33, 200-210. *See also* Prayer (prayer
  of the faithful)
    guidelines on 200
    intentions of 131
    nature of 203
    as preferred title for prayer of the faithful 131-32, 150
    structure of 200, 206-9
    use of 203-4
General Instruction of the Roman Missal 65, 114, 123, 129-31, 137, 144,
  147-51, 153-54, 164-65, 167, 195-98, 202, 204, 210, 214
GIA Publications of Chicago 250
Grail Psalter (revised) 218, 247-51
    opposition to 247
    role of Ladies of the Grail 248
    use of exclusive language in 247-49
    use of inclusive language in 247-50
    use of messianic language in 247-48, 250
Gregorian chant 100, 108
Gregory the Great, Pope 189
Griffiths, James H., Bishop 9-11, 22
Grimshaw, Francis, Archbishop 84
Guidelines for the Publication of Liturgical Books 139
Gurrieri, John A., Reverend 236

Hallinan, Paul, Archbishop 10-11, 14-15, 21-22, 62-63, 71, 83-84, 158
Health concerns 198, 255-59
Hierarchical nature of Church 51
Hispanic liturgy 14, 220, 243
Holy Communion. *See* Communion; Concelebration; Eucharist; Mass
Holy days of obligation 196
Holy Thursday 48, 55, 156, 196
Holy Week 5
Homily
    instructions, in place of, at ordinations 114-16
    importance of 226, 244

270

as Church in miniature 69

Participation aids 140-41, 158-59, 187-88

"Paschal mystery" 27, 61, 75, 86, 180-83, 197, 202, 210, 213, 222-27, 231

Pastoral Care of the Sick: Rites of Anointing and Viaticum 144, 156, 215, 228-29, 243

Pastoral-liturgical
  action 11-12, 64, 105
  institute (of scholars) 13

Patrologicae Cursus Completus: Series Latina 163, 182

Paul VI, Pope 1, 23, 80, 93, 113, 121, 123, 128, 140, 144, 167, 175, 186-89, 193-94, 217-18, 221-22, 240

Penitential rite(s) 147, 150, 161, 178-79, 183, 217, 228, 243, 246

Pentecost 141, 183, 230

Petitions 39, 149, 200-201. *See also* General intercessions; Prayer (prayer of the faithful)

Pilarczyk, Daniel E., Archbishop 247

Pius V, Pope 189

Pius V, Saint (1570 eucharistic rite of) 106

Pius X, Pope 5, 56, 106, 188

Pius XII, Pope 1, 5, 9, 59, 166, 188

Pontificalis ritus 114-15

Pontificalis Romani recognitio 113, 121

Popular publications 140-41, 158-59, 187-88

Porters 121, 125

Praenotanda 113, 193, 244, 246

Prayer(s). *See also* Eucharistic prayer
  bidding prayers 133, 203
  collect 32, 38, 39, 102
  common 133, 203
  evening prayer 174-75, 230
  lectio divina 28
  morning prayer 174-75
  opening prayer 147-49
  prayer after communion 145, 148, 151, 201
  prayer of the faithful. *See also* General intercessions
    content of 130, 200, 204
    in Mass 130
    other names for 133, 200, 203
    particularism in 133
    preparation and application of 75, 130-31, 201, 203-4
    in the service of the Word 102, 204, 206
    structure of 132, 200, 206-9
  prayer over the gifts (secret prayer) 38, 78, 100, 103, 140, 148, 151, 201, 209
  prayer over the offerings 32
  prayer over the people 152-53
  public prayer 39, 86
  presidential prayers. *See also* Sacramentary, The
    defined 140
    in English 82, 138-39
    manner of proclamation 36, 87
    in missalettes 139
    in popular publications 141-42, 159
    and prayer of the faithful 131

restriction to one 79
in *Roman Missal* 31, 156-57
silence preceding 36
silent prayer 25, 36, 39, 79, 149-51, 208
use of Latin in 25, 83
vernacular concession in 26, 88
Prayer of Christians, The 168, 173
Prayer of the Church, The 168
Preaching
    integration with Scripture 27
    liturgical 75, 244
    new appreciation for 87
    revolution in content, style 75
Presidential chair 79, 210
Priest(s)
    catechesis for 84
    as celebrant 39
    ordination rites for 113-18
    prayer-life of 28
    as reader 29-30
    role in concelebration 46-47, 118
    role in liturgical practice 74, 224
    unity of 50-52
Protestant denominations
    central role of Sunday in 241
    significance of communion from the cup in 58
Publishers (liturgical books) 138-39
Publishers (liturgical music) 119-20, 158-59, 211, 215

Quasten, Joannes 21

Reader(s) 121-26, 134, 184, 233
Regional liturgical commissions 11, 63
Riepe, Charles K., Reverend 64
Rite(s)
    of adult baptism 8
    of baptism for children 78, 181, 246
    of Christian initiation of adults (RCIA) 178, 191, 227, 242
    for the dedication of a church 5
    of funerals 78
    of marriage
        "human friendship" 229
        music in 215
        place of general intercessions in 129, 204
        revisions in 78, 134, 243
    of penance 147, 150, 161, 178-79, 183, 217, 228, 243, 246
    of tonsure
        definition 121
        future role of 124
        as a liturgical rite 125, 128
        and the subdiaconate 127
        suppression of 122, 125